# How to Design Websites

**Alan Pipes**

Laurence King Publishing

**LAURENCE KING**

Published in 2011 by Laurence King Publishing Ltd
361–373 City Road
London EC1V 1LR
United Kingdom
Tel: + 44 20 7841 6900
Fax: + 44 20 7841 6910
e-mail: enquiries@laurenceking.com
www.laurenceking.com

A catalogue record for this book is available from the British Library

ISBN: 978-1-85669-739-2

Design: Studio Ten and a Half
Typeface: Helvetica
Picture Research: Studio Ten and a Half and Alan Pipes
Printed in China

Front cover: Screenshot from itsnicethat.com appears courtesy of It's Nice That

# Contents

# Preface

Do designers need to learn code? Should they code their own designs? After all, architects don't build the houses they design, movie directors don't shoot and edit their own motion pictures, and even Damien Hirst doesn't paint his own spot paintings. It's only down at the craft level – of illustrators, potters, jewellers and the like – that designers actually make things these days.

Of course, in the past designers have had lots of excuses not to learn code. The internet was designed by scientists, for scientists. Tim Berners-Lee, the inventor of the World Wide Web, worked at CERN, the European Laboratory for Particle Physics. His main concern was to share research data with other professionals. When designers discovered the web, they had to adapt it to their needs, using workarounds and hacks to make the web do what they wanted it to do. And they still do, if they wish their layouts to make sense in older browsers.

But the amazing thing about modern computing is that it gives total control over the design process back to designers. Web designers can create entire websites without leaving their computer desks. It started with desktop publishing, when such programs as QuarkXPress enabled graphic designers to be responsible again for the whole design-to-production cycle, free from their layouts being reinterpreted and altered by outside typesetters, repro houses and printers. Musicians, who used to have to hire expensive studio time, can now create high-quality compositions in their own bedrooms. Photographers can produce stunning prints without the need for messy chemicals and darkroom equipment. Digital technology has democratized design. A solitary designer can take on the big studios and agencies on that mythical level playing field – and win.

Many designers will of course work for big studios, where the workflow is fragmented into distinct job descriptions; freelancers have to learn to do everything well. Splitting the duties among, for example, designers who mock-up pages in Photoshop and coders who then try to make them work is a backwards step into the days before computers, in that the design integrity can be lost when the coder is tempted to tweak the designer's concepts. This book, surprisingly, is not aimed at hardcore techie web designers – there are plenty of manuals out there for them. Of course, I'm not advocating that designers should code complex corporate and e-commerce websites themselves; there is nothing wrong with co-opting specialized help when you need it. But with an understanding of the medium and the tools of the trade – a working knowledge of HTML and CSS – you will produce, I argue, better, more thoughtful and ultimately more successful designs.

Coding, and conforming to standards, could be seen by some as constraining, but there are plenty of examples on the web of beautiful functional design achieved without resorting to Flash or type-as-image methods that play fast and loose with accessibility. Conversely there are sites on the web that may have impeccable coding but lack imagination, don't tell a story and are downright boring.

This book aims to be a hands-on guide to designing websites for anyone who needs a web presence – be they designers, makers, illustrators, artists or photographers – with the curiosity to want to take charge of the process. Above all, it is a practical and pragmatic handbook. Why reinvent the wheel? There are many generous and talented pathfinder people on the web who have already been along the learning curve and are waiting to help, with public-domain templates, plug-ins and helper programs, that will make 'coding' as painless as it can be – mostly just a matter of copying and pasting. This book aims to provide you with the framework and knowledge to design websites. You just need to add the all-important sparkling content – so go and create!

I would like to thank Jo Lightfoot at Laurence King Publishing for commissioning this book, editor John Jervis for his patience, support and sensible suggestions to improve the text, copy editor Kirsty Seymour-Ure for asking the sort of questions that require clear and concise answers that ultimately make the text easier to understand, Emily Asquith for a final look through the content to make sure all was ready for print, and designer Jessie Earle for adding lots of visual interest to my words and code – creating a book that is a joy to read.

Alan Pipes

# Hey

Search

## Fortune

*Diseño gráfico, Ilustración*

Fortune fue fundada en 1930. Sus cubiertas son dignas de colección.
Os dejo un link con un archivo bastante grande.

### Sobre Hey

**Categorías**
Arte
Audiovisual
Diseño gráfico
Diseño Industrial
Fotografía
Hey
Ilustración
Libros
Moda
Música
Set designer
Tipografía
Uncategorized
Web

Flickr
Twitter
Facebook
Contact

*heystudio.es*

---

# Hey

Search

## Johnny Kelly

*Audiovisual, Diseño gráfico, Ilustración*

Johnny Kelly vive y trabaja en el Reino Unido. Junto con su hermano Michael realizan proyectos de ilustración y animación.

### Sobre Hey

**Categorías**
Arte
Audiovisual
Diseño gráfico
Diseño Industrial
Fotografía
Hey
Ilustración
Libros
Moda
Música
Set designer
Tipografía
Uncategorized
Web

Flickr
Twitter
Facebook
Contact

*heystudio.es*

---

# Hey

Search

## Stefan Kanchev

*Diseño gráfico*

Stefan Kanchev (1915-2001). Pasión por los logotipos y símbolos.

Posted by Vero, 29.03.10
Comments *No Comments »*

*delicious, digg, mail*

### Sobre Hey

**Categorías**
Arte
Audiovisual
Diseño gráfico
Diseño Industrial
Fotografía
Hey
Ilustración
Libros
Moda
Música
Set designer
Tipografía
Uncategorized
Web

Flickr
Twitter
Facebook
Contact

*heystudio.es*

---

# Hey

Search

## Happy Socks

*Moda*

Happy Socks, una tienda sueca especializada única y exclusivamente en calcetines. Nos pedimos un par de cada!

### Sobre Hey

**Categorías**
Arte
Audiovisual
Diseño gráfico
Diseño Industrial
Fotografía
Hey
Ilustración
Libros
Moda
Música
Set designer
Tipografía
Uncategorized
Web

Flickr
Twitter
Facebook
Contact

*heystudio.es*

# Introduction and background

1

With the web well into what the community describes as version 2.0, it has never been easier to create a worldwide presence. The internet is now a key part of almost everyone's life, and for graphic designers particularly it is part of their toolbox and a source of potential income. But what is the best way of designing websites?

You will probably already have a Facebook profile to keep in touch with friends, you might store your photographs on a site such as Flickr, and you likely use Twitter or MySpace – so you already know the basics. You may even have a blog, which is probably the quickest and cheapest way to create a personal website (Fig **1.1**) and can be customized beyond recognition (see Step-by-step 1 on pages 46–49). Every designer should have one, whether it be standalone or the 'news' segment of a more conventional website. Sooner or later, however, especially if you are thinking of creating websites for clients, you will have to learn some code.

People approaching website design for the first time may easily be discouraged by the complexity of web design programs such as Adobe Dreamweaver. It may be tempting to enrol on an expensive Dreamweaver course and embark on a steep learning curve to be able to design the simplest site. And while this will expand your skillset and help with job prospects, initially it is not always necessary. Learn a program, and you may be locked in to using that program to the exclusion of all others. Learn about web design and you can pick and choose the tools to use. In Chapter 2 we jump right in at the deep end and demonstrate how you can hand-code a simple website in less than a day.

**1.1** A WordPress blog (weblog) is a quick and easy way to have a web presence – standard design templates can be customized to distinguish your site from all the others, as in this blog from Barcelona-based graphic designers Hey Studios

# What is the internet?

The internet is simply a global network of computers, and a means of connecting your computer, TV or mobile device to other computers. It is merely a medium. But on the internet we find lots of useful tools, the main ones being email (electronic mail), the World Wide Web (WWW) and, to a lesser extent these days, Usenet newsgroups.

Email allows you to send and receive messages and digital attachments – anything from computer-generated images, scanned photographs and artwork to sound samples – to and from anywhere in the world.

The World Wide Web (WWW) is a collection of 'pages', probably running into several billions by now, viewed using a browser such as Safari or Firefox and containing text, images, sound, movies and, most importantly, 'hot links' to other pages. You can also use some WWW pages interactively to communicate with, say, online stores or galleries. Webmail (e.g. Gmail, Hotmail) enables you to access your email on a browser from any computer.

Newsgroups are online bulletin boards or discussion groups that enable you to have conversations with other people. This role has largely been taken over by web-based forums.

For the designer, the internet is a cheap and fast way to send artwork to the client and the printer. It is also an inexpensive and effective way to advertise yourself and your work worldwide. Third, it is a potentially huge source of new clients and job opportunities (Fig **1.2**).

**1.2** Long-established Los Angeles-based design community website QBN (Quality Broadcasting Network) is a resource centre and discussion board for news, chat and – with companion site krop.com – creative industry jobs and portfolio housing

## The evolution of the internet

In 1962, the US military set up ARPAnet (Advanced Research Projects Agency) with the aim of improving the military's use of computer technology. ARPAnet initially connected together four computers at sites around the USA, the first node being installed at the University of California in Los Angeles in September 1969. This was made possible by 'packet switching', in which messages are broken down into 'packets' and sent off by different routes towards their destination, where they are eventually reassembled. Paul Baran of the Rand Corporation had published such a scheme in 1964. The National Physical Laboratory in the UK set up the first test network based on these principles in 1968.

ARPAnet was designed from the outset to be both resilient and decentralized, so as to ensure that communications would keep flowing even if parts of the network were destroyed – in a nuclear war, for example. By 1971 approximately 20 nodes had been installed. International connections to the ARPAnet were made in 1973: to University College, London, and the Royal Radar Establishment in Norway.

In September 1973, Bob Kahn and Vint Cerf started work formulating the international standard set of rules for network communication, the Internet Protocol Suite TCP/IP, based on two protocols: Transmission Control Protocol (TCP) and Internet Protocol (IP). These were finally published in September 1981, became the standard internet protocols in January 1983, and are still used today.

The internet was opened up to commercial networks, such as CompuServe and America OnLine (AOL), in 1991, and continues to grow. The number of computers on the internet reached a million in 1992. At the time of writing, more than 1.5 billion people worldwide use the internet.

# Email and domains

In October 1963, computer-consulting company Bolt, Beranek and Newman (BBN) published a paper demonstrating that users could communicate remotely with computers using ordinary telephone lines. BBN had already patented the modem earlier that year.

In 1971, Ray Tomlinson of BBN sent the first-ever network email, over two computers connected by ARPAnet: he is also responsible for the @ sign in an email address. By the second year of ARPAnet's operation, the main traffic was news and personal messages. Researchers were using the network not only to collaborate on projects and trade notes on work, but to gossip. People had their own personal user accounts on the ARPAnet computers, and their own personal addresses for electronic mail. It was not long before the invention of the mailing list, with which a message could be broadcast to anyone subscribing to a particular list.

Email addresses take the form username@site.dom, in which username is your name or a chosen nickname, site locates your ISP (Internet Service Provider), or server computer, and dom is a domain type, possibly including subdomains. These are all separated by full points.

Top-level domain types include .com for commercial organizations and .edu for educational institutions. Note that most of the sites in the .com and .edu domains are in the USA. Outside these functional domains, sites in the USA have the .us domain, with subdomains for the 50 states, each generally with a name identical to the state's postal abbreviation (note that .ca can be both California and Canada, depending on the context). Within the .uk domain, there is a .ac subdomain for academic sites and a .co domain for commercial ones. See page 18 for how to choose your own domain name and the advantages of doing this.

Email and messaging in its broadest sense now include webmail (e.g. Hotmail, Gmail), as well as Facebook and Flickr messaging and Twitter tweets.

**TIP**

**Country codes**

Each country has its own two-letter domain: Spain, for example, is .es, Germany is .de, India is .in, Austria is .at and so on (full list at www.iana.org). If your name ends with 'es', for example, you may be able to buy a domain such as alanpip.es with which to impress your friends. Some countries, however, will issue such domains only to people or organizations resident in that country, so check with your domain supplier. Other unusual country domains have been appropriated by particular industries or trades, for example domains ending .tv for Tuvalu (a Polynesian island), are popular with companies in the television industry.

# Newsgroups

Usenet (Unix User Network) was established in 1979 – long before the World Wide Web appeared – between Duke University and the University of North Carolina for the exchanging of news and views. The original programs were written by graduate student Steve Bellovin. These were then rewritten and extended by Steve Daniel and Tom Truscott.

Usenet is an example of a client–server architecture. You (the client) connect to a machine (the server) where the Usenet postings are stored. You can look at the headings of postings in the newsgroups of interest, and then request the full text of a particular posting (message or article) to be forwarded to a newsreader program on your machine. You may then read or store the article, reply directly to the poster via email, or post a follow-up article (starting or joining a 'thread'). You can also initiate a new subject heading with a new posting. The program keeps track of which articles you have already read.

At the time of writing, there were more than 100,000 different newsgroups, many of them inactive, covering everything from keeping fish (rec.aquaria.freshwater.goldfish) to font design (comp.fonts). They have largely been superseded by forums on the World Wide Web (see below), which share many of the attributes of newsgroups, such as topics and threads, but are mostly overseen by a moderator, and you may need to register and join before you can participate in discussions.

## Netiquette

Network etiquette, or netiquette, is something that a newbie (new user) will come across sooner or later. Newbies are encouraged to lurk for a while (a lurker is someone who reads but never posts) and to consult the newsgroup's FAQ (Frequently Asked Questions) list before posting for the first time.

Postings that are off-topic often elicit a flaming, or bashing. Cross-posting (posting the same message to numerous groups) is particularly frowned upon, but real venom is reserved for spamming (from the Monty Python 'Spam' song in the sketch of the same name). Spam initially described a carelessly inappropriate message or advertisement posted to many different groups or individuals, and is now a general term for unwanted or malicious mass-marketing. Messages set all in capitals (interpreted as 'shouting') or with over-long signatures (especially ones containing so-called ASCII art – pictures made up of text characters) are discouraged, but it is considered very bad form to criticize a poster's poor grammar or spelling. The latest versions of email and news-reading programs have useful 'kill files' and spam filters, which weed out unwanted messages.

# The World Wide Web (WWW)

While a consultant for CERN (the European Laboratory for Particle Physics) in 1980, Tim Berners-Lee wrote a hypertext-based program called 'Enquire-Within-Upon-Everything'. In 1990, he coined the name World Wide Web (WWW) and, with Robert Cailliau as co-author, he developed the first WWW program. In 1993, CERN placed this software in the public domain.

That same year, a group of graduate students from the University of Illinois at Champaign-Urbana developed Mosaic, a software package that used the WWW protocol. Mosaic was a major factor in the explosion of business interest on the internet, because it made the internet accessible to inexperienced users. Many other browsers have evolved since Mosaic's development, including its direct descendant Mozilla Firefox and Microsoft's Internet Explorer.

The World Wide Web is a huge collection of interconnected pages. Many sites encourage or require you to register (giving them valuable marketing information). Your ISP or college may provide you with disk space on their server for a home page and there are many sites around the world that offer free space. These can be used as test areas to develop your web design skills.

The WWW is based on a client–server model where the client (your browser) communicates with the servers (the sites storing the web pages you want to view) using mainly HTTP (Hypertext Transport Protocol). HTML (Hypertext Markup Language) is used to create and communicate the page. The address of a page, or its URL (Uniform Resource Locator), is generally of the form: http://www.yourisp.com/username/index.html.

Technically, the 'www' part of the URL is a subdomain, and as such could be anything you choose: 'www1' and 'www2', for example, are used by large organizations to share traffic among different servers. The 'www' at present distinguishes a web address from, say, an FTP address (see page 17), but is largely redundant and you will see more and more websites abandoning it in the future. Try typing in your URL without the 'www' and it will probably work just as well.

## Web standards

What are standards and why are they important? Without standard weights and measurements everyday life would be chaos and the mass-production of goods impossible. Time was standardized when the users of railways demanded accurate timetables. So it is with web standards – they ensure everyone is singing from the same hymn sheet.

## Abbreviations and emoticons

Because of the need to conserve bandwidth, and for speed of typing, many abbreviations are in common use. Here are a few you may encounter:

# BTW
by the way

# FYI
for your information

# IMHO
in my humble opinion

# LOL
laugh out loud

# RT*M
read the * manual (clean version!)

And because gestures or inflections of speech are impossible on the net, symbols made from text characters, called emoticons or smileys, have evolved. These are particularly useful to avoid causing offence – your harmless joke may be taken literally, but a ;-) smiley makes everything okay! The most common are opposite (turn your head 90 degrees to the left).

# Designing for the World Wide Web

There are two kinds of standards: de facto standards, which are introduced by commercial companies or research organizations and eventually become accepted by the community – PDF (Portable Document Format) is an example; and standards established by international committees of experts and interested parties. In web design that means the W3C (World Wide Web Consortium) founded by Tim Berners-Lee in 1994 and based jointly at MIT and other locations around the world. The W3C doesn't actually invent the standards – the technical specifications for various developments come from many different sources and the W3C has the role of endorsing the best of them. Recommendations are discussed and after a lengthy process become published standards.

When a website is said to comply with web standards, it means that the site or page has valid HTML, CSS and JavaScript, according to the published standard, and that this can be tested by the W3C's validation services. Commercial companies such as Adobe often develop programs ahead of standards and thus code produced by proprietary software such as Adobe's web design program Dreamweaver may not be totally standard. The standards committees are forever playing catch-up with commercial developments and this is something everyone has learned to live with.

The World Wide Web is a wonderful opportunity for the graphic designer, but it does have some curious challenges. For a start, until recently you did not have a great deal of control over how your designs and layouts would be seen. It is only possible to specify fonts that the user already has installed on their computer, and you can be reasonably certain only that they will have a subset of the most common fonts (see p90). You also have little control over what size they will be viewed at or the measure used. You have to accept that your design is going to appear differently on different browsers and on different machines (for an example of fluid design that works with these variables see Fig **1.3**.) On the upside, some designers find these constraints liberating, plus you don't have to worry about the resolution and format of images (everything is 72dpi) or about print production. Moreover, since the RGB (red, green, blue) colour model is used, which has a bigger gamut than CMYK (cyan, magenta, yellow, key or black) used in print, you can choose from more colours. The web is in many ways an ideal publishing medium: it is inexpensive (almost free), global, instantaneous, and, despite what was said earlier, extremely versatile.

So what is there left for the designer to do? Basically what all graphic designers do all the time: communicate the client's message in the most effective way; make it easy for the user to navigate around the site; and make the pages distinctive, attractive, eye-catching and entertaining. The web is a great leveller – college students and graduates have (almost) exactly the same tools available to them as the most prestigious design groups working for the largest multinationals.

Perhaps the biggest difference between designing for print and designing for the web is that the layouts for a book or magazine are, broadly speaking, designed in a linear fashion: readers are expected to start at the beginning and work their way through to the end. In interactive media such as the WWW, the reader is encouraged to leap from one hot link to another, so the organization of pages is important. The reader may enter any page in your site from an outside link, so every page must be self-contained with all the navigational aids necessary to help them carry on surfing. An initial concept plan with flowcharts and maybe a storyboard is essential. WWW designers need directorial skills too – with sound and animation available, you may well be asked to coordinate the efforts of a whole team of other professionals.

**1.3** Norwegian designers Commando Group use a fluid design for their website – when you increase the window size, the content moves to fill the space

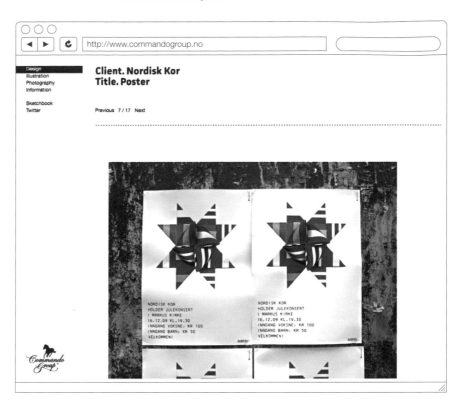

# Hosts and hosting

As mentioned earlier, the websites you create have to 'live' somewhere. It might be possible to configure your home computer to become a server, but it would have to be connected to the internet 24 hours a day. Your service provider would probably not allow it (or charge you a lot for the privilege) and, in any case, to host a domain (see page 18) you would need to run at least two servers. It is far easier – and cheaper – to use a third-party hosting service. Your ISP, the company you connect to the internet through, probably allocates you some disk space for personal use, and this is fine for a home page or a simple non-commercial site. But if you suddenly become a success and start getting lots of hits, with your site starting to use more of their bandwidth to cope, they will soon be contacting you for more money.

One of the earliest third-party hosting services was GeoCities, a Utopian attempt to set up an online community. Founded by David Bohnett and John Rezner in 1994 as Beverly Hills Internet, it was taken over by Yahoo! in 1999 and closed in 2009. GeoCities was organized thematically into 'neighbourhoods': for example, computer-related sites were located in Silicon Valley, entertainment sites were assigned to Hollywood, and artists and writers lived in SoHo. The idea was that neighbouring homesteaders would interact with each other, providing a virtual support and networking community. It was ahead of its time, anticipating the interactive nature of Web 2.0, and in 1999, at the peak of the dot-com boom, GeoCities was the third most-visited website on the WWW. But being a free service, it failed to make any money for its new owners, and Yahoo! has since been encouraging GeoCities users to migrate to its paid hosting service.

However, there are still numerous free hosting services, for example, www.110mb.com and www.freevirtualservers.com (Fig **1.4**). The reason for choosing these particular examples is because they offer something called SSI (Server Side Includes), which we will be looking at in Chapter 6 (see page 134). Make sure that any hosting service you decide to use also offers FTP access (see opposite) and gives you the amount of space, bandwidth and reliability you need – you may have to make small one-off payments or upgrade to a monthly paid contract to get all the features you require. Some free hosts will put advertisements on your site, or ask that you purchase a domain from them (see page 18).

One downside of using free hosting is that they are sometimes used to host illegal pornography and other criminal sites. When certain ISPs detect this is happening, they may blacklist the IP (Internet Protocol) address of that part of the

**1.4** There are many 'free' hosting and domain sites on the internet, but, like low-cost airlines, they may start off being free but to become functional their one-off fees and upgrade subscriptions can begin to add up

host's server that you may be sharing with the criminals – every website has a numerical address of the form 174.142.109.139 – and your site will go down (disappear from view) until the host weeds out and expels the perpetrators, and the ISP deems the host is safe enough to allow its customers to see.

# FTP: Uploading and downloading

When you have finished designing your website, you will need to transfer it from your computer to the host's server. Although most free hosting services provide a browser-based form-style system to do this, you might only be allowed to upload files one by one, which can become very tedious and time-consuming. FTP (File Transfer Protocol) is a long-established means of transferring files between computers and its most obvious use is to upload your files to the host server.

FTP has other uses too. There are many sites around the internet from which users can download programs, documents and images. Mirror sites keep copies of the files from the main sites, and if there is one geographically closer to you, it may well be faster and more responsive than the main site. You may also wish to upload large files to a client's computer – several print-resolution images, for example – and large email attachments can easily exceed the capacity of someone's inbox. Most web design programs, such as Dreamweaver, have built-in FTP; Apple's OS also has FTP available. There are also standalone FTP programs, such as Transmit and Fetch (Fig **1.5**).

Programs such as Transmit do one simple job well, showing two columns of files: 'your stuff' (corresponding to what is on your hard drive) and 'their stuff' (corresponding to what is on the host's server). To upload files, connect to the hosting server using the address and password supplied (see page 18), and simply drag and drop files from your stuff to their stuff; to download files, simply drag and drop files from their stuff to your stuff. The log-in details for different hosts are stored as a list of favourites.

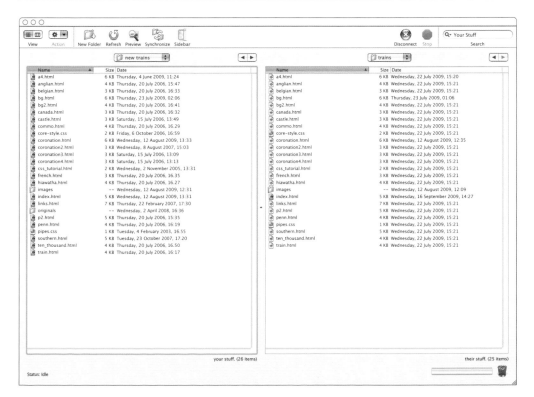

**1.5** An FTP (File Transfer Protocol) program such as Transmit focuses on one task, uploading and downloading files from your computer to others. Its main use is to upload your website files to a host's server

# Domains

So, let's take the plunge and open an imaginary account for a photographer with www.freevirtualservers.com. After the usual form-filling and choosing of passwords (if you write them down keep them in a safe but secret place) we discover that there is a small one-off set-up fee, and that they require you to buy a domain from them. We were going to buy a domain anyway, so after checking with them that janedoephotography.co.uk is available, we pay for two years. You can also check the availability of domains on www.who.is, where we found that www.janedoephotography.com is already taken (Fig **1.6**).

From their welcome email we receive the settings we need to put into the FTP program, which are as follows:

**Server address: ftp.janedoephotography.co.uk**
**(or 67.18.242.98)**
**FTP username: t15jane**
**FTP password: ********
**Starting directory: /public_html**

However, until we reach the end of Chapter 2, we do not yet have a website to upload, so will leave it there for now.

Domains ending in .co.uk (i.e. UK-based companies) and other .uk domains are looked after by an organization called Nominet. This private, not-for-profit membership company was founded in 1996 after its predecessor, a voluntary 'Naming Committee', was unable to cope with demand. Customers registering a domain, however, do not normally approach Nominet directly, but apply via a 'registrar' such as www. freevirtualservers.com. Once registered you will be asked by Nominet to confirm your details and will later receive a Registration Certificate.

In the United States, domains ending in .com and other top-level domains were registered exclusively with Network Solutions, Inc. (later taken over by VeriSign) until 1997 when monopoly legislation forced them to reduce their 'excessive' fees and open up registration to competition. Thus, the difference between 'wholesale' and 'retail' registrar companies is not as clear-cut as it is in the UK. Overseeing these companies is an organization called ICANN (Internet Corporation for Assigned Names and Numbers). The leading ICANN-accredited registrar is Go Daddy, followed by eNom, Tucows (also known for its website directory of shareware) and Australian company Melbourne IT.

Although it is convenient to buy both web hosting and domain hosting from the same vendor, it is often safer to use two separate companies, to avoid hidden costs if at a future date you decided to move the website and/or domain to another hosting company. Using a hosting service without

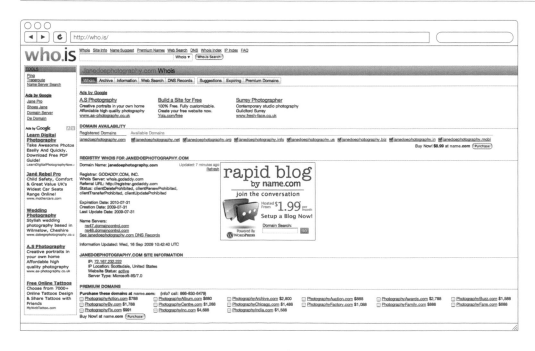

**1.6** Who.is can be used to check whether a domain is still available to buy – it also gives details of who owns a particular domain

having to buy a domain from it means you can store several websites using the same hosting account, all in separate folders on the server.

For example, you might set up a free hosting account with www.freewebhostingarea.com and the address of your website would be http://janedoephotography.ueuo.com. This may be good enough for you to start with, but you then might buy a better domain from Go Daddy or Freeparking, such as janedoephotography.net (be aware that all obvious straightforward domains, such as jane-doe.com, will probably already have been snapped up). Domain names can include only letters and numbers, plus hyphens – no spaces or fancy characters allowed. So try a few combinations, until you find one that works for you. For example, at the time of writing this, jane-doe-photography.com is still available.

## Linking to your website

Once you have registered the domain, you can link it to your website in one of two different ways. The first is called web forwarding.

After logging on, I navigate to My Domains>Maintain a Domain, then click on Edit Domain Name Properties. You will see that the domain is being redirected to the home page's 'real' address, for example from http://www.belengomez.com/ to http://homepage.ntlworld.com/urbantree/belen-gomez/ index.html, where the website is hosted. A user typing www. belengomez.com into a browser, or finding it via a search engine, will be unaware that a redirection has taken place. If you decide to change hosts, all you need do is change the address in the Use Web Forwarding box. This technique also works with email: redirect your mail to your domain – for example info@belengomez.com – and your mail will always find you – see the tip box on page 21.

One disadvantage of simple web forwarding is that your actual website is 'masked' in a frameset that can confuse the search engines, hence there are fields available for adding description and keyword meta-tags. You can see the code for these frames if you View Source in the browser (Fig **1.7**). For better control, we can use the Manage Your Own DNS Zone File section (Fig **1.8**). Here we need to enter the IP address of the new web server (which you must find out from your new host), of the form 72.1.201.156, plus maybe the names of their primary and secondary name servers. For example, the name servers for the web hosting company 1&1 are of the form ns59.1and1.co.uk and ns60.1and1.co.uk. Every domain must

**1.7** The disadvantage of simple web forwarding is that your website will be 'masked' by the domain host's frameset, which could confuse the search engines

http://www.uniqlo.com/uk/

HELP | NEWSLETTER | PRODUCT SEARCH
CREATE AN ACCOUNT | LOGIN | SHOPPING BAG

**UNI QLO**    MEN    WOMEN

> **WOMEN**

- **Special Collections**
  - › HEATTECH
  - › Fleece
  - › +J
  - › Ultra Light Down
  - › Cashmere
  - › Merino Cashmere
  - › Wool Outerwear
  - › Smart Casual
  - › UJ - Jeans

- › **New In**
- › **Limited Offer**
- › **Sale**

- **+J**
  - › 2010 Spring & Summer Collection
  - › 2010 Autumn & Winter Collection

- **Outerwear**
  - › Jackets
  - › Coats
  - › Blazers
  - › Down
  - › Other outerwear

- **Bottoms**
  - › UJ Jeans
  - › Jeggings
  - › Skirts
  - › Smart Trousers
  - › Casual Trousers
  - › Cropped Trousers and Shorts
  - › Other bottoms

- **Shirts**
  - › Shirts
  - › Flannel Shirts
  - › Blouses
  - › Other shirts

- **Dresses**
  - › Dresses

- **Tops and T-shirts**
  - › Long Sleeve T-shirts
  - › UT
  - › Sweats and Hoodies
  - › Fleece
  - › Other tops and T-shirts

- **Knitwear**
  - › Sweaters
  - › Cardigans
  - › Polonecks
  - › Cashmere
  - › Merino Cashmere
  - › Other knitwear

# Women's Clothing

**The Worldwide movement For Comfort And Style. UNIQLO Jeggings**     £19.99

**WOMEN'S 100% CASHMERE FROM £49.99**

**Pure Cashmere**

MADE FROM 100% PURE CASHMERE, THESE HIGH QUALITY SWEATERS ARE A SEASONAL ESSENTIAL

**WOMEN'S MERINO CASHMERE FROM £24.99**

**Merino Cashmere**

WOMEN'S MERINO CASHMERE - A SEASONAL WARDROBE ESSENTIAL

**WOMEN'S SUPER LIGHT WOOL JACKET FROM £59.99**

**Wool Outerwear**

INCREDIBLY LIGHT AND WARM. UNIQLO'S WOOL OUTERWEAR

**WOMEN'S DOWN JACKET FROM £59.99**

**Down Jacket**

Authentic down with a resilient fiber that moisturises the wearer's skin.

**WOMEN'S BOYFRIEND JEANS £29.99**

**Boyfriend Jeans**

WOMEN'S BOYFRIEND JEANS FROM JUST £29.99

**WOMEN'S SMART CASUAL JACKET STYLE FROM £49.99**

**Smart Casual**

CREATE A SMART CASUAL LOOK

LIMTED OFFER

**WOMEN'S FLANNEL SHIRTS £19.99**

**Flannel Shirts**

BETTER THAN EVER . NOW WITH A GREATER VARIETY OF CHECK PATTERNS, DESIGN DETAILS AND DRESSES

**HEATTECH TECHNOLOGY WEAR**

HEATTECH is the smart way to stay warm and comfortable in cold weather. Developed by UNIQLO and Toray Industries, the world's leading fiber maker, this revolutionary material keeps you warm by retaining body heat. Now you can dress more luxuriously in cold weather by taking advantage of this sheer, innovative fashion technology from Japan. Open up exciting possibilities. Give yourself a fashion edge with HEATTECH.

**WOMEN**

**FROM £6.99**

**Heattech**

HEAT-GENERATING. HEAT-RETAINING. WARMING BY WEARING HEATTECH. UNIQLO'S FAVOURITE WINTER WARMER IS BACK!

**1.8** With DNS control, the address that appears in the address bar of the browser is that of your domain and nobody is the wiser as to where it really resides. Large multinational stores like Uniqlo, however, are more likely to have their own real or virtual servers

# Web design for graphic designers

exist on at least two different servers (known as primary and secondary). With this method, the individual addresses of each page of the website using the better domain will appear in the address bar of the browser.

Larger companies and organizations are more likely to have their own servers, or to rent virtual servers from a third-party host, so they will have fewer problems displaying the domain name as they would like it. Virtual servers exist in their own enclosed space within a bigger server, bridging the gap between inexpensive or free shared web hosting, as described earlier, and much more expensive dedicated servers that only a multinational could afford.

**Use your domain email address**

It is surprising how many people buy a domain for their website but never get round to using the email that comes with it. Using your domain for email a) looks more professional than using a Hotmail, Gmail or similar account and b) means that if you change your ISP or leave college, you won't have to inform all your friends and contacts that you have a new email address. If you have bought a domain, such as janedoephotography.co.uk, then your email can be anything@ janedoephotography.co.uk, where anything means anything. Most people would choose info@janedoephotography.co.uk, or a more personal jane@janedoephotography.co.uk. Just go into the Manage Domains part of your domain host's site and set the email forwarding to your current 'real' email address. As with a PO Box number, the host forwards to your address and if you later move, you just set it to your new address and your email stays the same.

So far, we have not talked about design. Graphic designers used to working in print will notice a few challenges when moving to web design. When you design a brochure, for example, you can be sure that every one of them will look the same once printed. The fonts will be the ones you chose, in the sizes you specified, and all the elements will be in the positions you placed them. In web design, you have less control. The fonts will be whatever the end-user has installed on their computer, although there are methods to expand the range of fonts available (see Chapter 4). The layout might be different depending on the size of the screen, the browser used, or whether the computer is a Mac or a PC.

That's the bad news. The good news is that the web has many advantages over print. It is instant, so you can publish as soon as everything is in place. And if you make a mistake, you will not have to pay for a new print-run – corrections can be made quickly and uploaded at any time. All the images are in RGB, which has a bigger gamut than CMYK, so will be more faithful to your vision, and at 72dpi, they will be much smaller files than print-resolution pictures. But best of all, the text can be made interactive, by adding hot links to other pages or sites, and there is the possibility of adding sound and movies to the mix. Your customers worldwide will be able to give feedback, via email or comments on blog entries – and you can sell and distribute your merchandise through an e-shop. There is no expensive equipment to buy or hire either.

Designers previously had to resort to tricks and workarounds to get the results they wanted (and to some extent, they still do). The web was invented by scientists to share academic knowledge, and presentation was not a big priority. However, with the advent of CSS (Cascading Style Sheets: see Chapter 3) there is now a great toolbox that designers can use to realize their designs. Before, to have control over, say, which fonts appeared, text would have to be turned into pictures, which meant that files were bigger and also, with no real text, virtually invisible to the search engines. Or some designers would use programs such as Adobe Director, more suited to audio-visual applications like CD-ROMs or DVDs, to produce what were effectively online slide shows. Adobe Flash (see Chapter 6), a program similar in feel to Director but more geared towards animated websites, is still used to achieve similar interactivity, but the end-user has to download a plug-in to view it. Using Director, which also required downloading a ShockWave plug-in, was disastrous for any form of accessibility, such as talking websites for visually impaired people. It also made printing off pages a problem.

Layout was another challenge. Apart from the strategy of turning page layouts into large pictures containing images and text, the limitations of web design could be overcome by using framesets (now largely out of fashion, except for some special cases that will be discussed later) or tables, spaced out using invisible transparent image files, usually GIFs. Dreamweaver worked this way until recent versions embraced CSS.

## Successful design

To make a website that is so appealing and exciting that viewers will want to return to it over and over again is the Holy Grail of web design. Of course, the content – the pictures and words – is paramount, but how it is presented is also vitally important. How you achieve the perfect match of content and presentation is down to the fundamentals discussed throughout this book: layout, colour schemes, typography and usability.

Although it may not be spelt out explicitly, the box model of layout used by CSS harks back to the Swiss International style of the 1960s, with its grid-based designs. There is something pleasing about the edges of images and blocks of text lining up along the lines of an underlying grid, and the consistency it commits you to is also a positive discipline. Design theory books talk about the Golden Section and the Rule of Thirds when laying out material in a harmonious way. In web design this is not so easy – the canvas you have to work on is dictated by the shapes and sizes of users' computer screens, or their mobile device – and with fluid design, their relative sizes and positions can also change as a user resizes a browser window.

The best you can do is place the important elements above the 'fold' in the top of the screen area. Within that space, you can size text areas and images in proportion to one another. Keep out any clutter, especially fussy background images, and restrict yourself to just one or two fonts (Fig **1.9**). A consistent image width can also prevent a jarring change of layout as users move from page to page.

Usability guru Steve Grug implores web designers: 'Don't make me think!' He says that the test of a good website is that it should be self-evident, obvious, self-explanatory. 'I should be able to "get it" – what it is and how to use it – without expending any effort thinking about it.' So be nice to your public and don't make them work too hard.

Making a design self-evident is not that difficult, but is ignored at your peril. Simple, clear navigation that uses straightforward names for links and headings, and concise text

**1.9** Graphic Safari is an example of a simple, uncluttered Blogger-powered blog that can be accessed from the main menu of the Milan-based design studio La Tigre (latigre.net) and is used to showcase a range of the studio's latest projects

that gets to the point straight away, may seem obvious but it is surprising how many designers seem to want to tease their audience, obfuscating content and hiding menus. People with time on their hands might appreciate the entertainment factor, but in reality most are on the web to obtain information quickly and may not 'get' your subtle concept.

Subtlety in the right context can be a good thing, however. Your target audience is a factor when choosing colour schemes. Says Leatrice Eiseman in Hillman Curtis's excellent and inspiring book *MTIV* ('Making the Invisible Visible'): 'What am I trying to sell to the viewer? Should I shout to gain their attention, or will a more subtle approach be more in tune with the intended message?' Good designers ask questions like this and try to put themselves in the place of the intended user. Put yourself in your followers' shoes and ponder what you can add to their lives. What works for an emo youth audience might be inappropriate for a high street bank – or maybe not? Rules, once learnt, can always be broken.

# Browser compatibility

A big bugbear that remains is browser compatibility. A browser, such as Safari or Firefox, comes between your website and the end-user. It translates and interprets your website, parsing the code, to produce a formatted web page. Because proprietary browsers are in competition with each other, all wanting to add features that the others don't have, they will all interpret your designs slightly differently. And those small differences could make or break your design. Older versions of Internet Explorer, for example, often cause difficulties, and workarounds have to be devised to cater for them. Because there are many end-users out there who do not upgrade to the latest versions of software, a good rule of thumb is to design your sites to work on the last two versions of major browsers. If you do not have all the browsers installed on your computer, or both a Mac and PC to test on, websites such as browsershots.org are useful (Fig **1.10**).

If your cutting-edge website renders improperly or not at all, your reputation will suffer, and visitors and potential customers will leave your site and may never return. A professional-looking site should make visitors feel comfortable, so they will linger longer, browse more pages – and be more likely to purchase the client's products and use your services.

Tough decisions have to be made: do you try to make your designs cross-browser, i.e. working in every single browser ever invented? Or multi-browser, i.e. working with the majority of modern browsers? In any case your design should be failsafe, so that if it does fail in a given browser, the end-user can still at least access the content in a structured way.

Modern methodologies of web design such as CSS aim to allow that anyway, by separating the content from its appearance. The ambition is to achieve 'elegant degradation' (also known as fail-safe) – the term comes from engineering, where a machine or system is designed to break down slowly rather than catastrophically. In web design, the layout and CSS should be such that if an older browser or user's computer doesn't support a particular tag or font, then the website will still make sense. It won't look as good, but the content will all be available, in the right order.

CSS is now recommended by the major supervisory bodies and organizations involved with the World Wide Web. It has great benefits with the newer browsers, as well as for mobile phones, iPods and netbooks. These generally have small touch screens, so websites viewed on them need to be both legible and useable. These considerations will be explored in greater detail later in the book.

CSS for layout will be discussed in Chapter 3, but first we shall look at the basics of HTML coding.

**1.10** Browser compatibility can be checked in a website such as browsershots.org – using the new features of the latest browsers can play havoc with older browsers, which may not be able to render the website at all

menu ▶

**Zeitguised**
**Boolean Taxidermy**
- - - - - - - - - - - - - - - -
The "Boolean Taxidermy" is a personal project. Progressing one of Zeitguised main design concepts, the boolean camera - making use of 3D CG space in a uniquely digital way.

Click to open

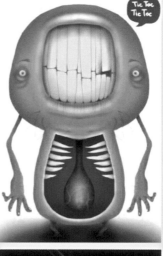

Tic Toc Tic Toc

minilogue

c

Hypnotized
Giant, hairy super furry story

POLICE

Source of http://www.blinkart.co.uk/

```
<!DOCTYPE HTML PUBLIC "-//W3C//DTD HTML 4.01 Transitional//EN" "http://www.w3.org/TR/html4/loose.dtd">
<html xmlns="http://www.w3.org/1999/xhtml">
<head>
<meta http-equiv="Content-Type" content="text/html; charset=iso-8859-1"/>
<meta name="viewport" content="width=1024, user-scalable=no" />
<title>Blinkart</title>
<script type="text/javascript" src="http://ajax.googleapis.com/ajax/libs/jquery/1.4.2/jquery.min.js"></script>
<script type="text/javascript" src="/js2/swfobject.js"></script>
<script src="/js2/jquery.swfobject.1-0-5.min.js" type="text/javascript" charset="utf-8"></script>
<link rel="stylesheet" type="text/css" href="http://yui.yahooapis.com/2.8.1/build/reset/reset-min.css">
<link rel="stylesheet" type="text/css" href="/css/blinkstyle.css">
<script>

function removeFlash(){
//alert ('removeFlash called');
$('#movieHolderInside').html('');
}

function insertLogo(swfFile, swfWidth, swfHeight, swfWhere, swfCount, swfBG, swfMovie, swfControls){
removeFlash();

var flashvars = {
showControls: swfControls,
movieWidth: swfWidth,
movieHeight: swfHeight,
movieFile: swfMovie
};
var params = {};
params.scale = "noscale";
params.wmode = "window"; //window //transparent

params.bgcolor = swfBG;
params.allowfullscreen = "true";
params.allowscriptaccess = "true";
var attributes = {};
attributes.id = "holder" + swfWhere;

swfobject.embedSWF(swfFile, swfWhere, swfWidth, swfHeight, "8.0.0", "", flashvars, params, attributes);

}
```

# 2

# Code

In this age of Web 2.0 – Facebook, YouTube, Twitter, MySpace – websites have become increasingly sophisticated. The code behind such sites as these is daunting – to see what it looks like, choose View Source from your browser's menu (Fig **2.1**). You may be surprised, then, to find that it is possible to create a simple website completely by hand, using only a text editor. Of course, it is also possible to walk coast-to-coast across the USA, but you may wish to do it only once! Similarly, it is a valuable exercise to try writing code by hand, without software help, but I promise you won't need to do it ever again.

**2.1** The great thing about web design is that you can see how websites are created by looking at View Source in your browser. However, for some sites code can look dauntingly complicated, as in this CSS-, Flash- and JavaScript-powered website for London-based Blinkart

# Getting started in HTML

The code or programming language we are going to use here is HTML (Hypertext Markup Language), or more strictly speaking, XHTML (Extensible Hypertext Markup Language), which became W3C (World Wide Web Consortium)-recommended in 2000. A website that conforms to an XHTML specification is said to be valid. Any document can be checked for validity with the W3C Markup Validation Service. One of the differences between HTML and XHTML is that the latter is case-sensitive: tags in XHTML should always be lower case. Other differences, such as the closing of 'empty' tags, will be mentioned as we encounter them. Be aware also that to write validating code you must make sure you use the terms and syntax exactly as they are defined – even if you are a French-speaker writing code for a French website – and note the American-English spelling of the words 'color' and 'center'.

There are several very good standalone wysiwyg ('what you see is what you get') web design programs, such as Dreamweaver, that claim that you can design web pages without ever having to come into contact with HTML code – after all, you don't need to be able to program in PostScript to lay out pages in QuarkXPress or InDesign. In practice, however, it helps to have a working knowledge of HTML to be able to troubleshoot the code if something peculiar happens in your design. Dreamweaver can toggle between the layout and code, or show them both in one window. Some programs never allow you to look at the code. One of these is Freeway, for the Mac, which has a QuarkXPress feel to it, with a pasteboard, master pages and text boxes. It can import Photoshop images and convert them to GIFs or JPEGs (more later). And when you have finished, the program 'compiles' and exports (and FTPs) the entire website.

Most websites are now so complex that it would not be economical to write the code by hand, and programs such as Dreamweaver are essential if you are working with free-form layouts using tables and frames, with mouse rollovers and other JavaScript effects, or developing database-driven e-commerce sites. Nevertheless, a knowledge of basic HTML will pay dividends.

## Putting a document online

Let's say you want to put a brief profile online to attract potential clients (Fig **2.2**). You will probably already have a version as a Microsoft Word or rich text file (RTF) document. To create the code we will use a text editor such as TextEdit on a Mac or Notepad on a Windows PC. More sophisticated word-processing programs such as Word often automatically anticipate what they think you want, and the first job, if your profile is in Word,

is to strip out any curly quotes, dashes and other formatting, to replace them with the feet (') and inches (") and simple hyphens that the code will understand.

A simple web page will comprise a text document plus GIF and/or JPEG files all in the same directory (equivalent to a Mac folder), or preferably with the images in a subfolder, named 'images'. You will also need a graphics program, such as Adobe Photoshop, that can export GIF and JPEG files. And finally, you will need FTP access to your host's server – you can create the pages on your computer, but for anyone else to be able to see them they must be 'published' by uploading them.

If you examine the source code of an HTML web page, you will see that all pages have the same underlying structure. They divide into two main sections: head and body. The first (home or start) page of a website is traditionally called 'index. html' (on Windows servers, index.htm and even default.htm are also allowable), and it looks like this:

```
<html>

<head>
<title> The text that appears top of the browser window is
here.</title>
</head>

<body>
Main content is here.
</body>

</html>
```

## Tags

The words in angled brackets (the < 'less than' and > 'greater than' symbols) are called 'tags' and usually come in pairs that enclose the text affected, the closing tag being preceded by a forward slash. An important exception is the tag for line break, which is placed at the end of a line. It used to be written `<br>`, but it is now written `<br />`. The tag `<html>` surrounds the entire document to tell the browser to expect an HTML document. Strictly speaking, the document should also have a '`DOCTYPE`' declaration at the top of the document, such as `<!DOCTYPE html>`. Apart from the title, anything appearing in the `<head>` section will be invisible to the viewer. What you see in the browser window will be contained in the `<body>` section. A complete list of tags is provided on page 165.

**2.2** Simple profile pages are an effective means of communicating skills and experience. Dowling Duncan, a graphic design company with offices in both the UK and the USA, have used a WordPress-powered website to produce a clear, simple and fast compendium of news and projects

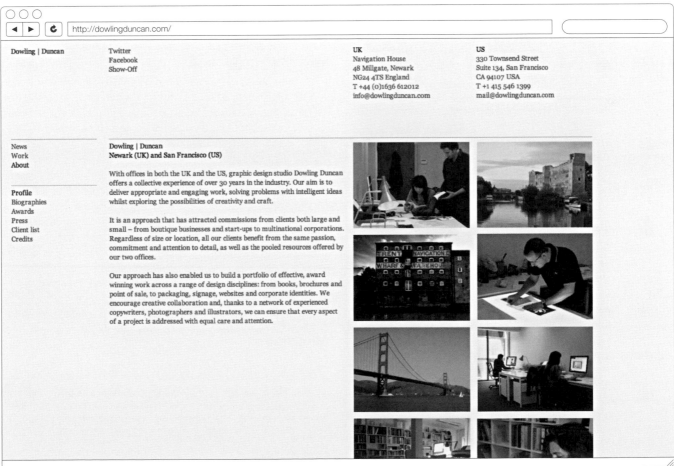

So, let's add some content. First give the page a meaningful `<title>`, one that will make sense to a search engine and will tell the viewer what it is they are looking at. Let's try 'Jane Doe Photographer'.

Here is our bare-bones 'About me' page. It could be longer, but as this is a demonstration project it will suffice.

Jane Doe Photographer

**About me**

I'm a freelance travel photographer, born in Delaware and currently based in New York. I specialize in abstracted landscapes and in architecture; my projects have taken me across Europe, Asia, and the Americas. I'm still waiting for my first invite to Australia or New Zealand!

I studied at **The New York Institute of Photography**, receiving an honorable mention in the student category from the **NY Photo Awards**. I've just been invited to take part in a group show at the **Dumbo Arts Center** next summer.

My clients include:
*Dover Post*
*Evening Tribune*
*Insight*
*Newark Post*
*Time Out New York*

Contact: jane@janedoephotographer.com

Check out my photographs on Flickr: www.flickr.com/people/ janedoephotographer

First we add `<p>` paragraph tags and `<br />` line breaks. Without these tags, all the lines of text would run into each other, creating one solid block. The browser would ignore all the line spaces and carriage returns you've carefully added to your text document to give it an attractive layout. So, when writing your code, use as much space as you like to separate the different sections.

```
<html>

<head>
<title>Jane Doe Photographer</title>
</head>

<body>
About me

<p>I'm a freelance travel photographer, born in Delaware and
currently based in New York. I specialize in abstracted
landscapes and in architecture; my projects have taken me
across Europe, Asia, and the Americas. I'm still waiting for
my first invite to Australia or New Zealand! </p>

<p>I studied at The New York Institute of Photography,
receiving an honorable mention in the student category from
the NY Photo Awards. I've just been invited to take part in
a group show at the Dumbo Arts Center next summer.</p>

<p>My clients include:<br />
Dover Post<br />
Evening Tribune<br />
Insight<br />
Newark Post<br />
Time Out New York</p>

<p>Contact: jane@janedoephotographer.com</p>

<p>Check out my photographs on Flickr: www.flickr.com/people/
janedoephotographer</p>

</body>

</html>
```

## Headings

There are six headings in html: `h1` through `h6`. The default for an `h1` heading is 24 pt Times bold. It is best always to start with an `h1` heading, then `h2` and so on, and not to skip levels. If you miss off the `</h1>` end tag, the whole document will be one big heading. Headings, like all the other tags, can be customized using CSS (see Chapter 3).

## Anchors and links

The best thing about the web is that you can create hypertext 'hot links', or hyperlinks, to other parts of your page, to other pages on your site, or to other unrelated pages on any another website anywhere in the world (see the tip box below).

A link has two ends – called anchors. The link starts at the source anchor, a hot spot on your page, and points to the destination anchor, which may be any web resource – an image, a video clip, a named spot on the same page or somewhere within your website, or an external HTML document. Anchors can be either local, relative ones pointing to another text file in the same directory, or absolute ones containing the full URL (Uniform Resource Locator) of the page you want to link to. An anchor is of the form:

```
<a href="url">the hot text</a>
```

where the URL is either relative (another page on the same site, for instance second-page.html) or absolute (for instance the URL of Jane Doe's Flickr site – http://www.flickr.com/people/janedoephotographer/). The `a` stands for 'anchor' and is used in different forms that we will see later; the `href` attribute defines the link 'address'. A link to Jane Doe's email address would be written:

```
<a href="mailto:jane@janedoephotographer.com">jane@
janedoephotographer.com</a>
```

A link to Jane Doe's Flickr site would be written:

```
<a href="http://www.flickr.com/people/janedoephotographer/"
target="_blank">Flickr</a>
```

Adding the optional `target="_blank"` to the link code opens the linked site in a new browser window of its own, leaving your site still in view.

**Retaining your visitors**

Adding external links to your website is generally a good thing. If you link to someone and they link back to your site, then the search engines will give you a higher rating. But you don't want people leaving your site as soon as they have arrived, so adding the expression target="_blank" to the link code opens the linked site in a new browser window of its own, leaving your site still in view.
`<a href="http://www.external-site.com" target="_blank">An external link</a>`

## Character formatting

You can also make words **bold** or *italic*. HTML, however, has two classes of styles: logical and physical. Logical styles, such as `<strong>`, are used to tag the text according to its meaning, while physical styles, such as `<b>` for bold, are used to indicate the specific typographical appearance of the text.

Logical tags are supposed to help enforce consistency in your documents. Remember, the WWW was developed by scientists used to academic papers, not by graphic designers with their own needs. Most browsers render the `<strong>` tag in bold text. However, it is possible that a browser might display the word in bright red instead. If you want something to be displayed in, for example, bold and do not want a browser's setting to display it differently, use physical styles.

Try to be consistent about which type of style you use. Whether you tag with physical or logical styles, do so within the whole document. Here are some of the logical styles:

**`<em>` for emphasis, typically displayed in italics**
**`<strong>` for strong emphasis, typically displayed in bold**

And here are some examples of physical styles:

**`<b>` bold text**
**`<i>` italic text**
**`<tt>` typewriter text, i.e. fixed-width font, for tabular matter**

## Entity codes

Three ASCII characters – the left angle bracket (<), the right angle bracket (>), and the ampersand (&) – are 'reserved characters' and have special meanings in HTML, and therefore cannot be used 'as is' in text. To use any of these in an HTML document, you must enter their code name or number instead (each starting with & and ending with ;) thus:

`&lt;` or `&#60;` for <
`&gt;` or `&#62;` for >
`&amp;` or `&#38;` for &

These 'entities' are also known as 'escape sequences'. Other non-standard keyboard characters and maths symbols also need to be turned into code: for example, a £ sign should be written `&pound;` or `&#163;`. Unfortunately this applies to accented characters too; 'crème brûlée', for example, needs to be written `cr&egrave;me br&ucirc;l&eacute;e`. Failure to substitute this code will result in spurious characters appearing in your text when the web page is uploaded to the server and interpreted by browsers. A full list can be found at www.w3schools.com/tags/ref_entities.asp, though most text editors aimed at helping with HTML, such as BBEdit or PageSpinner, will have them available.

## Images

To add or embed an image in a web page, we use the tag `<img src="picture.gif">`, where `picture.gif` is the file name of the image, in this case a GIF file. The `img` part says 'place image here', and `src` tells the browser that the source is an image in the same directory as the text file called `picture.gif`. Better practice is to be more organized and put all the images in their own subfolder named 'images', in which case the tag would be `<img src="images/picture.gif">`. When you come to FTP your files to a host server, you must ensure that the file hierarchy is exactly the same as it is on your hard drive otherwise the web page will not be able to find the images.

　　As an image tag does not have an end tag (just like a line break), strictly it should be written `<img src="images/picture.gif" />`. But we'll keep it simple for now. It is also useful to specify the dimensions of the image, in pixels, using `<width>` and `<height>` attributes, having checked its dimensions, and resized if necessary, in Photoshop. If you do this, the browser will leave a space for the image and display any text that follows without waiting for the image to load. The `<alt>` attribute allows you to describe the image in words (a text alternative) and is a courtesy to users with a browser that does not support graphics and to visually disabled people who rely on their computer to speak the websites out loud. This text description will appear if an image cannot be loaded, and often appears if a mouse is rolled over the image.

　　Other attributes define if an image has a border. For instance, when you use an image as a link, the default is a blue rectangular border. This can look odd, particularly on images with an irregular outline, so set the border to 0. For example:

```
<img src="images/littlehampton2.jpg" width="600" height="412"
border="0" alt="East Beach Cafe" />
```

displays an image without a border. If you were using a browser such as Lynx, or had images switched off, all you would see would be the text 'East Beach Cafe'. We can also add a caption, so the code for our new, improved home page looks like this:

```
<html>

<head>
<title>Jane Doe Photographer</title>
</head>

<body>
<h1>About me</h1>

<img src="images/littlehampton2.jpg" width="600" height="412"
border="0" alt="East Beach Cafe" />

<p>East Beach Cafe, Littlehampton</p>

<p>I'm a freelance travel photographer, born in Delaware and
currently based in New York. I specialize in abstracted
landscapes and in architecture; my projects have taken me
across Europe, Asia, and the Americas. I'm still waiting for
my first invite to Australia or New Zealand!</p>

<p>I studied at <b>The New York Institute of Photography</b>,
receiving an honorable mention in the student category from
the <b>NY Photo Awards</b>. I've just been invited to take part
in a group show at the <b>Dumbo Arts Center</b> next summer.</p>

<p>My clients include:<br />
<i>Dover Post</i><br />
<i>Evening Tribune</i><br />
<i>Insight</i><br />
<i>Newark Post</i><br />
<i>Time Out New York</i></p>

<p>Contact: <a href="mailto:jane@janedoephotographer.com">
jane@janedoephotographer.com</a></p>

<p>Check out my photographs on <a href="www.flickr.com/people/
janedoephotographer" target="_blank">Flickr</a>.</p>

</body>

</html>
```

　　The resulting page (Fig **2.3**) uses browser defaults (the font is Verdana). It may not look pretty and may alarm a website purist, but it does work – try it – and it was all made by hand.

## Adding comments

To add a note in the code to be seen by programmers only, use:

```
<!--This is a comment-->
```

This will be ignored when the browser renders the page. That's enough hand-coding for now. In the next chapter we'll learn to make attractive web pages with CSS – using software to help.

## Publicizing your pages

How do you tell the world that you have a website? You can send out postcards, and add your URL to your letterheads and to the signature on your email and newsgroup postings. And you can make it easy for people searching for your site to find it!

Search engines, such as Google, use various criteria to categorize websites; you can have some influence by using `<meta>` tags within the `<head>` section of your page, thus:

```
<meta name="description"
content="Jane Doe is a freelance photographer specializing in
abstracted landscapes and architecture">
<meta name="keywords"
content="photography, photographer, landscape, abstract,
architecture, architectural">
```

This will result in a 'hit' if you type in either 'architecture' or 'architectural'. As search engine robots have become more sophisticated, there is less reliance on such keywords, especially if they are repeated in the main body text.

SEO (search engine optimization) can increase the ranking of your web page in the search results. It is not an exact science, but factors that can help your hit rate include adding keywords and phrases subtly to the text on your home page, cross-linking pages within the site, and getting friends and colleagues to link to your site – you can even link to your site from your own blog. Tweeting about your updates on Twitter can also drive traffic to your site and make it look popular.

When choosing keywords, try to think like a potential client searching for someone like you. Anyone putting 'photographer' in Google will be given thousands of choices, and it's unlikely you'll be top of the list! Someone, however, may be looking for a local photographer, so include your home town in the keywords to narrow down the list. And add all your specialities, but not too many or it won't ring true. If they are looking for you in particular, and you have an uncommon name, then they will find you quickly. With a more common name, however, you'll have more work to do. Weave the keywords into some meaningful text on your home page – simply including a long list of keywords won't fool the search engine robots.

Another good way to publicize your blog or website is to participate in online forums or inspiration sites. If you are an illustrator, for example, Illustration Friday (illustrationfriday.com) sets a topic each week for you to tackle when you have a quiet moment. It gets your work seen by your peers (and perhaps by a potential client) and offers an opportunity to add a link to your site that will help in SEO. For web designers, there is Cargo (Fig **2.4**), cargocollective.com, and there are similar sites

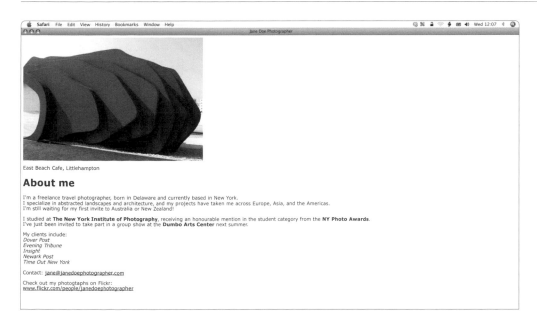

2.3 This simple web page uses all the defaults of the Safari browser: white background and blue hyperlinks, except that the default font Times has been changed to Verdana for clarity. The website was completely coded by hand using a text editor

**2.4** Cargo Collective is an experimental web publishing and content-management system showcasing creatives such as website designers, illustrators and artists, offering a quick way to gain a web presence and publicize your content. See also p145

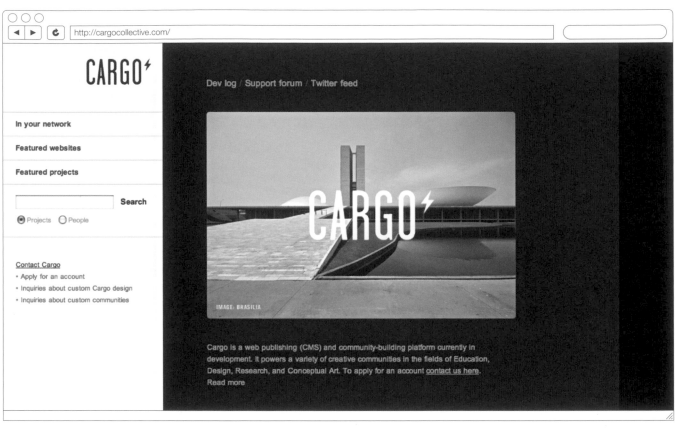

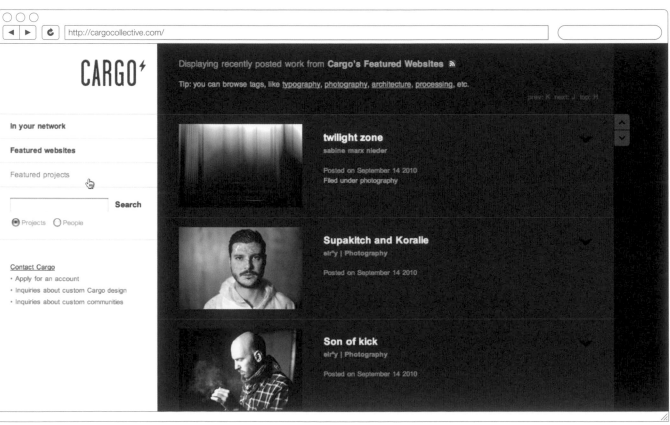

for photographers – some are text based, others give you an opportunity to upload work. Flickr groups also have discussion sections and most professional organizations will have a forum for members, and sometimes even non-members, to chat in about common concerns. The more you actively contribute to discussions on forums and mailing lists, the more exposure your work – and your website address – will receive.

## Testing your pages

Web pages are cheap and fast to produce and the temptation is to publish as soon as you possibly can. After all, if there are mistakes, they can soon be rectified and the original files at the server overwritten. Nonetheless, it is still good practice to test, test, and then test again.

You can view your emerging pages on a browser such as Firefox without going online, and this should be the first step. Then try viewing your pages on another browser, such as Internet Explorer. Try uploading your pages to a home page site and go online to check that they still look okay and that everything works.

If you designed the pages on a Mac, find a friend with a PC and see how they look on that platform, and vice versa. A PC might have a 96dpi monitor, so your text will appear larger and your 72dpi graphic will appear smaller.

**2.5** French website Fubiz is a great place to publicize yourself and your work. It describes itself as 'a daily dose of inspiration' providing WordPress-based galleries for the various design disciplines, and a mosaic view for random browsing

# Helper applications

## Open-source software

The big drawback with commercial proprietary programs (such as Dreamweaver and Freeway, discussed below) is that you have to buy them, although if you are a student there will be educational discounts available. Note that what you are buying is a licence to use the product – you never actually own it! An alternative is to use open-source or public-domain software, which is generally available free of charge. Other inexpensive programs may be 'shareware', and will be available for a donation or nominal fee. The best example of open source is the WWW itself, which Tim Berners-Lee gave to the world.

Every proprietary program has its open-source equivalents: Microsoft Word has LibreOffice; Adobe Photoshop has Aviary and The Gimp; and Dreamweaver has Nvu and KompoZer. Many are specific to the platform, but these examples are available for Windows, Linux and Mac computers. Open source means that the source code of the software is accessible to change or improve should you wish, with the approval of the community that is developing the program collaboratively. Open-source programs are licensed just like proprietary programs, granting you the right to copy, modify and redistribute source code (or content), but possibly also imposing obligations. Of course, most users won't want to develop the program, just use it, and they can be a viable option, but most will lack many of the features of the proprietary programs, and will have limited documentation and technical support.

## Dreamweaver

Dreamweaver is most probably the first program one thinks of for designing websites. Introduced by Macromedia in 1997 for the Mac, with a Windows version launched in 1998, it was acquired by Adobe in 2005, and in 2007 replaced Adobe's own product, GoLive, in their Creative Suite CS3. Just as Photoshop dominates image-processing applications, Dreamweaver now has a near monopoly on web design. Dreamweaver is described as a hybrid wysiwyg ('what you see is what you get') and code-based web design and development application. The window in which you place such elements as text and images looks much like a browser window, but it is possible to toggle to the HTML code, or have both aspects of the design – code and appearance – visible and updateable at the same time (Fig **2.6**). It uses syntax highlighting to display the code in different colours so that text is easily distinguished from the code. Like other HTML helpers, Dreamweaver is used to edit files locally on your hard drive, which are then uploaded to the remote web server using its built-in FTP or an external FTP program.

## Creating a site in Dreamweaver

Let's go back to Jane Doe's CV. First we simply copy and paste the text of the CV into the lower part of the split Dreamweaver window (Fig **2.7**). Immediately, the code in the upper part of the window is updated, with paragraph and line-break tags automatically inserted – they are coloured blue to distinguish them from our (black) text. You will also note that Dreamweaver has inserted various `DOCTYPE` header tags at the top to indicate that this is strict XHMTL. I have saved this file as index.html and told Dreamweaver where to put it. As in the previous example it is important to have the hierarchy and structure of the folders mirror the website, as it will be on the server.

Dreamweaver can help you with the hierarchy of your site, but you first have to tell it where your root folder is. The root folder is the main folder of a website that contains the home page index.html. There is no reason why images, for example, could not also be placed in the root folder but it is more organized to have them in their own subfolder within the root folder. It is best practice to create the necessary folders and subfolders, then size your images and place them in the correct folder, before you open Dreamweaver and begin on your site. By contrast, programs such as Freeway (see page 40) will happily assemble its own set of folders and files from resources that may be scattered all about your hard drive.

To make the email link work, highlight the email address and choose Insert>Email link from the top menu. A box will appear in which to paste the address (Fig **2.8**). To make certain words bold or italic, highlight the text using the mouse and press the **B** or **I** buttons in the bottom Properties window, just like you do in your favourite word processor. Note that in the code Dreamweaver uses the logical style tags `<strong>` and `<em>` by default. To add an `h1` heading, paste in the text, highlight it and choose Heading 1 in the Format pull-down menu (Fig **2.9**).

To insert the photograph, make sure it has been sized in Photoshop (resampled to 72dpi and to a width of 600px) and a copy placed in the images folder inside the website folder. Place the cursor where you want to position the image on the page, i.e. between the heading and the first paragraph, and choose Insert>Image from the top menu. You will be presented with a box with which to navigate to the image's location. Add the alternative text describing the image in the Image Tag

Accessibility Attributes box and press OK. The image should now appear, with size and alt text incorporated automatically. Set the border to 0 in the bottom window (Fig **2.10**) if desired.

All that remains is to add the link at the end of the CV. Highlight the text and type or paste in the URL of the website into the Link box in the bottom Properties window. Finally, set the Target to `_blank` so that the link will open in a new window (Fig **2.11**). The completed CV page can be previewed in a browser, such as Safari, to check all is well (Fig **2.12**), before being uploaded to the server by FTP and published on to the internet for the world to see.

As with most programs, there are many different ways of carrying out a particular action, including keyboard shortcuts for 'power users'. You will also note that we have only scraped the surface of Dreamweaver's functionality.

Of course, you can hide the code completely and just work in wysiwyg mode, but being able to access the code means that you can identify and sort out any problems at a glance. Try editing the code, press the Refresh button and see how the wysiwyg window has changed. As in the previous hand-crafted example, we have done no text formatting other than to make a few words bold or italic: we have relied completely on the defaults of the browser. In the next chapter we will learn how to change the layout and typography using CSS (Cascading Style Sheets).

**2.6** Adobe Dreamweaver screenshot showing it in split-screen mode, with the code in a window above the 'design' window – whichever you update is reflected in the other. You can write in wysiwyg mode, without ever seeing the code, or in full code mode, but split screen is a compromise that allows you to keep an eye on the HTML as you input content

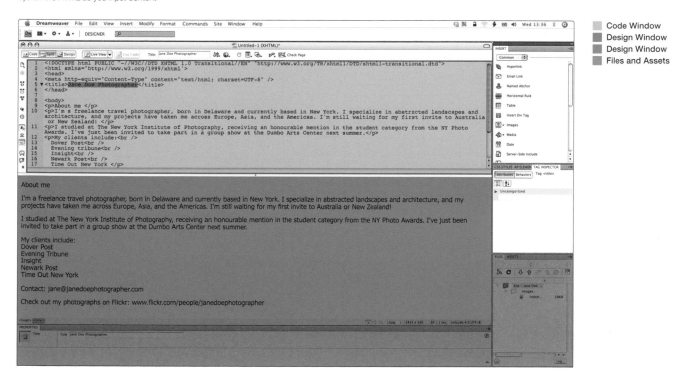

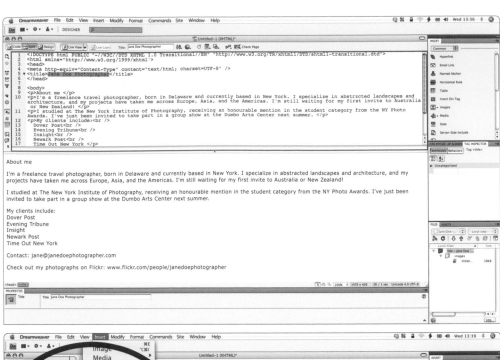

**2.7** This screenshot shows Dreamweaver in split-screen mode, with the code in the upper window and the wysiwyg content in the lower

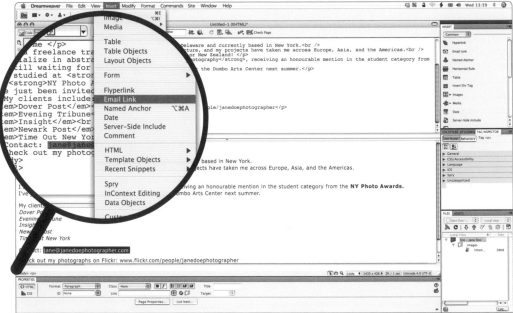

**2.8** In Dreamweaver, to make an email link, highlight the text and choose Insert>Email link from the top menu. Note that, by default, Dreamweaver uses `<strong>` and `<em>` rather than the `<b>` and `<i>` that graphic designers are more used to

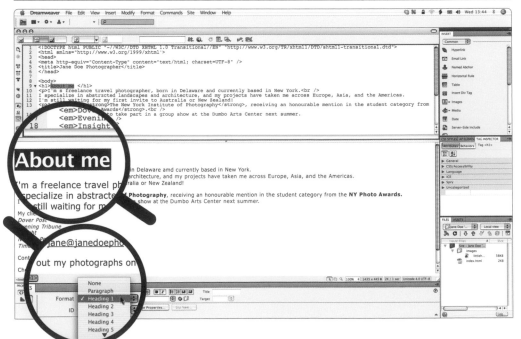

**2.9** To create headings in Dreamweaver, highlight the text and select from the pull-down menu in the Properties window, bottom of the screen

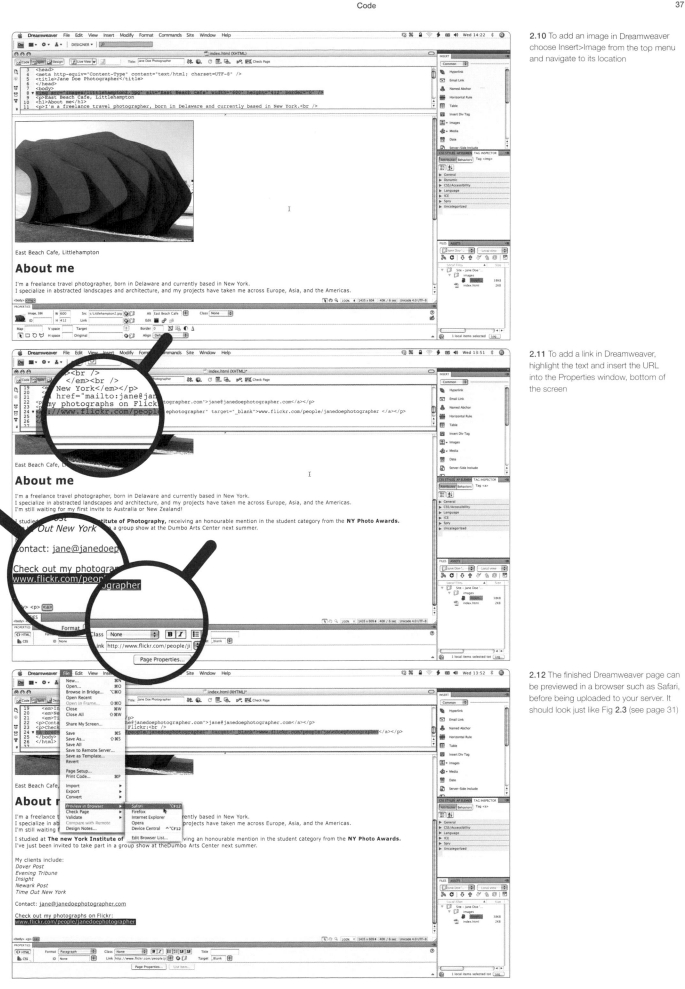

**2.10** To add an image in Dreamweaver choose Insert>Image from the top menu and navigate to its location

**2.11** To add a link in Dreamweaver, highlight the text and insert the URL into the Properties window, bottom of the screen

**2.12** The finished Dreamweaver page can be previewed in a browser such as Safari, before being uploaded to your server. It should look just like Fig **2.3** (see page 31)

**2.13** The clean, stylish lines of Spanish graphic designer Alejandro Gallego Lozano's portfolio website hide some quite complex code working behind the scenes – click View Source to take a look

**2.14** Swiss typeface design publisher MilieuGrotesque, the brainchild of graphic designers Alexander Meyer and Timo Gaessner, uses XHTML and JavaScript to produce a dynamic user experience

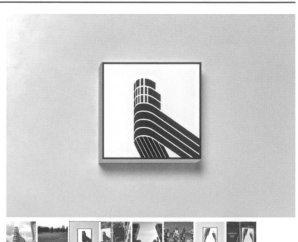

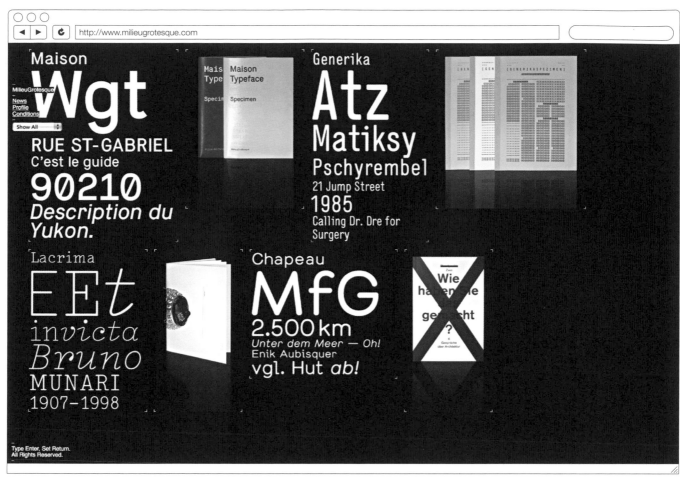

# Freeway

Freeway, from Softpress, is a Mac-only wysiwyg program that does not allow you to see the code at all. It claims to operate just like a desktop publishing application, such as InDesign or QuarkXPress, and – unlike many other wysiwyg web design applications – to produce syntactically valid code conforming to W3C standards, thus making it usable for websites where valid HTML code is obligatory.

Once more, let's begin by pasting in our text into a blank page (Fig **2.15**). First, create a text box using the HTML button above the window, as you would in QuarkXPress, and import or paste in the text we used in previous examples. It is actually quite difficult to design for browser defaults using Freeway, as it immediately asks you what colours and fonts you would like to use. Normally, using browser defaults, the page will be as wide and deep as the content dictates. Freeway, however, requires the page size to be specified.

Long pages, although often seen in blogs, are generally discouraged in web circles and should be split into many smaller ones, with links between them. The point at which the text meets the bottom of the browser window is termed the fold: anything below the fold requires scrolling using the sidebars of the window. If you do decide to put all the content on a long page rather than several shorter ones, ensure that the important information – and the navigation – is always above the fold and hence instantly available. For this exercise, all the content was contained in one page.

When we go to File>Preview in Browser, all the text appears above the fold, although the spacing needs adjusting (Fig **2.16**). The text can be tidied up using the Delete button and by introducing line breaks using Insert>New line in the top menu, or the keyboard shortcut Shift-Return. To make words bold or italic, highlight the words using the mouse and click the **B** or **I** buttons on the Inspector palette, top right. To activate the email link, highlight the address, and select Edit>Hyperlink from the top menu, choose External, mailto: from the drop-down menu and paste in the address (Fig **2.17**).

To fit in the photo, we will first make the page bigger by putting W: 700px and H: 1200px in the Inspector and moving the text box down the page. First, however, we will create another text box for our heading. Now, we are unable to use an `h1` heading unless we go into CSS, and we don't want to do that yet, so we will merely make it bold. Use the Graphic tool on the top menu to create a graphic box and import the image. Freeway remakes the image so it is not necessary to

have it already in a particular folder. So, import the image and using the contextual menu (ctrl-click on the Mac), choose Fit Box to Content – because we have already sized our image (Fig **2.18**). Alt text can be added via the Page menu. The title 'About me' is added in the Inspector, and any meta tags can be incorporated using the pop-up form found at Page>Meta Tags. Finally, we add the link to the Flickr site using the same method used for the email link: by choosing Edit>Hyperlink (Fig **2.19**). The various text and graphic boxes have here been quickly aligned by eye and using guides that can be dragged from the side rulers; to use Freeway properly, the alignment and positioning should ideally be according to a predetermined layout. We can now preview the page in Safari (other browsers are available) to check all is well (Fig **2.20**) before publishing the site via the File menu. The published 'site' can now be uploaded to your server using Freeway's built-in FTP or an external FTP program, such as Transmit.

Although Freeway keeps you well insulated from the code, we can take a peek at it using another helper program, which we will encounter in the next section, PageSpinner (Fig **2.21**). You will notice that it is considerably more complex than in earlier examples and has introduced CSS elements almost against our will – all that material in the head and tags such as `<span class="style1">` in the body. This is no bad thing, so long as the code complies with standards. Quite sophisticated websites, incorporating JavaScript actions (see Chapter 6), can be created quickly using Freeway, and if you really don't want to know, you need never see the code that makes them work (Figs **2.22** and **2.23**).

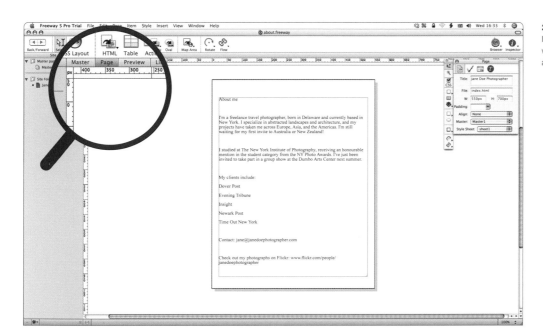

**2.15** Freeway acts in a similar way to InDesign or QuarkXPress – it is completely wysiwyg, using text and image boxes – and no code to be seen

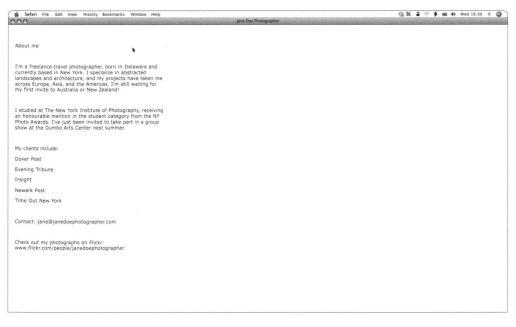

**2.16** A Safari preview of the Freeway document reveals that the formatting of the text needs some tweaking. Green guidelines dragged from the side rulers allow you to align boxes and images, see Fig **2.18**

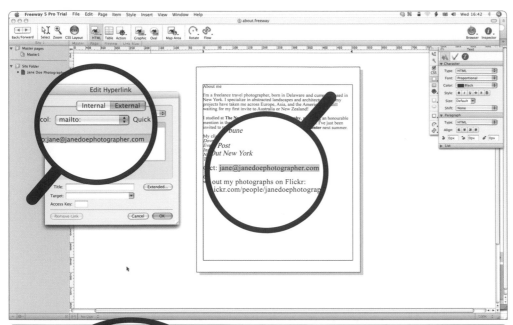

**2.17** To add an email link in Freeway, highlight the text and select Edit>Hyperlink from the top menu

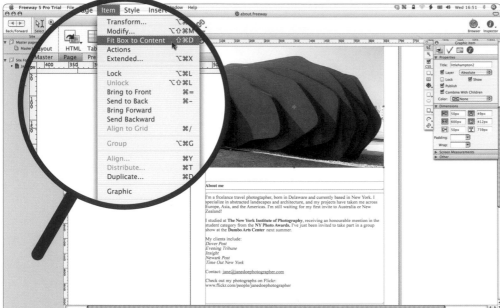

**2.18** Freeway reformats images on the fly, so there is little need to organize them first into folders

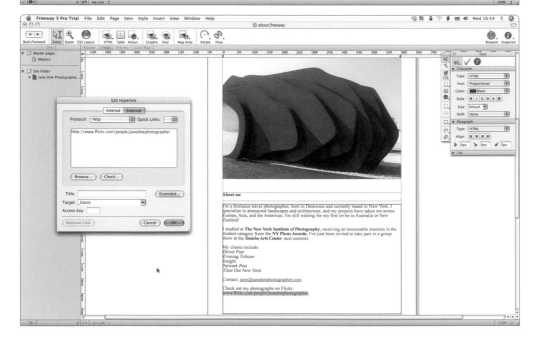

**2.19** Add the Flickr link like you did the email link

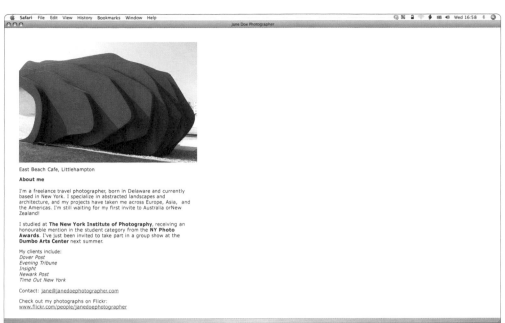

East Beach Cafe, Littlehampton

**About me**

I'm a freelance travel photographer, born in Delaware and currently based in New York. I specialize in abstracted landscapes and architecture, and my projects have taken me across Europe, Asia, and the Americas. I'm still waiting for my first invite to Australia or New Zealand!

I studied at **The New York Institute of Photography**, receiving an honourable mention in the student category from the **NY Photo Awards**. I've just been invited to take part in a group show at the **Dumbo Arts Center** next summer.

My clients include:
*Dover Post*
*Evening Tribune*
*Insight*
*Newark Post*
*Time Out New York*

Contact: jane@janedoephotographer.com

Check out my photographs on Flickr:
www.flickr.com/people/janedoephotographer

**2.20** The Freeway document can be previewed in a browser such as Safari

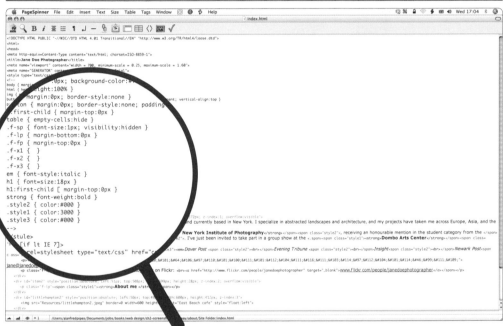

**2.21** The code that Freeway generates, when revealed in another program, PageSpinner, has more complexity than we required, including CSS tags when they weren't strictly necessary

**2.22** Children's book illustrator Rebecca Elliott used Freeway to develop her site, happy not to have to learn JavaScript – this is the home page

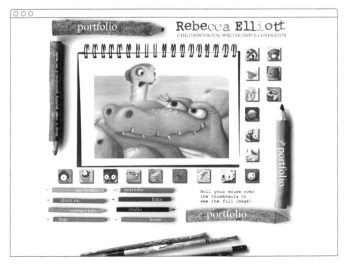

**2.23** This is the portfolio page: the central picture changes as the mouse rolls over the thumbnails

## PageSpinner

The final helper application we will look at in this chapter takes us back to basics and hand-crafted code, albeit with some automated assistance. PageSpinner, from Optima System, belongs to a class of HTML programs that includes BBEdit made by Bare Bones Software and WebDesign from Rage Software – basically text editors with added features aimed at helping to write HTML, such as syntax highlighting and actions that make adding and formatting tags much easier than manually typing them out. A new page from PageSpinner already includes the most fundamental tags, along with a DOCTYPE.

So once again, lets paste our CV text between the `<body>` tags and the title between the `<title>` tags (Fig **2.24**). To make words bold and italic we highlight the text and press the **B** or **I** buttons on the top menu. In Preferences we can choose whether these actions produce logical `<strong>` or physical `<b>` styles. To create an h1 and h2 heading, we again highlight the text and choose Header 1 or Header 2 from the Size menu. To make the email a link, highlight the text and enter the email address into the HTML Assistant window. There is also an HTML Examples window available for guidance (Fig **2.25**).

To add the Flickr link, again highlight the text and hit the 'chains' button at the top – this will pop up the HTML Assistant

where the link and target can be entered. Don't forget to add paragraph and line breaks: highlight the whole paragraph and hit the 'paragraph' ¶ button to add `<p>` tags, and place the cursor where you want line breaks and hit the 'bent arrow' button. Line breaks are not necessary for headings, but the bold subheads do require them. To add the image, place the cursor under the h1 heading and hit the 'picture frame' button. Navigate to the image (it should already be in an images subfolder in your root folder) and add an alt tag in the HTML Assistant (Fig **2.26**). The page can now be previewed by pressing the 'eye' button at the bottom left of the window or in the browser of your choice via the 'M' button at the top (Fig **2.27**). And that's it: nice clean code and a simple website painlessly created (almost) by hand.

There are many ways to design a profile: this has been the most stripped-down, basic example, getting you used to different helper programs. In the next chapter we will at last start to do some actual designing, when we put CSS to work for graphic design-style typography and layout.

**2.24** Text editor PageSpinner uses syntax highlighting to allocate different colours to different tags, thus making troubleshooting easier

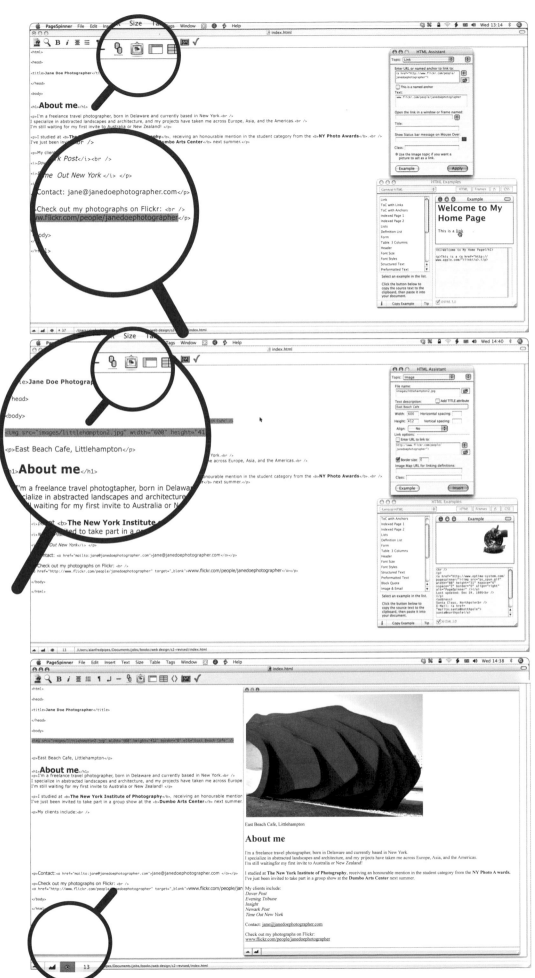

**2.25** To add a link in PageSpinner, highlight the text, hit the 'chains' button on the menu bar and the HTML Assistant will pop up

**2.26** To add an image in PageSpinner, place the cursor where you want it, hit the 'picture frame' button and navigate to the image you prepared earlier

**2.27** The PageSpinner document can be previewed at any stage by hitting the 'eye' button at the bottom left of the window, or viewed in a browser of your choice

# Step-by-step 1
## Instant websites: a customized blog

### Step 1.

Register with WordPress. Other blogging platforms include Blogger, LiveJournal, Posterous, Tumblr and TypePad, but for this exercise log on at wordpress.com (wordpress.org is the address of the original self-hosted version) and fill in the registration form. The username of janedoephotography was available so a blog (**right**) is automatically created with that name (it can be changed later). The URL of your blog is http://janedoephotography. wordpress.com/ – later you can always register your own domain and either simply redirect it to the blog or 'map' your domain so that your blog's address would be janedoephotography.com without the .wordpress.com portion.

### Step 2.

WordPress automatically puts a dummy posting, complete with a comment, on your blog that you can either delete or edit (**above**). Editing it will give you a taste of how to add content to your blog, so here we will replace the text. You can type directly into the top box, or prepare your text in a word processor and copy it in (**right**). To make a word italic, for example, highlight it and press the **I** button above the box. To create a link to another website, highlight the words you would like to work as the link, hit the 'chain' button and paste in the full URL, e.g. http://en.wikipedia.org/ wiki/Angus_McBean. Two other important things to do now are to set the category and tags. The category you select will become your menu item, e.g. landscapes, still lifes, portraits. Each posting will have just one category. Tags further describe the posting, so you can have more than one per posting.

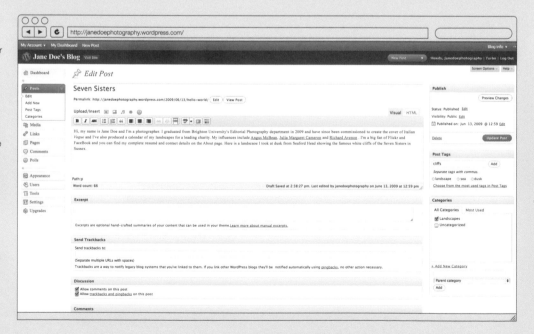

A blog (short for weblog) is fundamentally a kind of diary or journal, with the entries, or postings, appearing with the most recent first, at the top of the page. Previous postings are archived automatically and tidied away. The great thing about blogs is that they can be customized so that their appearance looks less like what you might think a blog looks like and more like a conventional website. With a little imagination, you can even create a portfolio website quickly and painlessly. For an instant web presence, blogs take a lot of beating.

The other advantages of a hosted blog are:

- they are free
- you don't need to worry about hosting or FTP
- you don't need to learn any HTML
- you don't need to buy and learn to use any software
- people can comment on your postings

Here we shall set up a blog for Jane Doe, an imaginary photographer.

## Step 3.

To add an image, click the 'picture frame' button above the box you were just typing into and find the image on your hard drive (it is best to prepare your images first in Photoshop or another image-processing program to be 72dpi and not more than 550 pixels wide). WordPress will resize them to 450 pixels wide. Add any caption information in the form and click the Insert into Post button. Press the blue Upload Post button on the right and take a look at the first proper posting on your site (**right**).

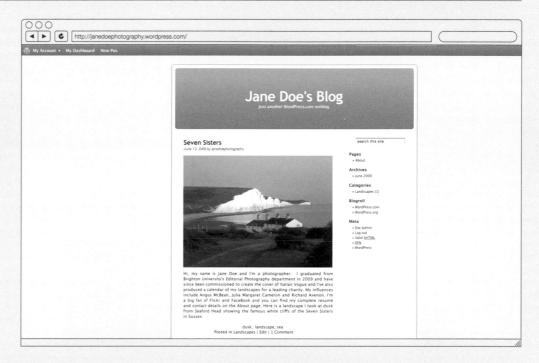

## Step 4.

Now to change its appearance with some customization. The default look and feel for WordPress is a template called Kubrick by Michael Heilemann. There are many other templates to choose from, but let's stick with this for now. Return to My Dashboard and click the Appearance button on the left menu. The simplest way to change the appearance of your blog is to change the header. Click Custom Header and you will find you can either simply change the colour from blue, or replace it completely with a banner of your own. Now you can be creative and create an image 740 x 192px to fill the space. I'm sure you can do better than my attempt. Import it and click the Hide text button. I have also added a second posting and category (**right**).

## Step 5.

Next we will tidy up the navigation. Back at My Dashboard, under Appearance, is a menu item called Widgets (**right**), where the items on the right-hand side of this template can be edited. I have changed Blogroll to Links and Categories to Menu. Note that when you click on a Menu (Category) item a page will be created on the fly containing all the postings defined by that category – here, all landscapes. The menu will grow as you add new categories. Tags are arranged in a 'cloud', the largest words denoting the most popular tags, with the most recent ones listed first. External links can be added by clicking the Links button upper left of the control panel. Another feature of WordPress is that at the bottom of the page is a link to an RSS (Really Simple Syndication) feed, so followers can keep track of when your blog has been updated. In WordPress you can create standalone pages too, for a CV or résumé, contact details and perhaps an FAQ (Frequently Asked Questions).

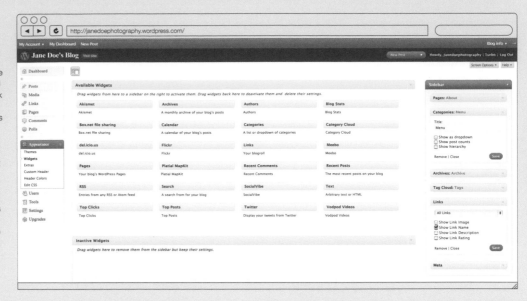

## Step 6.

So, without spending a penny or using a single line of HTML, you have created a credible web presence, which will be instantly publicized throughout the blogging community (**right**). You can add its URL to your email signature and begin to make it known in many other ways, before eventually search engines like Google will find and list it.

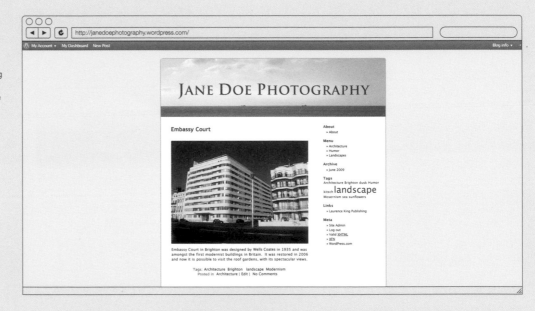

## Example.

Artist and maker Lesley Buckingham writes and illustrates fairy books under the name of Betty Bib (**right**). She set up a customized blog – Betty Bib's Fairyware (http://bettybib.blogspot.com/) using Blogger, to communicate and interact with her fans around the world. She also uses it to promote her books, greetings cards and handmade fairies, with links to Amazon and her Etsy online shop.

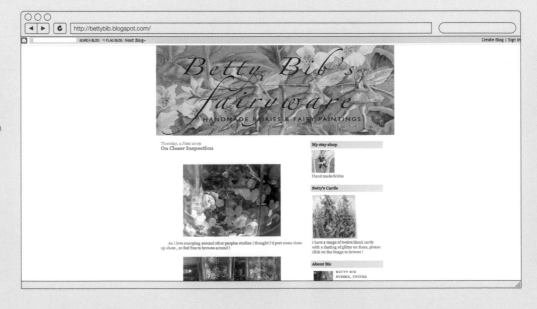

Shinning Star is a charming Blogger-powered blog where Mayu from Tokyo describes her travels and documents photos of her life

Effektive is a graphic design studio based in Glasgow. Their WordPress blog was created as a design archive of inspiring work, design agencies' portfolios, general news, 'meanderings' – and, as here, a way to advertise updates to their main site

http://mayumayumayu.blogspot.com

Share   Report Abuse   Next Blog»                                                                     Create Blog   Sign In

# Shinning Star☆☆

You can only live once!! Crazyにやりたいことして今を一生懸命生きよう。 Learn from yesterday, Live for today, Hope for tomorrow...

### About Me

☆Mayu☆
Tokyo, Japan

☆2009年☆ 自分のやりたかった世界を駆け巡る仕事が実現しつつある中、その仕事・責任に不安と負荷を感じるこの頃。2009年は仕事・プライベートともに充実したものにします！あと、常に感謝の気持ちを忘れずに。 人生の目標は外見的にも内面的にも良い女・できる女！！自分磨きです。 海外経験は多く、小さい時にTaiwan4年、U.S.3年住んでいました。大学時代はSeattleに1年留学。 他 旅行やホームステイで London, Paris, NY, Chicago. LA, SF, Sydney, Vancouver(BC), Vienna, Budapest, Prague, Thailand, Cancun, Malaysia, Italy, Spain, Portugal, China, Vietnam, Cambodia, Singapore, Australia (only Sydney & Uluru), Bali... I think that's all...

View my complete profile

### Labels

Travel (58)
Pictures (51)

Sep 6, 2010

## Top of Japan, Mt. Fuji

My biggest memory of this summer is Mt. Fuji.
2 days, total of 15 hours walking, I finally reached the top and came back down.
It was hell; hot in daytime, freezing at night and on the top, rocky path, full of people in lines, little oxygen that make you headache, and the worst was going down. Walking step by step with your knees and feet hurt incredibly on the path you cannot see the end...
I cannot do this again, but I wanted to do this once in my lifetime and I finally did it.

I appreciate to this person who went with me, with his support I probably couldn't finish to the end. I am glad to share this wonderful experience with him.

# Trailblazer 1
## Joshua Davis

Joshua Davis was an early adopter of Adobe (formerly Macromedia) Flash, the author of *Flash to the Core* (2002) and was featured in the seminal book *New Masters of Flash* (2000). He moved from Colorado to New York in 1992, and it was at the Pratt Institute in 1995, while studying illustration and painting, that Davis began writing HTML. Soon he was also experimenting with Flash. From 1998 to 2001 he worked with the web production company Kioken Design, where he created the website for Barneys in New York (Fig **1**).

In 2002 he joined up with developer Branden Hall to form The Department of Notation Studios, a media development studio, disbanded in 2006 when Hall left to form Automata Studios Ltd in Washington D.C. With Hall, Davis developed a coding framework called Hype, designed to make Flash – and ActionScript – fun, allowing beginners to express themselves playfully while learning how to program. His big break came in 2003 when he was asked by Adam Jones of rock band Tool to redesign their website.

Since 2007, Davis has lived and worked in New York. He is a professor at New York's School of Visual Arts, runs his own design studio, and continues to lecture and lead workshops at design conferences around the world.

Davis was influenced by abstract expressionist painter Jackson Pollock, not so much for his visual style but the way he was disconnected from the process: 'he always identified himself as a painter, even though a lot of the time his brush never hit the canvas'. Davis writes code that randomly distributes, arranges and distorts his artwork, to generate new work. It's a process he calls 'Dynamic Abstraction', and can be seen on his experimental gallery Once Upon a Forest, in his 'stained glass' artwork, on his iPhone app Reflect and on his diverse merchandise, which includes cups and saucers, bags for stationery company Miquelrius and bedding for homeware designers Umbra.

Lately, Davis has become a fan of WordPress (Fig **2**), saying that WordPress plug-ins have taken the place of complex Flash snippets to bring interactivity and a network-based experience to web design. 'I can install WordPress in 11 minutes, and right out of the box I have access to thousands of plug-ins that can be modified to suit your visual needs, and a level of social-networking functionality that we all expect to have on a site. Try the same thing in Flash – it won't just take 11 minutes. And it might even be longer than 11 days.'

'In terms of layout, I'm always looking for the most efficient way to present content, so that the work is the object that shines and the layout is a quiet vehicle to deliver the content.

Fig 1

WordPress has a community of people creating features that make it easier for a guy like me to update easily, while at home or on the road, from my phone. I can upgrade WordPress and you would have no idea it had happened. I can tear down my current theme and create a new one, and the content sitting in my database wouldn't care less. This project exists as a singular entity and is able to adapt to the changing displays in which it's viewed.'

He's created websites for clients such as Motorola, Sony, Nokia and Volkswagen, he was the winner of the 2001 Prix Ars Electronica Golden Nica in the category 'Net Excellence' and has exhibited at Ars Electronica in Austria, Tate Modern, the Institute of Contemporary Arts and the Design Museum in London, Centre Georges Pompidou in Paris, P.S.1 Contemporary Art Center, MoMA and the Smithsonian's Cooper-Hewitt, National Design Museum, both in New York.

www.joshuadavis.com
www.once-upon-a-forest.com

**Fig 1** Flash-based website for clothing store Barneys of New York (2000)

**Fig 2** Most of Davis's previous websites, such as Praystion and Dreamless, now all redirect to his WordPress-based studio site

**Fig 3** Kaleidoscope (2006) for the Motorola Krzr mobile phone website

**Fig 4** JD Reflect (2009) is a generative art app for the iPhone. Says Davis: 'Chance is not always pretty, but it is fun. Take a walk, or rather design, in my shoes.'

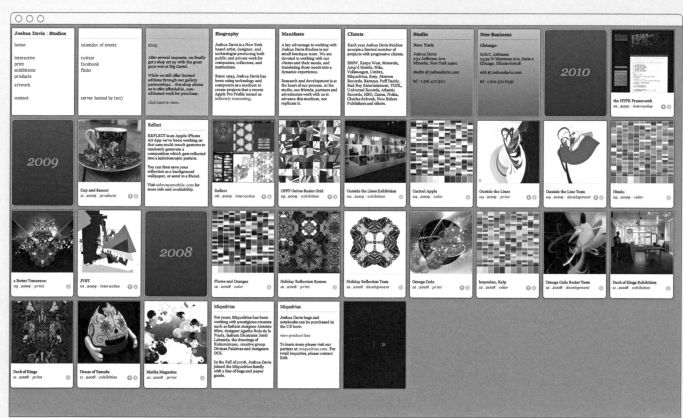

Fig 2

Fig 3

Fig 4

**Figs 5 – 11** The experimental website Once Upon A Forest is explained in a comment in its code, which can be seen by choosing View Source from your browser's menu. He writes: 'For me, the art form is not in the few days it takes me to write the program. The art is the few weeks I will spend living with the work, waiting for the work to evolve. Running functions, re-running functions, always waiting to capture that moment in time – the beautiful accident.'

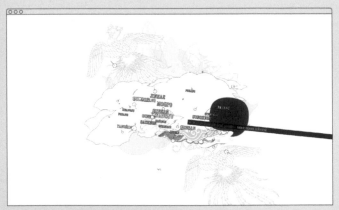

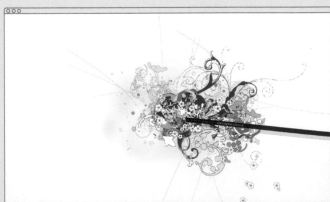

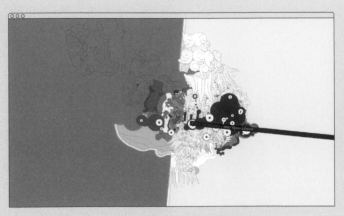

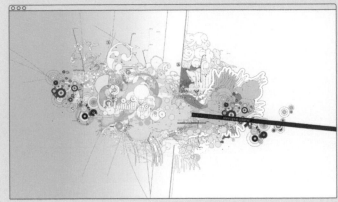

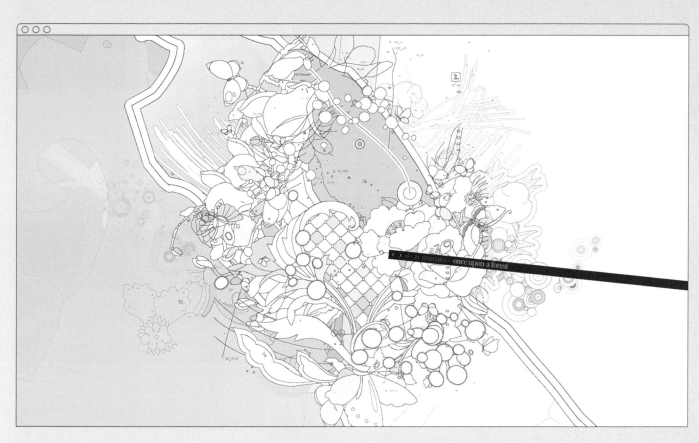

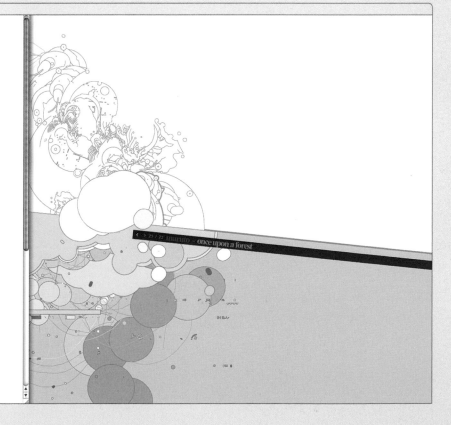

"Dynamic Abstraction"

Among modern artists I conceptually identify with Jackson Pollock - not that I'm a particular fan of his visual style, but because he always identified himself as a painter, even though a lot of the time his brush never hit the canvas. There's something in that disconnect - not using a brush of tool in traditional methods - that says a lot about the concept of dynamic abstraction, because in that loss of control there can be beauty in randomness.

Pollock might argue that it's the process of abstraction that's dynamic, not the end result, which in his case is a static painting. In my own work, the end result is never static; by making room for as many anomalies as possible, every composition generated by the programs I write is unique to itself. I program the "brushes," the "paints," the "strokes," the rules and the boundaries. However it is the machine that creates the compositions - the programs draw themselves. I am in a constant state of surprise and discovery, because the program may structure compositions that I may never have thought of to execute or might take me hours to create manually.

For me, the art form is not in the few days it takes me to write the program. The art is the few weeks I will spend living with the work, waiting for the work to evolve. Running functions, re-running functions, always waiting to capture that moment in time - the beautiful accident,

"Residue"

I've often wondered how work influences the next project. How colors and forms make their way into future works - building on this idea of "flow", or continuation of style and process.

The body of work on this site is navigated in a linear format, starting with the most current composition and then offering the ability to navigate backwards to a prior composition. However, as you navigate, an imprint of prior work is left - giving us the ability to see how new works played upon prior compositions.

The system has the ability to store 5 projects at a time, slowly fading out prior projects as you press forward. If you were on the 5th composition the system would look like this...

20 % transparent - composition 1
40 % transparent - composition 2
60 % transparent - composition 3
80 % transparent - composition 4
100 % transparent - composition 5 - current position

Upon pressing forward to the 6th composition, the system would look like this...

removed - composition 1

20 % transparent - composition 2
40 % transparent - composition 3
60 % transparent - composition 4
80 % transparent - composition 5
100 % transparent - composition 6 - current position.

The challenge... is for me to try to build work that somehow flows or plays on what was previously created. How will new themes play with related or conflicting new themes? How will space be used? How will color be introduced and evolved? How will possible collaboration with other artists and designers fit into the system without stepping outside of the flow?

◄ ► ⟳  http://www.cinematek.be

# CINEMATEK

IN DE KIJKER
CINEMATEK?
KALENDER
PROGRAMMA
EXPO
BIBLIOTHEEK
EDUCATIE
DVD
PRO

NI I Fr
Wegwijzer
Nieuws
Sitemap
Account

Zoeken
in de website ▼
Zoektermen 🔍
Mandje
Kalender

CINEMATEK
Baron Hortastraat 9
1000 Brussel
02 551 19 19
info@cinematek.be

Bibliotheek
Ravensteinstraat 3
1000 Brussel
02 551 19 30
bib@cinematek.be

## CLASSIC
### TWELVE ANGRY MEN
### 28.10 - 19:00

Twelve angry men (Sidney Lumet)

SPOT OP CONGO

De initiatieven van CINEMATEK n.a.v. 50 jaar Congo

## CYCLUS
## AVANT-PREMIÈRE
### PAUL PANDA FARNANA
### 30.10 - 19:00

Avant-première ingeleid in het Frans door de regisseuse Françoise Levie

## CYCLUS
### DENNIS HOPPER

25.10

CINEMATEK

19:00 > Bwana Kitoko

18:00 > Whirlpool

20:00 > The plough and the stars

FLAGEY

18:00 >

---

◄ ► ⟳  http://www.cinematek.be

# CINEMATEK

IN DE KIJKER
CINEMATEK?
KALENDER
PROGRAMMA
EXPO
BIBLIOTHEEK
EDUCATIE
DVD
PRO

SPECIALE VERTONINGEN
CYCLI
REEKSEN
BELGISCHE FILM
DOCUMENTAIRE
HET ZILVEREN SCHERM
JONGE FILMFANS
CURSUS & LEZINGEN
STILLE FILM
CINEMATEK -> FLAGEY
EXTRA-MUROS

NI I Fr
Wegwijzer
Nieuws
Sitemap
Account

Zoeken
in de website ▼
Zoektermen 🔍
Mandje
Kalender

CINEMATEK
Baron Hortastraat 9
1000 Brussel
02 551 19 19
info@cinematek.be

Bibliotheek
Ravensteinstraat 3
1000 Brussel
02 551 19 30
bib@cinematek.be

◄ Oktober ►

| M | D | W | D | V | Z | Z |
|---|---|---|---|---|---|---|
| 27 | 28 | 29 | 30 | 01 | 02 | 03 |
| 04 | 05 | 06 | 07 | 08 | 09 | 10 |
| 11 | 12 | 13 | 14 | 15 | 16 | 17 |
| 18 | 19 | 20 | 21 | 22 | 23 | 24 |
| 25 | 26 | 27 | 28 | 29 | 30 | 31 |

## CYCLUS
### CHARLES BUKOWSKI, DICHTER VAN DE GOOT
### 01.09 > 29.10

Factotum (Hamer)

Charles Bukowski, de gedoemde schrijver bij uitstek, maakte van de wanhoop en zelfvernietiging krachtige poëzie. Het is geen sinecure om de unieke en groezelige sfeer van zijn uitzonderlijke teksten voor het grote scherm te adapteren. Marco Ferreri, Barbet Schroeder, Bent Hamer en de Belg Dominique Deruddere zijn er wel in geslaagd, ten bewijze deze cyclus.

## CYCLUS
### WONDERLIJKE WOODY ALLEN

## CYCLUS
### SIMONE SIGNORET & YVES MONTAND
### 01.09 > 30.10

Les Sorcieres de salem (Rouleau)

Hoewel ze maar een handvol films samen gedraaid hebben, waren Yves Montand en Simone Signoret hét iconische acteurskoppel van de Franse cinema tijdens het derde kwart van de twintigste eeuw. Het was een relatie die veel stormen kende, maar ze allemaal overleefde. 25 jaar na de dood van Signoret duikt CINEMATEK in het verleden voor een retrospectieve van het werk van deze twee enorme persoonlijkheden.

## CYCLUS
### FOREVER GODARD
### 03.09 > 31.10

## CYCLUS
### PETER LORRE DE EEUWIGE SLECHTERIK
### 01.09 > 31.10

M, eine stadt sucht einen mörder (Lang)

Peter Lorre, de meest gezochte slechterik van de klassieke cinema, stelde zijn talent ten dienst van onsterfelijke films als M van Fritz Lang, **The man who know too much** van Hitchcock, **Casablanca** en **The Maltese falcon** (met als tegenspeler Bogey), **Arsenic and old lace** van Capra, **Silk stockings** met Fred Astaire en **The raven** van Roger Corman, alle te zien in FLAGEY

## CYCLUS
### DENNIS HOPPER
### 08.09 > 30.10

# Layout

3

With CSS (Cascading Style Sheets), designers at last have a sound, simple method for producing layouts that will be both standards-compliant and accessible to all. If you already know some HTML, then you can forget many of the tags you may have been using, but you will have to learn about two new ones: `<div>` and `<span>`, of which more later. Until recently, designers had few options when it came to laying out web pages. They had to use either framesets or tables – using spacers (transparent single-pixel GIF images resized to a specified width and height) to attempt any form of controllable layout. Both methods are unsatisfactory for various reasons, as will be described in this chapter, and have been replaced by CSS.

**3.1** The Belgian movie museum Cinematek is a permanent exhibition space for the Royal Film Archive's collections. The design and art direction for their website is by BaseDesign, with development by Tentwelve, both Brussels-based. It uses CSS with some JavaScript to produce a clear but visually engaging user experience

**3.2** It's not immediately obvious that London-based illustrator Richard Sanderson's website relied on frames to make the top title and menu appear on every page. Look at the toolbar, however, and you'll notice that the URL never changes, making bookmarking a particular page impossible. It has since been converted to CSS (**below**)

# Frames
# and tables

## Using framesets

A frameset divides a web page into different segments, each frame containing and displaying a separate HTML document. Repeating parts of a layout, such as the navigation, can appear in one frame, while variable content is displayed in another. Headers and sidebar menus remain in fixed positions if the content frame is scrolled up and down. This can be very convenient – to add an item to the sidebar menu, for example, you need only update one file, whereas on a non-frameset website each individual page would have to be edited (Fig **3.2**). However, SSI (Server Side Includes) and scripting languages such as PHP can also be used to accomplish this aim without the disadvantages of frames (more on SSI and PHP in Chapter 6).

The `<frame>` tags replace the `<body>` tags thus:

```
<frameset cols="85%, 15%">
  <frame src="url of page 1">
  <frame src="url of page 2">
  <noframes>
    Text displayed in browsers that do not support frames.
  </noframes>
</frameset>
```

The `<noframes>` tag is a courtesy to users with browsers that do not recognize framesets.

There are several big drawbacks to framesets. They can break the link between the content and its URL, making it difficult for other sites to link to particular pages or bookmark a particular frame of content. Visitors arriving at your site from search engines may open an 'incomplete' page intended for display within a frame and hence with no apparent navigation to allow you to move elsewhere in the site. Framesets do not usually print the way users expect, and clicking an external link on a frames-based page could result in someone else's pages appearing within your frameset ad infinitum. Finally, if the screen resolution or browser window size is too small, then each frame will develop scroll bars, making the page look cluttered and messy. So although frames were included in the XHTML 1.0 specification, they did not make it through to XHTML 1.1.

## Using tables

A table is a grid of rows and columns, rather like a spreadsheet. Designers produce layouts by filling some cells with content, with other, empty cells acting as spacers – except they have to contain something or else they will collapse. This is where the 'invisible' transparent GIF comes in. Images can be expanded or contracted to any rectangular shape or size by means of the height and width attributes. For file-space-saving reasons a 1px clear GIF is used, resized to the amount of blank space required in the layout. David Siegel is credited as being the inventor of the spacer GIF in his 1996 book *Creating Killer Web Sites*. The code:

```
<img src="images/dot_clear.gif" width="8" height="8">
```

would thus produce a space 8px by 8px. Because the GIF is transparent, the cell can be given a background colour that will show through.

A table layout takes the form:

```
<table>
<tr> <!-- row 1 -->
        <td>item</td>
        <td>another item</td>
</tr>

<tr>  <!-- row 2 -->
        <td>a third item</td>
        <td><img src="images/dot_clear.gif" width="8"
    height="8"></td>
</tr>
</table>
```

The tag `<tr>` indicates the row, `<td>` the cell. The `<table>` tag can have several attributes:

```
<table border="1" cellspacing="10" cellpadding="3"
summary="description of the table">
```

Most of these are now invalid in strict XHTML and have been replaced by CSS. Tables can be nested in other tables to produce quite complex layouts, and until recently this was how such programs as Dreamweaver generated layouts. It worked – but was very cumbersome to code.

The only way to publish exact layouts on the web is to link to a PDF (Portable Document Format) file, a slow, unsatisfactory method, requiring users to install plug-ins or to download and view in a PDF reader (some browsers allow you to view PDFs in HTML, but do a poor job; and it defeats the object anyway).

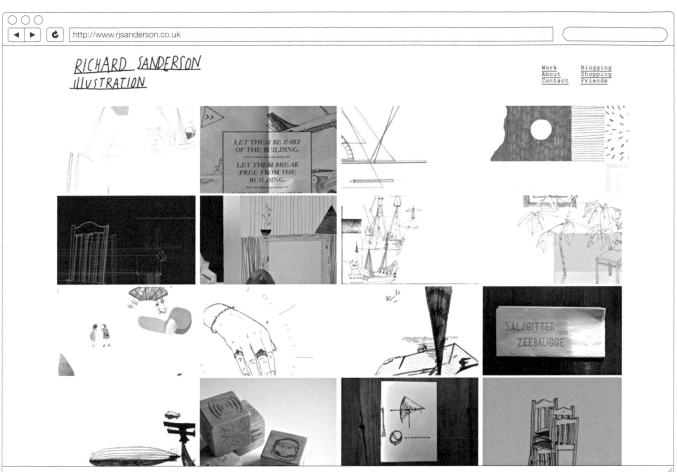

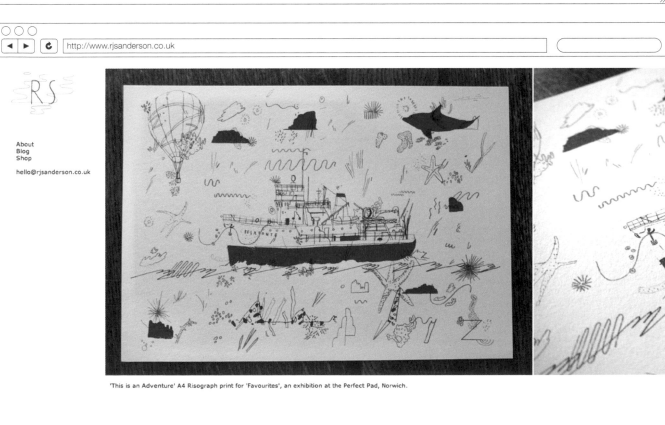

'This is an Adventure' A4 Risograph print for 'Favourites', an exhibition at the Perfect Pad, Norwich.

http://www.thegridsystem.org

Hide Grid

Join The Forum

# The Grid System

The ultimate resource in grid systems.

*" The grid system is an aid, not a guarantee. It permits a number of possible uses and each designer can look for a solution appropriate to his personal style. But one must learn how to use the grid; it is an art that requires practice. "*
Josef Müller-Brockmann

Search

## Articles

### Long Live the 12-Column Grid
When I first crossed the great divide from print to web, one of the earliest things I tried to do was introduce a flexible multi-column grid (you know, like a magazine).
07.May.2010

### Web Design with Grids
People, including myself, are building sites using grids. Now it seems to me that when you're design-ing in a browser you want to be able to follow the grid's principals all the way through the process.
07.May.2010

### Applying Mathematics to Web Design
Because of its beautiful nature, mathematics has been a part of art and architectural design for ages. But it has not been exploited much for website design.
02.Mar.2010

**View All Articles →**

## Tools

### Fluid Grid
A web grid system that allows designers to use the screen real estate on large monitors and retain great design on smaller ones.
07.May.2010

### Griddy
A small JQuery plugin thats creates a simple, customizable overlay on top of any element.
07.May.2010

### #grid
A tool that inserts a layout grid in web pages, allows you to hold it in place, and toggle between displaying it in the foreground or background.
02.Mar.2010

**View All Tools →**

## Books

### Universal Principles of Design
Universal Principles of Design is the first compre-hensive, cross-disciplinary encyclopedia of design.
04.Nov.2009

### Designing for the Web
A Practical Guide to Designing for the Web has written explanations of the core principles of graphic design in relation to the web.
08.Oct.2009

### The Way of Typography
The book also goes into depth on how to create grid systems by hand with only pencil, straightedge and compass.
18.Sep.2009

**View All Books →**

## Templates

### The Golden Grid Template
A PSD template based on the CSS framework The Golden Grid by Vladimir Carrer.
02.Mar.2010

### Photoshop 4 Column Grid
A free 4 Column Photo-shop grid template for a 1024x768 screen resolu-tion by Ray Gulick.
08.Jun.2009

### InDesign 568x792 Grid System (12)
By Dario Galvagno. Adobe InDesign file with a grid system for a 568pts x 792pts page that is divided into 12 columns and rows using the Golden Ratio. Includes a 12pt baseline grid.
16.Apr.2009

**View All Templates →**

## Blog

### Forum is back up!
Sorry for the downtime on the forums. They're back up now.
07.May.2010

### Sushi & Robots
Beautifully personal port-folio by Jina Bolton that reveals the site grid and baseline grid.
07.May.2010

### Bisgrafic
Lovely grid site design by Barcelona based Bisgrafic.
07.May.2010

**View All Blog Posts →**

## Inspiration

Ace Jet 170
AisleOne
Athletics
BBDK
Blanka
Build
Corporate Risk Watch
Counter Print
David Airey
Design Assembly
Dirty Mouse
Experimental Jetset
Form Fifty Five
Grafik Magazine
Grain Edit
Graphic Hug
I Love Typography
Lamosca
Mark Boulton
Minimal Sites
Monocle
Neubau
NewWork
OK-RM
Original Linkage
Robin Uleman
SampsonMay
Schmid Today
September Industry
Souleills
Subtraction
Swiss Legacy
The International Office
Thinking for a Living
This Studio
Toko
Typographic Posters
Visuelle
Xavier Encinas
Year of the Sheep

## About
Made popular by the International Typographic Style movement and pioneered by legends like Josef Müller-Brockmann and Wim Crouwel, the grid is the foundation of any solid design. The Grid System is an ever-growing resource where graphic designers can learn about grid systems, the golden ratio and baseline grids.

Created by **Antonio Carusone**, graphic designer and author of the design and typography blog **AisleOne**. Special thanks to **Duane King** for his help and wisdom.

If you want to say hi or for general inquiries, send an email to: **hello@thegridsystem.org**

Have an article, tool, template or news you want to submit? Send an email to: **submit@thegridsystem.org**

## Subscribe
Want to stay updated with the most recent content? Subscribe below via email for daily updates or to the RSS feed.

**Subscribe by Email**
**Subscribe to RSS**

## Archives
May 2010
March 2010
January 2010
December 2009
November 2009
October 2009
September 2009
August 2009
July 2009
June 2009
May 2009
April 2009
March 2009
February 2009
January 2009
December 2008
November 2008

## Goodies
LegiStyles
AisleOne Store
Wallpapers
The Grid System Group
Inter-Typo-Style Group
Wim Crouwel Group

## Colophon
Made on a **Mac**
Set in **Helvetica**
Themed in **Futurosity**
Hosted by **Media Temple**
Powered by **Wordpress**

# CSS (Cascading Style Sheets)

CSS has been used for years to style fonts and colours. Before CSS, to assign typographic characteristics to, say, all `<h1>` headings, designers had to use the `<font>` tag to mark up each occurrence of that heading type, making document code complex and difficult to maintain, and increasing file size. Fewer HTML tags in a document reduces page download times and bandwidth. The only drawback to CSS at present is in uneven browser support, so hacks or workarounds sometimes have to be introduced to cater for older versions of browsers such as Internet Explorer. In 2006, the W3C (World Wide Web Consortium) declared CSS to be superior to previous methods. The `<font>` tag is now 'deprecated', which means that it is tolerated in older websites, but it is to be avoided in new-builds.

In CSS, presentation is separated from structure, such that a single standalone CSS document can define colour, font, text alignment, size and many other attributes. Change the CSS document and every page attached to it is automatically updated. But it can do much more, and designers are now using CSS for layout, with `<div>` (for 'division') tags to position 'containers' of design elements. Localized design changes are handled by a `<span>` tag, like the span of a bridge.

CSS separates design from structure and content. The content and structure is in the HTML (or strictly speaking XHTML) documents; the design is in the CSS file (Fig **3.5**). So-called 'tableless' web design also improves accessibility: screen readers and voice software have fewer problems with CSS designs because the content follows a more logical structure. It is also possible to provide multiple layouts for different devices, such as netbooks (small, light and cheap laptops, often with touch-screen interaction) and mobile phones, by having a dedicated CSS file for each.

Why 'cascading'? Styles can be specified inside a single HTML element, inside the `<head>` element of an HTML page, or in an external CSS file. Multiple external style sheets can be referenced inside a single HTML document. And a single CSS document can be shared by many HTML pages. All the styles will 'cascade' into a new 'virtual' style sheet, in order of priority:

**1 an inline style inside an HTML element;**
**2 an internal style sheet contained within the `<head>` tag;**
**3 an external style sheet;**
**4 the browser default.**

Thus an inline style, such as

```
<p style="color: #009900; margin-left: 20px">
This is a green indented paragraph.
</p>
```

for a paragraph with a different colour and left margin from the rest, will override a style declared inside the `<head>` tag, which in turn will override an external style sheet. If the CSS should fail completely, your website will degrade gracefully – that means you will still have a legible document, but displayed using the browser's default styles (usually Times on a white background, with blue underlined links).

An external style sheet is merely a text file with the suffix .css, for example `style.css`. The instructions in a style sheet are called statements, or rules, and have two parts: a selector (an HTML tag), and a declaration enclosed by curly brackets { }. The selector tells a browser which elements in a page will be affected by the rule; the declaration tells the browser which set of properties to apply (Fig **3.4**).

```
selector {property: value;}
```

**3.4** A style, or rule, contains two parts: a selector, which tells the browser to style an `h1` heading in this case, and a declaration, which in turn contains properties and their values

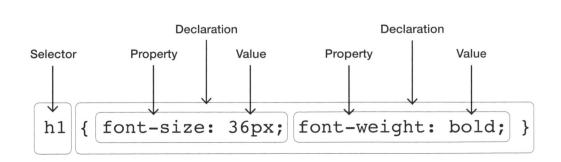

Selector — Declaration — Property — Value — Declaration — Property — Value

```
h1 { font-size: 36px; font-weight: bold; }
```

A statement with a selector for the `<h1>` heading, for example, with multiple properties, might look like this:

```
h1 {
  font-family: Verdana, Helvetica, Arial, sans-serif;
  font-size: 36px;
  text-align: center;
  color: #333333;
  font-weight: bold;
}
```

Properties are separated by semi-colons; the final one is optional but worth putting in, in case you want to add any other attributes in future. Size can be measured in px (pixels), as here, or in points, ems (equal to the current font size), exs (the x-height of a font), picas, inches or millimetres (see Chapter 4). Colours are generally defined in hexadecimal RGB. Doubled-up numbers such as 00FF55 can be abbreviated to three figures, 0F5. W3C also has 16 colour keywords that will validate: aqua, black, blue, fuchsia, grey, green, lime, maroon, navy, olive, purple, red, silver, teal, white and yellow.

Similarly, all other HTML tags can be styled. The syntax is very precise, but there are programs available, such as Style Master and CSSEdit, with every possible permutation of properties, accessed by pull-down menus, to take care of writing the code for you. To style the body text, for example, the body tag `<body>` and the paragraph tag `<p>` will be given certain typographic properties. To create a minor variation of a tag, such as a caption to an image that you may want to look smaller than the body text, a class attribute is used. In the style sheet it will look like this:

```
p.caption {
  font-size: 10px;
}
```

In an HTML document, the `<p>` tag for the caption will be modified thus:

```
<p class="caption">This is a caption</p>
```

Other classes, not related to an HTML tag, just have a dot in front of their ID, for example `.clearboth` (see page 65). There will be more about typographical CSS in Chapter 4.

The important thing to remember is that the HTML document holds the content in some sort of logical structure. All paragraphs should be contained within `<p>` tags and headings should be identified hierarchically, with `<h1>` for the main heading, `<h2>` for a subheading, `<h3>` for a sub-subheading and so on. Try

**3.5** Zen Garden is a demonstration project by Dave Shea that shows how identical content can look very different when styled by different designers – the HTML code remains exactly the same, the only thing that changes is the external CSS file

to avoid using `<bold>` for subheads, even though it may look identical to an `<h2>`; an `<h2>` heading can have its own individual styling in the CSS. Even if they are not as attractive, such websites should elegantly degrade, if the CSS should somehow fail, and should continue to make sense in various generations of browsers.

The external style sheet, `style.css`, is associated with the HTML page by adding a link in the `<head>` section. There are different ways to do this. The most common is to add:

```
<link rel="stylesheet" type="text/css" href="style.css" />
```

More complicated style sheets – multiple style sheets for different languages or different versions for printing, for example – can be called in using the `@import` statement:

```
<style type="text/css">@import url("style.css");</style>
```

The most common use of `@import` instead (or along with) `<link>` is because older browsers don't recognize `@import`, so you could use it to hide styles from them.

One drawback to using `@import` is that if you have a very simple `<head>` with just the `@import` rule in it, your pages may display a flash of unstyled content as it is loading. This can be jarring to your viewers.

# Layout in CSS

The main building blocks used in CSS page layouts are `<div>` elements, or boxes, each with a unique ID so that we can identify them and give them positioning properties in the style sheet. A `<div>` tag has no inherent visual or structural properties, it is just an empty vessel waiting for you to give it meaning. A web page layout will typically comprise a header or banner, the main content, a navigation bar or menu, either horizontally under the banner or vertically in the left column, perhaps a sidebar in the right-hand column, and a footer (Fig **3.6**). For a simple two `<div>` website with just a header and area for content, the HTML might look like this:

```
<!DOCTYPE html PUBLIC "-//W3C//DTD XHTML 1.0 Strict//EN"
"http://www.w3.org/TR/xhtml1/DTD/xhtml1-strict.dtd">
<html xmlns="http://www.w3.org/1999/xhtml" xml:lang="en"
lang="en">

<head>
<!--This file was created on 29/2/2011 by me-->
<title>Simple layout</title>
<link rel="stylesheet" type="text/css" href="style.css" />
</head>

<body>
<div id="wrapper">

 <div id="header">
 <p>This is the header</p>
 </div>

 <div id="content">
 <p>This is the main content area</p>
 </div>

</div>
</body>

</html>
```

Note the complicated-looking `DOCTYPE` declaration at the beginning, which states that this is a valid strict XHTML 1.0 web page, and will thus validate at http://validator.w3.org/ and receive a seal of approval. A website does not necessarily have to validate for it to work, but being standards-compliant can avoid problems later and assist accessibility (see page 72). Note also the link to the external CSS document. The wrapper contains the whole page, constraining its width, and enables the website to be centred in the browser window, for example.

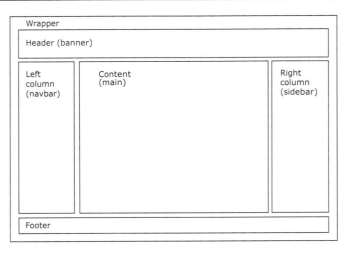

**3.6** A schematic diagram of a typical web page, which will generally have a header containing a banner, sidebars for navigational menus and other standard matter, a central area for content (which may include nested `<div>`s), and perhaps a footer for copyright and contact information. This kind of layout is known as the 'box model'

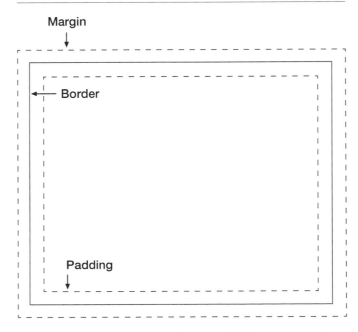

**3.7** A CSS `<div>` box can have a border (solid, dotted or invisible), margins outside the box to keep it at a distance from other elements, and padding within the box to keep content away from the border. It can also have a fill colour or contain a background graphic

The part of the CSS code that defines the layout will look like this:

```css
#wrapper {
 margin: 0 auto;
 width: 922px;
}

#header {
 width: 900px;
 padding: 20px;
 border: 0px;
 height: 100px;
 margin: 10px 0px 0px 0px;
 background: #cccccc;
}

#content {
 width: 900px;
 border: 0px;
 background: #e6e6e6;
 margin: 0px 0px 10px 0px;
 padding: 10px;
}
```

In CSS, the `<div>` IDs are always preceded by a hash mark, #. Note that the borders of the boxes here are measured in pixels, as are the margins (the space around the box) and padding (the space inside the border) (Fig **3.7**).

---

**TIP**

Use a shortcut

Instead of writing out all four attributes of margins (and padding), viz:

```css
#example-div {
 margin-top: 2px;
 margin-right: 3px;
 margin-bottom: 4px;
 margin-left: 5px;
}
```

you can write them all in one line, remembering the clockwise order in which the margins are defined: top, right, bottom, left.

```css
#example-div { margin: 2px 3px 4px 5px; }
```

If all the margins are the same, you can write:

```css
#div { margin: 5px; }
```

---

So, adding our content to the code results in:

```html
<!DOCTYPE html PUBLIC "-//W3C//DTD XHTML 1.0 Strict//EN"
"http://www.w3.org/TR/xhtml1/DTD/xhtml1-strict.dtd">
<html xmlns="http://www.w3.org/1999/xhtml" xml:lang="en"
lang="en">

<head>
<!--This file was created on 29/2/2011 by me-->
<meta http-equiv="Content-Type" content="text/html;
charset=UTF-8" />
<title>My home page</title>
<link rel="stylesheet" type="text/css" href="style.css" />
</head>

<body>
<div id="wrapper">

 <div id="header">

 <h1>My world</h1>

 </div>

 <div id="content">

 <img src="forest-walk.jpg" alt="My Sunday Forest Walk"
width="500" height="375"  />

 <p class="caption">My Sunday Forest Walk</p>

 <p>This is my getting there slowly home page.</p>

 <p>My favorite artist of all time is
 <a href="http://www.elvisnet.com">Elvis</a>.</p>

 <p>You can find more musical links on my
 <a href= "music.html">Music</a> page.</p>

 <p>This page was last updated on 29 February 2011.</p>

 </div>

</div>

</body>
</html>
```

**3.8** The HTML part of the website, as seen in PageSpinner

**3.9** The CSS part of the website, as seen in Style Master

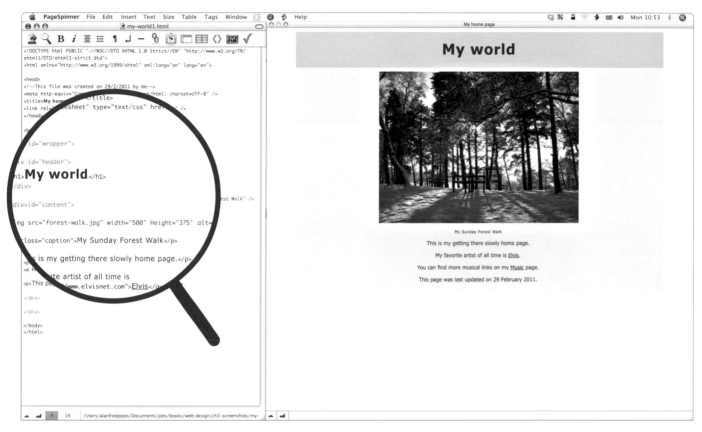

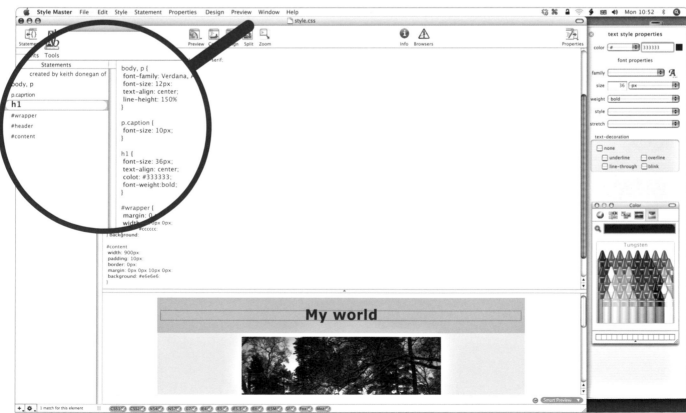

The CSS will look like this:

```
body, p {
  font-family: Verdana, Arial, Helvetica, sans-serif;
  font-size: 12px;
  text-align: center;
  line-height: 150%;
}

p.caption {
  font-size: 10px;
}

h1 {
  font-size: 36px;
  text-align: center;
  color: #333333;
  font-weight: bold;
}

#wrapper {
  margin: 0 auto;
  width: 922px;
}

#header {
  width: 900px;
  padding: 10px;
  border: 0px;
  height: 70px;
  margin: 10px 0px 0px 0px;
  background: #cccccc;
}

#content {
  padding: 10px;
  border: 0px;
  margin: 0px 0px 10px 0px;
  background: #e6e6e6;
}
```

```
a:link {
}
a:visited {
}
a:hover {
}
a:active {
}
```

**Hover**, for example, changes the colour of the link or its background when the user's mouse rolls over it (more in Chapter 4). These need to be in the specific order: link, visited, hover, active – or they may not work properly.

**LoVe? HA!**

The four states of a link can be given different colours: the default is an underlined blue (#0000FF) for the link, which turns red (#FF0000) when clicked (a:active) and changes to purple (#800080) once visited. The a:hover, which changes the colour as the mouse rolls over, is ignored. All of these can be changed to your colour scheme using CSS, but these states must be defined in the correct order: link, visited, hover and active. A good way to remember it is to use the mnemonic 'LoVe? HA!'.

## The float property

We can use `<div>` tags to divide up a page into logical sections, but how do we put the blocks of content into position? The above example simply had one `<div>` below another, in what is known as normal flow – but now we want to position a menu column to the left of the content area and under the banner.

There are three main kinds of layout: liquid (or fluid); fixed-width, or absolutely positioned; and elastic. A liquid layout is one where the sections and content will move to fill the browser window if it is enlarged or decreased in size; and elastic, where as the text size is increased, the sections, measured in ems, will increase in size as well.

A fixed-width layout may sound as if it gives you more control, but it can annoy users with small screens, who will have to scroll up, down and side-to-side to view all the content, while those with large screens could see lots of wasted space. Most fixed-width sites will be 760px wide, aimed at users with 800 x 600 screens. But as more people buy 1024 x 768 monitors, 960px would be a better width to choose as it can be divided into halves, thirds and quarters.

An elastic design is based on the font size of the end-user's computer. If you size the divs in ems, then a short-sighted user increasing the font size will make all the page elements wider

To save having to repeat definitions, the selectors **body** and **p** have been grouped, using a comma. Don't worry about the various properties for now, they will be explained in detail later. The finished page now looks a lot more interesting (Fig **3.8**), and merely changing the CSS will change the whole appearance of the website, with the content staying the same. The CSS as seen in Style Master is shown in Fig **3.9**.

For links, this design still uses the browser defaults. We can go on to define link properties using what are known as 'pseudo-classes'. CSS pseudo-classes are used to add special effects to some selectors, thus:

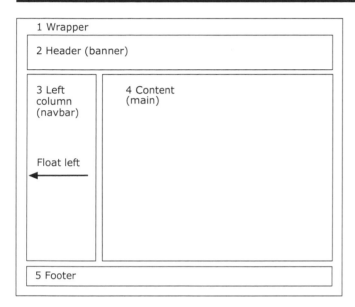

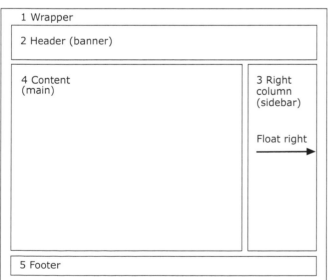

**3.10** To create a two-column liquid design, float the sidebar either to the left (top) or right (bottom). The numbers indicate the order in which the chunks of html code should be written

as well, keeping everything in relative proportion (more in Chapter 4). Remember that a user's screen resolution will affect how much of your website they can see. On an older low-resolution screen, everything will appear larger, as each pixel will be bigger, but the user may have to scroll horizontally to see all the content. As more people have higher-resolution screens, this will not be such a problem.

If you float an element, it becomes a block box, which can be moved horizontally left or right, with other elements wrapping around. The markup values are **float: left, float: right** or **float: none**. An image, for example, can be pushed to the right, with text flowing around it, using the CSS:

```
img {
  float: right;
}
```

This general instruction would apply to all images, pushing them to the right. It would be better to create a specific class:

```
.thumbnail {
  float: left;
  width: 180px;
  margin: 0px 30px 0px 0px;
}
```

Further thumbnails would float left until they push against their neighbour and there is no more room on the page, then they would start a new row. Applying a float left to a **<div>** creates a sidebar that could be used for the site's menu, thus:

```
#leftcolumn {
  width: 130px;
  float: left;
}
```

Any elements following a floated element will wrap around it. To cancel this effect you can apply the **clear** property, which has four values: **clear: left, clear: right, clear: both** or **clear: none**. The CSS for a class called 'clearboth' would be:

```
.clearboth {
  clear: both;
}
```

The HTML would look something like this:

```
<br class="clearboth" />
```

If the sidebar floating left is given a specific width, the main content block flowing to the right of it will just expand to fill up the rest of the browser window, making this a liquid design. In the HTML, the code for the floated element must appear before the code for the element wrapping around it, even if the sidebar is floated right (Fig **3.10**). Floats should always be given a width, either a fixed size in px or ems, or a percentage of the browser window width. Thus, if the sidebar is set at 20% and the browser window is 700px then the menu will be 140px wide. If the user expands the browser window to 1000px, the sidebar will also expand, to 200px wide, maintaining the overall proportions of the page. With a fixed-width wrapper, the layout will not change when the browser window changes size.

Unless you add a set height to the sidebar and the menu is quite short, it is possible that the main content could wrap underneath the sidebar, ruining the layout. To avoid this, add a right float to the main content `<div>`. A three `<div>` basic layout would look like this (Fig **3.11**):

```
<!DOCTYPE html PUBLIC "-//W3C//DTD XHTML 1.0 Strict//EN"
"http://www.w3.org/TR/xhtml1/DTD/xhtml1-strict.dtd">
<html xmlns="http://www.w3.org/1999/xhtml" xml:lang="en" lang="en">

<head>
<!--This file was created on 29/2/2011 by me-->
<meta http-equiv="Content-Type" content="text/html;
charset=UTF-8" />
<title>My home page</title>
<link rel="stylesheet" type="text/css" href="style.css" />
</head>

<body>
<div id="wrapper">

 <div id="header">
 <h1>My world</h1>
 </div>

 <div id="leftcolumn">
 <p><a href="index.html">Home</a><br />
 <a href="about.html">About me</a><br />
 <a href="music.html">Music</a><br />
 <a href="links.html">Links</a><br />
 <a href="contact.html">Contact</a></p>
 </div>

 <div id="content">
 <img src="forest-walk.jpg" alt="My Sunday Forest Walk"
 width="500" height="375" />

 <p class="caption">My Sunday Forest Walk</p>
 <p>This is my getting there slowly home page.</p>
 <p>My favorite artist of all time is
 <a href="http://www.elvisnet.com">Elvis</a>.</p>
 <p>You can find more musical links on my
```

```
<a href= "music.html">Music</a> page.</p>
<p>This page was last updated on 29 February 2011.<br />
</div>

</div><!--end of wrapper-->
</body>
</html>
```

The CSS will look like this (Fig **3.12**):

```
body, p {
 font-family: Verdana, Arial, Helvetica, sans-serif;
 font-size: 12px;
 text-align: center;
 line-height: 150%;
}

p.caption {
 font-size: 10px;
}

h1 {
 font-size: 36px;
 text-align: center;
 color: #333333;
 font-weight: bold;
}

#wrapper {
 margin: 0 auto;
 width: 922px;
}

#header {
 width: 900px;
 float: left;
 padding: 10px;
 border: 0px;
 height: 70px;
 margin: 10px 0px 0px 0px;
 background: #cccccc;
}

#leftcolumn {
 border: 0px solid #ccc;
 background: #dddddd;
 margin: 0px 0px 0px 0px;
 padding: 10px;
 height: 535px;
 width: 200px;
 float: left;
}

#content {
 padding: 10px;
 border: 0px;
 margin: 0px 0px 10px 0px;
 background: #e6e6e6;
 }
```

**3.11** A three `<div>` layout comprising a header, sidebar (left column) and main content area. The sidebar floats left; the content floats right. This is the HTML component as seen in PageSpinner

**3.12** A three `<div>` layout comprising a header, sidebar (left column) and main content area. The sidebar floats left; the content floats right. This is the CSS component as seen in Style Master

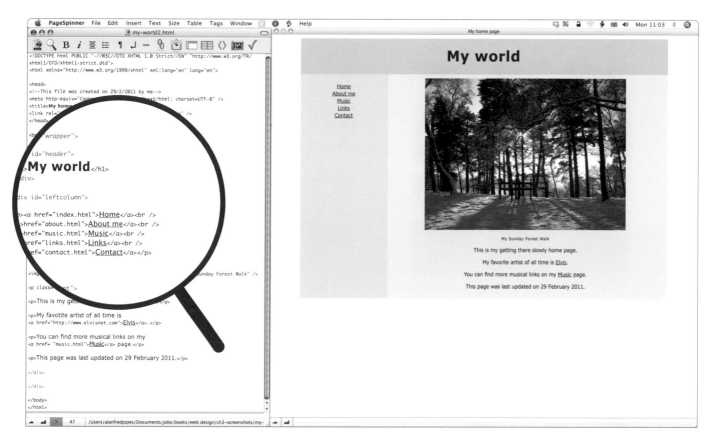

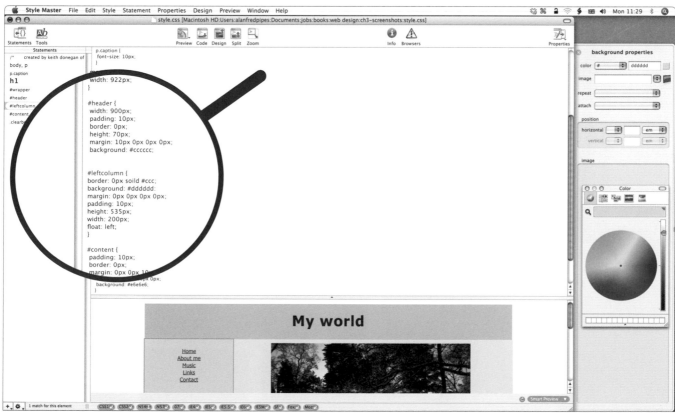

**3.13** The home website of Barcelona-based graphic designers Hey Studios (see their blog on page 8) uses strict XHTML and JavaScript to produce a deceptively simple but effective portfolio site

**3.14** Established in 2003, Brazilian design studio Nitrocorpz works in print, illustration, branding, animation and interactive projects. Their colourful grid-based website uses JavaScript and CSS to present their portfolio of projects in both English and Portuguese

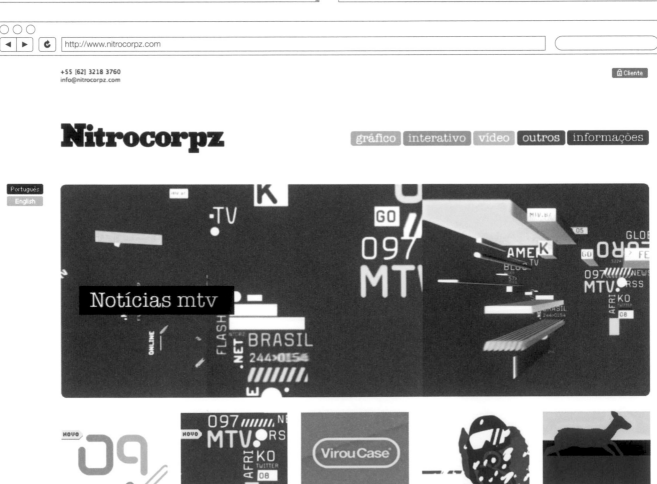

# Navigation

As discussed, in the simple box-model the menu is generally placed down the left column – the navbar. The menu of links to other pages is a form of navigation, the means by which your users will move around the site. Navigation is important so it's useful to draw a diagram of all the connections that will be made through your site – a user should be able to get to where they want with the minimum number of clicks. The menu could be anywhere in the layout, and some Flash-based sites tease the user by hiding the hot links around the page. The most logical places, however, are either along the top, under the logo/banner, or down one of the side columns, 'above the fold'.

If the website is of a set width, the number of menu items that can be displayed in a horizontal menu will be limited, although a submenu for each item can be created as a pull-down or pop-up menu, which appears as the mouse rolls over the menu item. If you are not sure how many items will be in your menu, or there are likely to be additions in the future, it is better to consider a vertical menu – in the left-hand column for users used to Western languages. Submenus can be pop-ups or simple indented lists that appear when a menu item is clicked. Always include a way to get to the home page, and on long pages add a link or button that takes the viewer back to the top of the page.

To do this, add the following internal anchor at the top of the content just below the `<body>` tag:

```
<a name="top"></a>
```

and at the bottom of the page, and at intermediate points if it is a very long page, add the code:

```
<p><a href="#top">^top</a></p>
```

This can work the other way round too: a menu at the top of the page could take visitors directly to the start points of various headed sections below.

In a complex site, with many levels of navigation, it may be useful to include 'breadcrumbs' to remind users where they are located within the site, especially if they have been brought to a specific page by a search engine. The term comes from the trail of breadcrumbs left in the woods by Hansel and Gretel in the Grimms' fairytale. They typically appear horizontally across the top of a web page, usually below title bars or headers. For a portfolio page, for example, it would take the form:

Home page > Portfolio > Landscapes > Abstract landscapes

allowing the user to return to a particular section, subsection or to the home page with one click of the mouse.

3.15 The navigation for the website of Portland-based illustrator and designer Gavin Potenza is top right of the window and comprises just four menu items – Work, Weblog, Résumé, Profile – which show up on every page; you can always return home by clicking his name at top left. A central submenu takes you to different aspects of his portfolio

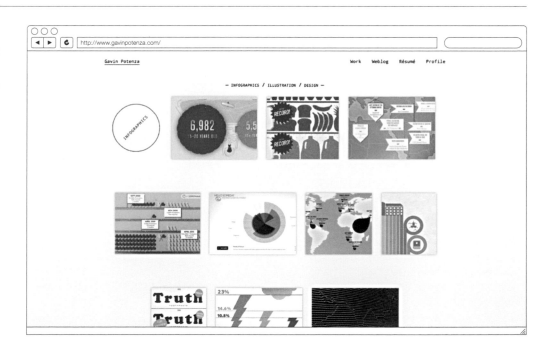

**3.16** Most designers will want some sort of portfolio site, comprising thumbnails and pages (or pop-up windows) containing a larger version of the image. This can be achieved using an image plus caption `<div>` combo, as in this website by Geneva-based graphic design studio Gavillet & Rust

# Nesting divs

Say you want to add a portfolio page to your website: a page of thumbnails that when you click on one you are taken to a page with a larger image on it? The thumbnail and its caption can be contained within a `<div>`, but as there will be more than one of them and `<div>` IDs have to be unique, this is best achieved using a class, for example:

```
.thumbnail {
 float: left;
 width: 180px;
 margin: 0px 30px 0px 0px;
}
```

Remember that margins are defined in the clockwise order, top, right, bottom, left, so here we have added a 30px space to the right of the `<div>`. The HTML for each thumbnail/caption combo would look like this:

```
<div class="thumbnail">
<img src="thumbnail-1.jpg" width="180" height="200" border="0"
alt="Sunflowers" />
<p class="caption">Sunflowers</p>
</div>
```

Adding a link to a page called big-image-1.html that will contain the larger image, we have:

```
<div class="thumbnail">
<a href="big-image-1.html"><img src="thumbnail-1.jpg"
width="180" height="200" border="0" alt="Sunflowers" ></a>
<p class="caption">Sunflowers</p>
</div>
```

This chunk of code is repeated for each of the different thumbnails, changing the image name and caption each time. If you want to limit the rows to three thumbnails across (Fig **3.16**), then add a `clear` after the third chunk of code:

```
<br class="clearboth" />
```

The portfolio layout will be developed in Step-by-step 3 and we will improve the typography in Chapter 4.

This introduction shows that CSS is very versatile and need not be daunting – and that web design is a rare field in which the graphic designer can have complete control over design and production. But why reinvent the wheel? The web is full of people who have already written basic layouts that can be freely used as long as credit to source is included in the code. Check out, for example, www.code-sucks.com (from which the above examples were adapted) and www.oswd.org.

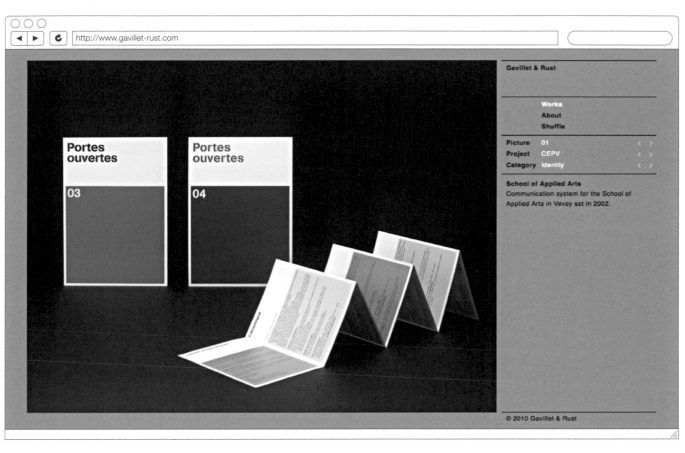

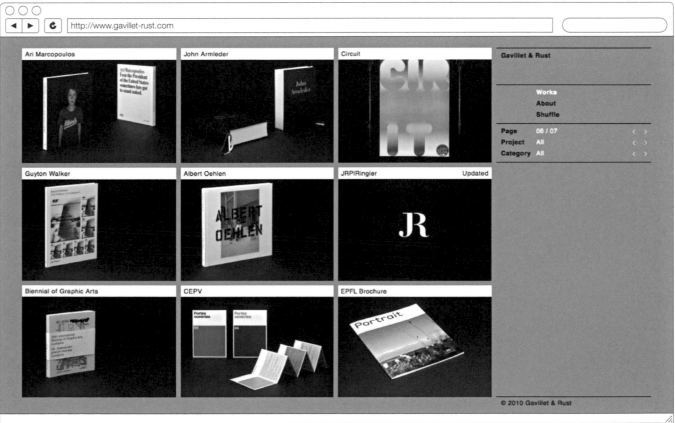

# Accessibility

By the 1990s, people were becoming much more aware that some members of society – those with disabilities – simply did not have access to many of the places most able-bodied people take for granted, so much so that certain requirements to avoid discrimination due to disability were enshrined in law. In the United States, the Disabilities Act of 1990 defined a disability as 'a physical or mental impairment that substantially limits a major life activity'. Major life activities are defined as including 'seeing, hearing … learning, reading, concentrating, thinking, communicating and working'. The UK's Disability Discrimination Act 1995 (both acts have been amended since) and laws in other countries cover similar ground.

So, along with changes like providing ramps into shops and public buildings for wheelchair users, employers, with certain exceptions, must have accessible computer equipment and public organizations are expected to provide information in alternative formats (such as large print). The UK government issued a consultation document in 2008, *Delivering Inclusive Websites*, making it a legal obligation for web designers to ensure that blind or partially sighted people can access official sites. If your website makes it impossible or unreasonably difficult for a disabled person to access information or services (the example often cited in guidelines is of a public flight reservation and booking service), you could be sued and told to take down your site. In the USA, Section 508 of the US Rehabilitation Act is a comprehensive set of rules intended to help web designers make Federal sites accessible to people with disabilities, including employees and the public.

There are four main categories of disability to consider:
• vision impairment
• motor difficulties
• cognitive and learning difficulties, including dyslexia
• deafness or hardness of hearing

Users with vision impairment may use screen-reader software or may need to magnify text and images, viewing only a portion of the page at a time. Users who are quadriplegic might use speech-recognition software and people with less severe motor disorders may have issues with mouse control, navigation or forms. Elderly users could have a combination of reduced vision, restricted mobility and decline in memory.

To date there have been no legal actions taken against a website, but it is only a matter of common decency to make websites accessible and inclusive, not just because it may be difficult to change your website some time in the future when someone complains, but it also makes sound business and moral sense to be accessible – there are 50 million people in the USA with a disability, and many of them use the internet – do you really want to turn your back on potential users?

It is not difficult to be helpful. Basically, if your site is built to W3C standards, which means valid HTML and CSS that passes AA-level conformance with the WAI (Web Accessibility Initiative) WCAG (Web Content Accessibility Guidelines) – see www.w3.org/TR/WCAG10/ – then you will at least be making an effort, and improving the compliance of your website. In 2002, the European Parliament set the minimum level of accessibility for all public sector websites to be at level AA by December 2008.

## Practical steps

What this means in practice is that you need to provide alternatives for people who have hearing or vision disabilities, and make sure your website does not rely on a single sense or ability of the user, with the proviso that some users may need additional accessibility-related software or peripheral devices.

The first step to accessibility is to add a DOCTYPE (document type definition) right at the top of your code – your website won't validate without one. In this book we have been striving to use strict XHTML – in English – and the DOCTYPE for that would be:

```
<!DOCTYPE html PUBLIC "-//W3C//DTD XHTML 1.0 Strict//EN"
"http://www.w3.org/TR/xhtml1/DTD/xhtml1-strict.dtd">
```

There is also a transitional version of XHTML that is less strict and allows deprecated (phased-out) tags and older styles of usage to work in older browsers.

```
<!DOCTYPE html PUBLIC "-//W3C//DTD XHTML 1.0 Transitional//EN"
"http://www.w3.org/TR/xhtml1/DTD/xhtml1-transitional.dtd">
```

It is possible that your website may validate with one DOCTYPE and fail with the other.

Other factors to consider include having sufficient contrast in colour schemes for individuals with low vision and colour blindness (see Chapter 5), and text-only versions of pages that incorporate multimedia, such as audio, video and Flash. Use relative units, such as em or percentage lengths, rather than absolute units, such as pt or cm (see Chapter 4). Above all, make sure that documents are marked up with the proper structural elements – when content is organized logically, it will be rendered in a meaningful order if style sheets are turned off or not supported. When in doubt – keep it simple.

One possible drawback to using floats, for example, is that the text in the floating elements will appear above and before the main content, so that a visually impaired person using a screen reader will have to listen to all the items in the menu every time they access a new page. This can be worked around by placing divs within divs (like the old nested tables), with say the content and sidebar within another wrapper, thus changing the source order and making the content come first. But there again, most screen-reader users do expect the navigation to come first and may find content before the navigation disorientating – so it may not be such a problem after all. Common-sense, meaningful headings, structural labels and links that enable users to skip content and move on to relevant sections are much more useful.

Why text-only content? Text can be converted to synthesized speech or Braille, making the information accessible to people with a variety of sensory and other disabilities. A simple example is the <alt> tag of an image, which must convey the purpose of the image, not just its description, to be really effective. Conversely, non-text equivalents of text, such as pre-recorded speech, or a video of a person translating the text into sign language, can make websites accessible to individuals with cognitive disabilities, learning disabilities and deafness.

Once you have done as much as you can to consider the needs of disabled people, validate your pages using W3C's Markup Validation Service http://validator.w3.org/ and W3C's CSS Validation Service http://jigsaw.w3.org/css-validator/ and perhaps think about adding an accessibility statement such as:

> This <website name> is committed to ensuring access for people with disabilities. Each page on our website will conform to the Web Content Accessibility Guidelines (WCAG) Level Double-A.

along with information for users (Fig **3.17**) on how they can configure their browsers to customize and enhance their experience (increase text size or change the background colour, for example). The BBC website http://www.bbc.co.uk/accessibility/ is a good example. Finally, a 'human review' by real users with disabilities will provide you with valuable feedback about any accessibility problems and how they can be solved.

Here is an accessibility checklist:

- Add a valid DOCTYPE.
- Keep the content simple, avoiding jargon and complex words.
- Avoid justified text, as users with dyslexia find this more difficult to read than if the text is left-aligned.
- Use a sans-serif font such as Verdana or Arial – these are easier to read on screen.
- Avoid images of text, which cannot have their appearance altered by the user.
- Ensure that font size can be increased.
- Ensure that links have a large clickable area.
- Use descriptive links – avoiding the use of 'click here', for example. This is important for screen-reader users.
- Provide a site map to allow users to gain an overall feel for the layout and allow direct access to any page on the website.
- Put a 'Back to Top' link between sections and provide 'skip links' for users accessing the website via the keyboard.
- Ensure that all functionality is available through the keyboard, by tabbing for example, as well as via the mouse.
- Use images and icons for users with cognitive impairments.
- Provide meaningful alternative <alt> text for images.
- Allow for colour flexibility – some dyslexic users, for example, find it more comfortable to read text on certain coloured backgrounds.
- Use good contrasting colours.
- Ensure that any distracting animations can be paused, skipped or switched off.
- Provide a consistent design throughout the website.
- Make use of white space to separate design elements.

http://www.disabilityartsonline.org/

Accessibility | Skip to: content | navigation | Remove images | ◯ Change the way this site looks          Search DAO with Google™ [          ] [Search]

# Disability Arts Online

● **Home**

● **News**

● **Features**

● **Blogs**

● **Listings**

● **Directory**

● **About dao**

● **Contact us**

● **Site map**

**Join our mailing list**

ARTS COUNCIL ENGLAND

You are here:  Home > Accessibility for this site

## Accessibility for this site

2 March 2009

### Accessibility

The new DAO website attempts to strike a balance between access and a clear, but visually striking layout. We wanted to allow the art that DAO represents to take the centre stage. What we have come up with takes the look of a pencil sketch of a layout.

DAO has been built with findability, accessibility and usability in mind, so we hope you can find, access and use the information you need. This page explains the accessibility features available on the web site. We are always happy to receive feedback via the helpline about accessibility on the web site.

### Access Keys (shortcuts)

You can navigate to the sections this site using your keyboard. Available shortcuts are:

Home = 1

Features = 2

Blogs = 3

Listings = 4

Directory = 5

About DAO = 6

Contact us = 7

Join our mailing list = 8

Accessibility for this site = 9

To use the access keys, you press the "Alt" key and the number or letter above, then press "Enter". On a Mac you press the "Ctrl" key and the number or letter.

### Hearing websites

There are some programs available which allow your computer to talk to you.  Windows Narrator is a basic screen-reading program, offering speech feedback for all menus and dialog boxes, Windows Explorer and Notepad but will not speak out a whole Word documents or web page. There are however, a number of text to speech programs available any selected text to be spoken back to the user.

(Window's Narrator is currently only available for Windows 2000 and XP)

### Mac OS:

Go to '**System Preferences**' and select '**Universal Access**'. From here you can turn on the text to speech function.

### Page Layout

The DAO website has been designed to change according to the device you are viewing it on. So you should find the text easy to read and the layout easy to follow.

Equally, users of screen reading software, should find the site layout easy to navigate and the image descriptions informative.

### Text size

You can control the size of the text and change fonts if you wish. Here's how:

To change the text size in Internet Explorer (a typical Windows browser):

- Select View in the menu bar
- Select Text Size
- You'll get a list of different font (text) size options –choose the size that's appropriate for you.

To change the text size in Safari (a typical Mac OS X browser):

- Select the View menu from the Finder bar
- Select Make Text Bigger and choose the size that's appropriate for you.
- In addition to text size – the font type (i.e. Arial, Verdana, etc) is also selectable via the browser.

To display web page text in a different font in Internet Explorer:

- Go to the Tools menu and click on Internet Options
- On the General tab, click Fonts
- In the Web page font and Plain text font lists, click on the fonts that you want to use.

### Magnifying the screen

You could try magnifying the screen if increasing the text size does not make text easy to read.

### Mac OS users:

Go to '**System Preferences**' and click on '**Universal user**'.  Here you can magnify the screen and have the option to turn on the 'text to speech' function.

### Windows users:

All recent versions of Windows include magnification software.  This allows you to greatly increase text size, but is restricted to a small portion of the screen.

To use Windows magnifier click on the '**Start**' menu, then select '**Programs**', '**Accessories**', '**Magnifier**'.  The settings dialog box will appear; from here you can adjust the magnification as desired.

### Using different stylesheets

Web developers, Surface Impression have used internationally standardised web design code. By using Strict HTML 4, combined with CSS 2.1, different Stylesheets affect how the site will appear in different browsers and on different computers. For more information about this, you can click one of the icons at the bottom of the page to visit the 'W3C' website.

You can find free tools to help you create your own stylesheet on the web.  By doing this you can specify the text colour, font type and size, background colours etc. to suit you.  Once you have created your own stylesheet you can apply it to our website.

### Internet Explorer:

Click on the '**Tools**' menu, then on '**Internet Options**'.  This brings up a dialog box.  Select '**Accessibility**' to bring up another dialog box.  From here you can attach your stylesheet by ticking the '**Format documents using my style sheet**' checkbox.  Click on the '**Browse**' button and select the stylesheet you want to use.

### Opera:

Go to '**File**', '**Preferences**' and select '**Page Style**' from the list on the left hand side.  From the drop down menu next to '**Default Mode**', select '**User Mode**' from the list.  Click on the '**Choose**' button under '**My Stylesheet**' to find your stylesheet and attach it.

For more information on viewing web pages...

If you have any comments or feedback regarding accessibility or even accessible features you'd like to see on the site, please visit the 'Contact Us' page and let us know.

Contact us

Friendly URL: http://www.disabilityartsonline.org/Accessibility_for_site

**3.17** If you have made your website accessible, then tell your readers about it with instructions on how to change text size, for example, as on this Disability Arts Online website

# Usability

The term 'accessibility' is used to describe the degree to which a website can be understood by as many people as possible. 'Usability', however, describes the extent to which a website can be used with effectiveness, efficiency and satisfaction within a specified context of use (Fig **3.18**). There is obviously a good deal of overlap: ideally an accessible site should be usable, and vice versa.

Usability guru Jakob Nielsen (www.useit.com) has set out guidelines for usability but has been criticized by some graphic designers for not taking into account design factors such as eye appeal. If you look at websites such as amazon.com or ebay.com, they may not use cutting-edge design, but they are very successful in what they set out to do, presenting a reasonably pleasant and efficient user experience. While usability might not dictate the design of your website, keeping the principles of usability at the back of your mind while designing can produce a more elegant and functional design. As Nielsen points out: 'People have to be able to grasp the functioning of the site immediately after scanning the home page – for a few seconds at most.' And remember that not all users arrive via the front page, especially if they have found your site through a search engine.

Here are some simple ways to ensure usability:

- Be concise – use short screen-size pages.
- Structure your text with two or three levels of headlines (a general page heading plus subheads).
- Use meaningful rather than cryptic headings – reading a heading should tell the user what the page or section is about.
- Use emphasis to make important words catch the user's eye – bold or coloured text – but avoid the less legible italics wherever possible.
- Put concise introductory paragraphs on the home page, full of keywords, describing the site content and stating the purpose of the website. This will also help the search engines.
- Restrict to one idea per paragraph (users may skip over any additional ideas if they are not caught by the first few words).
- Use lists, indents, summaries and plenty of bullet points.
- Many users don't like to scroll, so they will only read the top part of an article. Write in the journalists' 'inverted pyramid' style with the most important and interesting stuff at the beginning – as Walter Matthau asks Jack Lemmon in the newsroom movie *The Front Page*, 'Who's gonna read the second paragraph?' Interested readers will scroll down for greater detail.
- Make each page a self-contained entity: users come through many portals and can go anywhere they like – they will not necessarily read your text in your order.
- Use hyperlinks rather than repeating information found elsewhere.
- Place external links on a 'Further information' page rather than in the text. Grouping links to other sites at the end means readers are retained and rewarded.

**3.18** As this BBC blog points out, 77% of users will return to a website if it is easy to use, only 22% will return because it's their favourite brand

# Step-by-step 2
# A simple handmade XHTML/CSS website using a template

## Step 1.

The aim is to create a very simple but functional website that will conform to XHTML and CSS standards. First we download a public-domain template from www.code-sucks.com (**right**). It will be a two-column fixed-width layout comprising a header, menu sidebar and area for the main content (**below right**). It does not look much yet, but with CSS it can quickly be customized.

The template comprises two files: an HTML document called index.html, which we will open in PageSpinner, and a CSS document called main.css, which we will open in Style Master. Rename the folder they came in if you wish, to reflect the project. Add a subfolder called images, in which we will store our images.

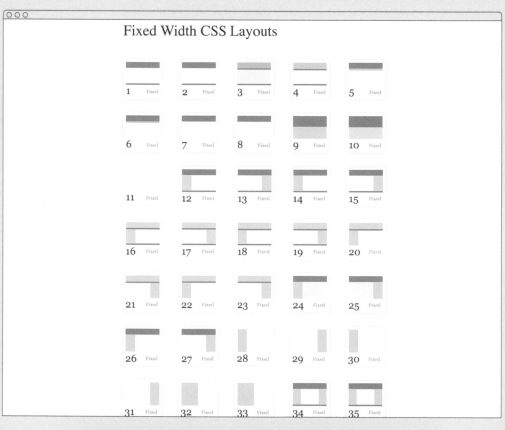

Coding by hand can be relatively painless when helper applications such as PageSpinner and BBEdit for XHTML or Style Master and CSSEdit for CSS are all available. There are also many generous developers on the net offering tried-and-tested templates and code snippets as open source for you to use, as long as the creator is acknowledged on the website – usually within the source code itself as a comment. All you need to provide is your content – words and pictures. If you can cut and paste, then you can create a website.

# Step 2.

First we shall create a banner in Photoshop, 920px wide and 120px high, to fit the header `<div>`. The template header is 900px wide with padding of 10px either side, so 900 + 10 + 10 = 920. This banner is added to the CSS as a non-repeating (tiling) background image by adding the following code to the `#header`:

```
background: url(images/banner.
jpg) no-repeat;
```

While in Photoshop use the eyedropper to choose a colour from the sky, in this case #c6d7d5, and paste into kuler (kuler.adobe.com) to create an analogous colour scheme (see Chapter 5) for the two columns (**right**).

The layout using this colour scheme can be tested in a browser (**below right**).

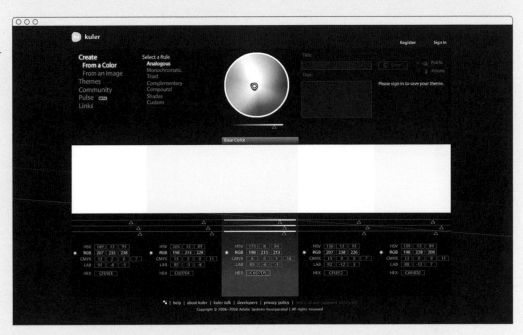

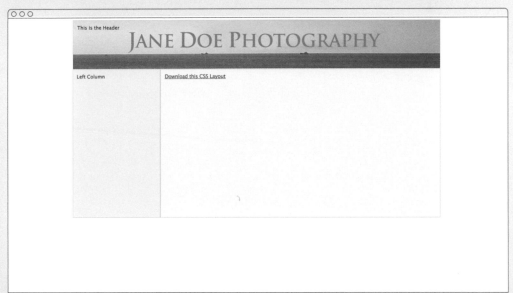

## Step 3.

Now to add some content. The menu will go in the left column and we will need the following pages: Home (where we are now), About me (for our biography or CV), Portfolio (to showcase our best work), Blog (for up-to-date news), Links (to other sites, in the hope that they will link back to ours) and Contact (so that potential clients can contact us). This code is placed between `<div id="leftcolumn">` and `</div>` (**top**).

The main text will appear in the right column, and to accommodate it, we raise the height of each column to 750px in the CSS.

The HTML code for the main content is shown **middle**.

Note the escape code `&copy;` for the copyright symbol. Note also that the text has yet to be formatted in the CSS – what you are seeing so far are the browser defaults (**bottom**).

```
<p><a href="index.html">Home</a><br />
<a href="about.html">About me</a><br />
<a href="portfolio.html">Portfolio</a><br />
<a href="blog.html">Blog</a><br />
<a href="links.html">Links</a><br />
<a href="contact.html">Contact</a></p>
```

```
<div id="rightcolumn">

<h1>Welcome to my new website</h1>

<img src="images/brighton_pav2.jpg" width="550" height="399"
alt="Brighton Pavilion">

<p>My name is Jane Doe and I specialize in architectural photography. Please take a
look at my portfolio and contact me if you have any questions.</p>

<p>All images are &copy; Jane Doe 2010</p>

</div>
```

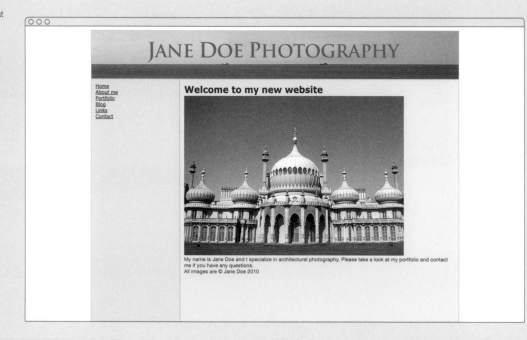

## Step 4.

To style the `h1` header, in Style Master hit the 'cog' button at bottom left and choose New Type Selector, then `h1` from the menu. We can then give it a colour, size, weight and font family, centre it and add some bottom margin, as shown **right**:

Similarly, we can style the `<p>` tag and the `<a>` links, remembering the mnemonic 'LoVe? HA!' (see page 64) to get the `<a>` tags in the correct order (far right). Kuler was used again for the colour scheme, starting with a colour sampled from the sea in the banner. Setting `text-decoration: none` removes the default underlining.

```
h1 {
  font-family: Verdana, Helvetica, Arial, sans-serif;
  color: #5a727d;
  font-size: 1.5em;
  font-weight: bold;
  text-align: center;
  margin-bottom: 1em;
}
```

```
a:link {
  color: #639194;
  font-size: 1.2em;
  text-decoration: none;
  font-weight: bold;
}

a:visited {
  color: #639194;
  font-size: 1.2em;
  text-decoration: none;
  font-weight: bold;
}

a:hover {
  color: #5c658a;
  font-size: 1.2em;
  text-decoration: none;
  font-weight: bold;
}

a:active {
  color: #5c8a81;
  text-decoration: none;
  font-size: 1.2em;
  font-weight: bold;
}
```

# Step 5.

We can also add a class for the photo captions to centre them.

```
p.caption {
  font-size: .9em;
  text-align: center;
}
```

The HTML would look like:

```
<p class="caption">Brighton
Pavilion</p>
```

Centring the image is not so simple – we need a workaround:

```
img.displayed {
  display: block;
  margin-left: auto;
  margin-right: auto;
}
```

The completed home page can be seen **top right**. The HTML document in PageSpinner can be seen **middle** and the CSS in Style Master at the **bottom**. What still needs to be done is to make up all the other pages. The simplest way is to 'save as' the new page, and replace the content. Remember also to add meta tags for the search engines to the head of the HTML document. When all is ready it can be uploaded to your host using FTP. In the next Step-by-step (see pages 102–5) we will create the portfolio page.

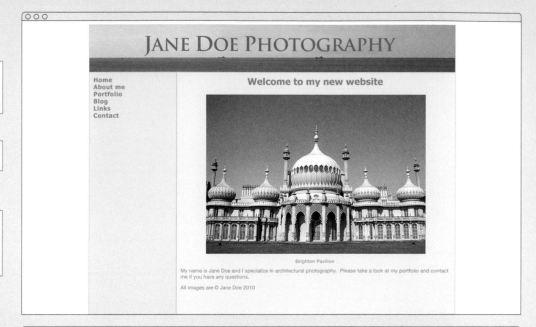

# Trailblazer 2
## Erik Spiekermann

Erik Spiekermann will always be celebrated for designing the font Meta, but he was also an early pioneer of information systems and web design, with his clear grid-based websites in his trademark red and black. He was an early adopter of blogging, and his domain spiekermann.com now redirects straight to his (red and black) blog.

Spiekermann was born in Stadthagen, Germany. He funded his own studies, in art history at the Free University in Berlin by setting metal type and operating a printing press in the basement of his home. After seven years working freelance in London in the 1970s, principally for Wolff Olins and Pentagram, he returned to Berlin, founding MetaDesign with Dieter Heil and Florian Fischer in 1979, where he worked on projects for Audi, Skoda, Volkswagen, Lexus, Heidelberg Printing, Berlin Transit and Düsseldorf Airport. In 1984, the company was bought by Sedley Place Design, and Spiekermann left to work as MetaDesign Mk 2.

Spiekermann founded FontShop with his then wife Joan in 1989, along with partners Neville Brody in the UK and the late Ed Cleary in Canada. This was followed by his own-brand FontFont label. In 1992 Spiekermann co-founded MetaDesign West in San Francisco, with Terry Irwin and Bill Hill, ostensibly because he needed 'a work excuse to spend more time in California'. In 2001 Spiekermann left MetaDesign again and started UDN (United Designers Network), with offices in Berlin, London and San Francisco. UDN was renamed SpiekermannPartners in 2007, and in 2009 it merged with Amsterdam-based Eden Design & Communication to create EdenSpiekermann, a company that employs 100 people in Amsterdam and Berlin.

Meta began life as a corporate typeface for the German post office to try end the 'chaos' created through the use of dozens of versions of Helvetica in the organization, but ended with the client's decision to stick with Helvetica, because to change would 'cause unrest'. Spiekermann also designed Officina and a Charles Rennie Mackintosh-inspired typeface for Glasgow City of Architecture and Design 1999.

No conference about type and typography is complete without an appearance by Erik Spiekermann. Newcomers in the audience are struck first by his bilingual articulation and then by his humour, at once acerbic and self-deprecating. His ability to communicate ('not called speaker-man for nothing') has speeded his international recognition. Spiekermann's speciality is creating order from chaos: information design. This is achieved through care in type selection, sometimes type creation, and especially through typographic clarity. He says:

Fig 1

'What I believe is that, after all the hype about the New Economy, we are going back to the original reason for being on Earth: to find ways to improve our lives, and the way we live together, and to preserve this planet. As graphic designers, we contribute to this by making things easy to use and pleasant to behold. That can be a website, a timetable, a magazine or even a legible and beautiful typeface.' Large-scale websites involve teamwork and Spiekermann is always proud to credit those involved in their design and production.

Erik Spiekermann is Honorary Professor at the University of the Arts in Bremen and Past President of ISTD, the International Society of Typographic Designers. In 2006, the Art Center College of Design in Pasadena awarded him an Honorary Doctorship for his contribution to design and in 2007 he was the first designer to be elected into the Hall of Fame by the European Design Awards for Communication Design. Also in 2007 he was awarded Honorary Royal Designer for Industry by the Royal Society for the encouragement of Arts, Manufactures & Commerce, London. In 2009 he became the European Union's Ambassador for the European Year of Creativity and Innovation.

http://spiekermann.com/
www.edenspiekermann.com/
Erik Spiekermann and E. M. Ginger, *Stop Stealing Sheep & Find Out How Type Works*, Adobe Press 1993
Fay Sweet, *MetaDesign: Design from the Word Up*, Thames & Hudson 1999

**Fig 1** The WordPress-powered Spiekerblog uses Spiekermann's trademark red rectangles bleeding off the top of the screen and a tabbed menu. Like many other bloggers he embeds YouTube or Vimeo videos to make the content more dynamic. It is available in German and English, though the content is not always the same. Both Spiekerblog and the edenspiekermann site subscribe to the paid service Typekit so they can use typefaces other than websafe fonts on their pages. Body type is set in Espi Slab Regular, headlines in Espi Sans Bold, Twitter Feeds in Espi Sans Regular and Bold. Espi is their inhouse version of FF Unit and FF Unit Slab.

**Fig 2** The website for his design studio edenspiekermann uses JavaScript and CSS to provide a clear, accessible website, available in English, Dutch and German. When news and photographic agencies ddp (Deutscher Depeschendienst) and German Associated Press merged to form dapd nachrichtenagentur, edenspiekermann were involved early in the process, helping with the naming of the new company. The new corporate design was launched not only through publications and business cards, but also through office templates, bringing the brand to everybody's desk and computer.

**Fig 3** SoundPrism is a musical instrument for the iPad developed with Fraunhofer Institute for Digital Media Technology and Audanika GmbH. Edenspiekermann gave strategic advice, designed the user interface for the app and the Audanika Microsite, and helped create a buzz on Twitter. The screenshot shows the new edenspiekermann website design in beta produced during a 'design-a-website-in-2-days-marathon' to make it leaner and slimmer.

**Figs 4 and 5** An example of Spiekermann's approach to information design is the website for the Berlin Philharmonic Orchestra. He says: 'I think we need complex information systems that enable the user to find everything effortlessly, while offering an aesthetically pleasing experience.' The website is powered by TYPO3, a free open-source Content Management Framework initially created by Kasper Skaarhoj. The team involved in the redesign include: Robert Stulle (Creative Director), Marcus Scheller (Interaction Designer), Sven Ellingen (Interaction Designer) and Claudia Baumgartner (Project Manager). It won a Webby award in 2009 for its usability, particularly the calendar section – see www.berliner-philharmoniker.de

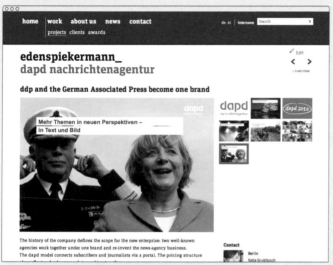

Fig 2

Fig 3

Fig 4

Fig 5

**A** ARKITIP MAGAZINE, L.A. **B** BABYPHAT BRANDBOOK BEAUTY BEN POGUE BIG #55 MAGAZINE BLONDIE, NY B&W **C** COLLECTIVE LUXURY, BEIJING - NY CONTACT US CRYING SKULL FOR BEAMS T-SHIRTS, TOKYO **D** DAVI SKINCARE **E** E&A - THE GLOSSY ZINE EDITORIAL EPOS VISA CARD ARTIST EDITION, TOKYO ESTEE LAUDER PRIVATE COLLECTION TUBEROSE GARDENIA EXISTENZIALIST **F** FALLING PINS FAT MAGAZINE FRAGRANCE FRIENDLY SKULL **G** GAS AS INTERFACE - BEAMS T-SHIRTS, TOKYO GIRLS GUCCI ENVY ME **H** HEARTS **I** IDENTITY INTERN F '09 **J** J.CREW  J.CREW COLLECTION **L** LARSIE LIL' WAYNE - BEST RAPPER ALIVE LIZ CLAIBORNE **M** MISC. CARDS MISC. TAPE MISC. TYPE **P** PILATES WITH MARINA TREJO PINK PRESS, PUBLICATIONS & EXHIBITIONS **S** SKINCARE STAN SMITH 2004

# Text and typography

**4**

In recent years, graphic designers working in print have been spoilt for choice with the number and variety of fonts they can use in their layouts. Yet it was not always so. Before digital desktop publishing, back in the days of hot-metal type and phototypesetting, only a few of the classic fonts were available and new fonts were rare – they represented a huge investment by the type foundries and were expensive for printers to buy. A similar situation exists for web designers today. Strictly speaking, if the users of your website do not own the fonts that you may have specified and already have them installed on their computers, then the browser will render your text in the default font.

This has led to web designers having to offer users a fallback position. As well as specifying a preferred font, you also have to suggest alternatives – with a last resort of one of the five generic descriptions of fonts: serif, sans serif, monospace, cursive and fantasy.

**4.1** The giant ABC typography of New York 'boutique studio' Studio Von Birken, founded by Katia Küthe and Philipp Müssigmann, may be a challenge at first, but once you discover the rules of engagement, then it's a delight to use. Click View Source to see how they have made extensive use of the `<span>` tag

# Selecting fonts in HTML

Old-school HTML used the `<font>` tag, which is now, in the parlance of web standards, 'deprecated'. It has not been totally eliminated, so as to ensure some backward compatibility with existing older websites and browsers, but its use is to be avoided and it may well be withdrawn in the future. The `<font>` tag's biggest disadvantage was that it had to be wrapped around every single scrap of text, increasing the file size considerably and making future maintenance problematic.

```
<p><font face="Verdana,Helvetica,Arial,Geneva,sans-serif"
size="2" color="#0000af">The text goes here.</font></p>
```

Now you can forget all about it. New-school HTML is much simpler, thus:

```
<p>The text goes here.</p>
```

The styling is now all done in the CSS code (either in the `<head>` of the document or preferably in a standalone external page):

```
p { font-family: Verdana, Arial, Helvetica, sans-serif; }
```

For simplicity, the size and colour properties have been omitted for now. This says to the user's browser: 'For any text enclosed by a `<p>` paragraph tag, please use the font Verdana, but if you have not got Verdana on your hard drive, use Arial (for PCs) or Helvetica (for Macs), and failing that, any generic sans serif font you can find.' Verdana, however, is a common font specially designed for the web and given away free by Microsoft, so in this case the alternatives may not have to be invoked. The final semi-colon (`;`) is optional, but is best left in as you may want to add other properties at a later date.

## Serif and sans serif fonts

In type there are two basic kinds of font: serif and sans serif (Fig **4.2**). Serifs are the marks at the extremities of the letterform, said to originate from the finishing strokes made by Roman stonemasons to the letters they carved, on the base of Trajan's Column in Rome, for example. *Sans* (French for 'without'), means that the typeface has no serifs and is more modern-looking. Sans serif fonts are more legible on screen – thin serifs can disappear or look too large on screen.

Serif faces include Times New Roman and Georgia. To define serif fonts the CSS would be:

```
p { font-family: "Times New Roman", Times, serif; }
```

Note that if the name of a font is more than one word, it must be contained within quotation marks.

Sans serif fonts include Helvetica (Microsoft's variant is Arial) and Verdana. A third category is the monospace font, in which all letters occupy spaces that have the same width, as they are on old-fashioned manual typewriters. A common example is Courier. Cursive fonts, also known as script, are like joined-up handwriting, such as Brush Script – the sort you see on wedding invitations. The generic fantasy category covers all the rest – fonts that are primarily decorative, including the one that designers love to hate, Comic Sans MS (Fig **4.3**).

Before we discuss fonts in more detail, let's go back to basics and set out some definitions.

**4.2** A sans serif face such as Verdana has no serifs terminating its extremities; a serif face such as Georgia, shown here, does

**4.3** The five generic font families of CSS: serif (e.g. Georgia), sans serif (e.g. Verdana), monospace (e.g. Courier), cursive (e.g. Brush Script) and fantasy (e.g. Comic Sans MS)

Serif

Serifs

Serif Sans-serif

Serif

Sans-serif

Monospace

*Cursive*

Fantasy

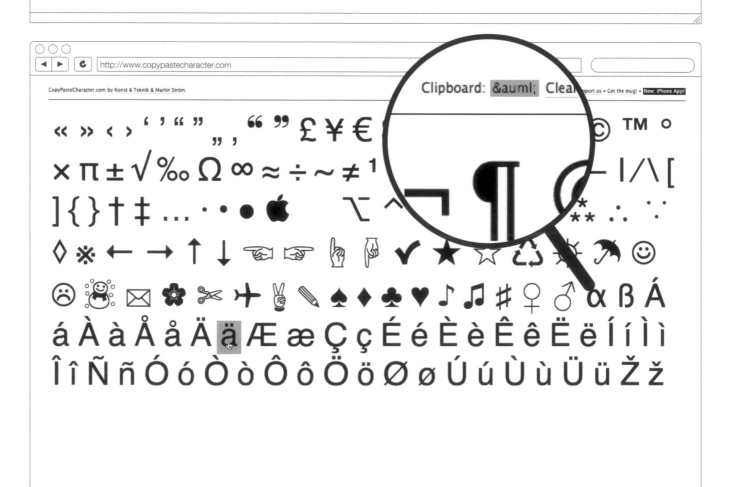

# Text

Before text came to mean a short message on a mobile phone, it meant raw copy, more likely nowadays to be called 'content'. Text is the 'meaning' part of type: just plain words plus the spaces between them, devoid of any information about the typefaces, sizes, measures or weights being used. It is always best to compose your text first in a text editor or word processor.

But be warned, programs such as Microsoft Word can in fact be too helpful. HTML can handle only the most common symbols and punctuation: curly quotation marks, apostrophes and em and en dashes left in the text may cause spurious characters to appear when the browser renders the page. So convert curly quotes and apostrophes to the symbols for feet (') and inches ("), or use the escape characters `&#34;` or `&quot;` or the more specific code listed to the right.

As we saw on page 29, some common symbols have been reserved for special uses in the code and cannot be used 'as is'. To the right are some common escape entities, as mnemonics and with their decimal equivalents (with hexadecimal versions in parentheses). Hexadecimal numbers (numbers in base 16, viz 0–9 plus a–f) are a throwback to the computer science origins of the internet. Computers are happiest dealing with binary numbers (numbers in base 2, namely 0 and 1) but these are unwieldy for humans, who prefer decimal (numbers in base 10, namely 0–9); hexadecimal (hex for short) numbers, however, translate directly to binary and as we shall see in Chapter 5 are also used to define colours (see page 114). Some browsers have trouble interpreting mnemonics (you will spot unexpected characters appearing when you preview your page), so the decimal or the hex equivalents must be used.

As mentioned in Chapter 2, a full list of code equivalents for common symbols can be found at www.w3schools.com/tags/ref_entities.asp. The big advantage of using a web-specific text editor such as BBEdit or PageSpinner is that they make it easier for you to add these essential codes, instead of having to type them out by hand.

Once you have input your text and turned it into web pages, print it out and proofread it away from the computer. Better still, get a colleague to read the proof – mistakes are often invisible to those who make them. Proofreading is vital now that designers are expected to set text as they are laying out designs.

& ampersand

```
&amp; &#38; (&#x26;)
```

£ British pound

```
&pound; &#163; (&#xA3;)
```

© copyright

```
&copy; &#169; (&#xA9;)
```

~ tilde

```
&tilde; &#732; (&#x2DC;)
```

– en dash

```
&ndash; &#8211; (&#x2013;)
```

— em dash

```
&mdash; &#8212; (&#x2014;)
```

' left single quote

```
&lsquo; &#8216; (&#x2018;)
```

' right single quote

```
&rsquo; &#8217; (&#x2019;)
```

" left double quote

```
&ldquo; &#8220; (&#x201C;)
```

" right double quote

```
&rdquo; &#8221; (&#x201D;)
```

… ellipsis (three dots)

```
&hellip; &#8230; (&#x2026;)
```

non-breaking space

```
    ( )
```

**4.5** An almost (some punctuation marks and foreign language letters have been omitted here) complete font, comprising roman, bold and italic. This example is Georgia, a serif font designed for the computer screen by Matthew Carter in 1993, named after a newspaper headline titled 'Alien heads found in Georgia'

# The language of type

The terms 'font' and 'typeface' are often used interchangeably these days. Strictly speaking, a font is defined as a complete set in one size of all the letters of the alphabet, complete with associated ligatures (joined letters), numerals, punctuation marks and any other signs and symbols (Fig **4.5**), collectively called 'sorts' (hence the expression 'out of sorts'). The word 'font', or 'fount' as it used to be spelt in Europe, derives from 'found', as in type foundry, and reminds us of the days when typesetting involved molten metal-type cast from moulds.

'Typeface', often shortened to 'face', is the name given to the look and design of the alphabet and its associated marks and symbols. Every typeface has a name. This can be the name of its designer, for example Garamond, Bodoni or Baskerville. It can take the name of the newspaper or publication it was originally designed for, for example Times New Roman or Century. Or it may just have a fanciful name intended to convey the 'feel' of the face, for example Optima, Perpetua or Futura.

In the days of hot-metal setting there would be a slightly different design – or font – for each physical size of type, optimized to work well at that particular size. In computer setting, however, it is common for one single design to be enlarged or reduced to make all the sizes. In a digital page-layout system or word processor on your computer, a menu item labelled 'font' will in fact display a list of the available typefaces.

A complete set of sorts will also include some or all of the following:
• alternative letters, for the ends of lines, for example, and ornamented or 'swash' capitals (but try to avoid setting whole lines of swash letters)
• diphthongs, such as æ and œ
• ligatures, such as fi and fl (in books of poetry, you may even see a ligature between c and t)
• accented letters for setting foreign languages, such as à (grave), é (acute), ô (circumflex), ü (diaresis), ç (cedilla), ñ (tilde)
• numerals or figures, which can be lining or non-lining (sometimes called 'old-style' numbers). Georgia, for example, uses old-style (non-lining) figures, whereas Times New Roman has lining figures (Fig **4.6**)

ABCDEFGHIJKLMNOPQRSTUVWXYZ
abcdefghijklmnopqrstuvwxyzfifl
.,:;&?!£$@ 1234567890

**ABCDEFGHIJKLMNOPQRSTUVWXYZ**
**abcdefghijklmnopqrstuvwxyzfifl**
**.,:;&?!£$@ 1234567890**

*ABCDEFGHIJKLMNOPQRSTUVWXYZ*
*abcdefghijklmnopqrstuvwxyzfifl*
*.,:;&?!£$@ 1234567890*

- punctuation marks, such as , (comma) and ; (semi-colon)
- reference marks, such as * (asterisk) and ¶ (paragraph)
- fractions and mathematical signs, also known as pi characters, such as + (plus) and = (equals)
- other signs and dingbats, such as & (ampersand) and © (copyright)

A font of roman type will comprise three alphabets:
- capitals, also called upper case, so named because of the position of the letters in a compositor's typecase (abbreviated to caps or u.c.)
- small letters, also known as lower case (abbreviated to l.c.)
- perhaps small capitals, which are capitals the height of a lower-case letter

Italic and bold fonts contain just two alphabets: capitals and lower case.

A family is a set of fonts related to the basic roman typeface, which may include italic and bold plus a whole spectrum of different 'weights'. These range from ultra light to ultra bold. It will also include different widths, ranging from ultra condensed to ultra expanded. Univers, for example, was designed by Adrian Frutiger in 1957 to have 21 fonts, in five weights and four widths. A series is a complete range of sizes in the same typeface.

This is well and good for graphic designers working in print, but for web designers all these variations may not be available and, as we have seen, some non-standard characters and symbols will have to be replaced by escape entities.

Fonts you can be confident are common to both PCs and Macs are sometimes called websafe fonts (Fig **4.7**). They all have bold variants and most have italic versions – for an up-to-date list of websafe fonts, check out www.ampsoft.net/webdesign-l/WindowsMacFonts.html.

**4.6** Lining and non-lining (old-style) numbers. The lining numbers are Times New Roman; the non-lining numbers are Georgia. Old-style numbers have more charm but lining numbers are easier to tabulate

1234567890

1234567890

**4.7** Common websafe fonts (those that are available on both PCs and Macs). Almost all websafe fonts will have bold variants, and most will also have italic versions available

**Sans serif fonts**

# Arial
# **Arial Black**
# Impact
# Lucida Sans
# Tahoma
# Trebuchet MS
# Verdana

**Serif fonts**

# Georgia
# Palatino Linotype /
# Book Antiqua
# Times New Roman

**Cursive fonts**
None common to Macs & PC

**Monospace fonts**

# Courier New
# Lucida Console

**Fantasy fonts**

# Comic Sans MS (no italic)

**Dingbats and symbols (no italic)**

Webdings

Symbol

# αβχδεφγηιφκλμνο

## Distinguishing typefaces

Each typeface has its own distinctive characteristics, called 'earmarks' (Fig **4.8**), named after the distinctive 'ear' on the lower-case g. These enable us to identify one design from another. To distinguish Helvetica from Univers, for example, look for the vertical downstroke in the capital G, the curly tail of the lower-case y, and the angled tail through the bowl of the Q (Fig **4.9**).

**TIP**

Identifying typefaces

When trying to identify a typeface, a good strategy is to start with the Q (a letter so infrequently used that typographers often have fun with it, making it their trademark), then the ampersand, then the J, G and W. Try the lower-case g, then a, j and y. For numbers, look first at 3, then 1, 7, 5 and 2.

Other features that help to distinguish different typefaces are the overall proportions (the relation of x-height to ascenders and descenders, for example), the stress (is it oblique or vertical?), the contrast between thick and thin strokes, the formation of the serifs. Are the characters wide and loose-fitting, or compact and tight? Some are easy: script and 'black letter' faces, for example, stand out from all the others.

Verdana, designed by Matthew Carter, and named after the verdant Seattle area, was designed specifically for website use. Microsoft released the initial version of the font in 1996 as part of its core fonts for the web collection and it has since been bundled with Internet Explorer. It is extended and has extra space between characters so they do not touch, particularly with letter combinations such as 'fi' 'fl' and 'ff', which would be ligatures in print. The bolds are very bold, so you can always tell the difference between bold and roman, yet the bold characters will not fill in, even at small sizes (Fig **4.10**). Special care has been taken with such letters as 1, i, I, l and J, adding serifs to the upper-case I and J so that they are easily distinguishable. The lower-case i is slightly shorter than the lower-case l, curves are kept to a minimum and lower-case

**4.8** The anatomy of type – knowing the names for the component parts and key measurements of letters is an aid to identifying and specifying typefaces. The example here is the serif face Georgia

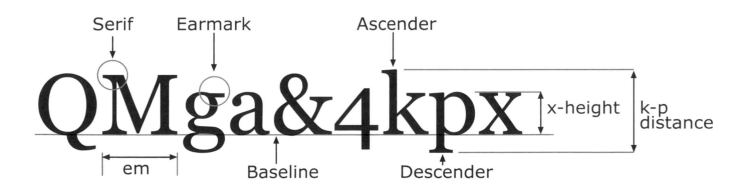

characters are a pixel taller than their upper-case counterparts at key screen sizes. Carter also designed Verdana's serif companion Georgia, which is larger than Times at the same point size, with a greater x-height.

## Increasing your choice of typefaces

Graphic designers frustrated by the lack of choice in fonts for websites have resorted to several tricks over the years. First they would substitute headings and menu items, for example, with the text in the desired font rendered as a graphic, and sometimes even whole pages rendered as one big GIF or JPEG. This plays havoc with the search engines, even if `alt` tags are used, and makes life difficult for anybody making changes in the future. Graphic 'text' also reduces the accessibility of your web page.

Mac OS X uses a graphics technology called Quartz to display true PostScript anti-aliased fonts on screen. Windows uses a similar technology called ClearType to accomplish the same thing. With this ability to display true versions of typefaces in web browsers, you would think typography on the web would be booming. But it is not, and why? Because no one has yet solved the problem of how to deliver custom typefaces to people who do not have them installed.

The fonts installed on most Macs and PCs are termed websafe fonts (see page 90). In CSS3, a CSS rule called `@font-face` enables you to use some specially licensed non-websafe fonts in your designs. You link to them as you would to an image. In the style sheet, the CSS code to style an `h1` heading, for example, using a TrueType font designed by Ray Larabie, would be:

```
@font-face {
  font-family: "Kimberley";
  src: url(http://www.princexml.com/fonts/larabie/kimberle.ttf)
  format("truetype");
}

h1 { font-family: "Kimberley", sans-serif }
```

**4.9** Univers was the most popular sans-serif face until desktop publishing came along and pushed Helvetica (and its PC equivalent Arial) into top spot. With the web came Verdana, optimized for screen viewing. Note that Arial has some features of Univers, in the capital G for example

GRgyQa&1

Univers 55

GRgyQa&1

Helvetica

GRgyQa&1

Arial

GRgyQa&1

Verdana

Browsers that support @font-face will render text using Kimberley while older browsers will use the default sans serif face. Make sure that the particular font you wish to use is freely available for use with @font-face.

Google has also entered the font arena with an open-source collection of fonts available free of charge. The Google font directory contains a range of fonts accessed by an API (application programming interface) enabled by the CSS3 @font-face standard. Available fonts are listed at http://code.google.com/webfonts and this will grow over time. To use the font Tangerine by Toshi Omagari, for example, add the HTML to the head:

```
<link href ='http://fonts.googleapis.com/css?family=Tangerine'
rel='stylesheet' type='text/css'>
```

and in the CSS:

```
h1 { font-family: 'Tangerine', serif; }
```

Text styled using these web fonts is searchable, scales crisply when zoomed, and is accessible to users with screen readers. The API takes care of converting the font into a format compatible with any modern browser (including Internet Explorer 6 and up), sends just the styles and weights you select, and the font files and CSS are tuned and optimized for web serving.

Another solution is to use sIFR (scalable Inman Flash Replacement) text, developed by Mike Davidson, based on the work of Shaun Inman. Flash (see Chapter 6) is vector-based, so can produce crisp lettering. By using a combination of JavaScript, CSS and Flash, sIFR replaces plain browser text with the designer's typeface of choice, regardless of whether or not users have that font installed on their systems. A JavaScript function (see Chapter 6) is first run to check that Flash is installed and then looks for whatever tags, IDs or classes you designate. If Flash is not installed (or if JavaScript is turned off), the (X)HTML page displays as normal and nothing further occurs. If Flash is installed, the script creates Flash movies the same size as the designated elements and

**4.10** Verdana, designed by Matthew Carter in 1996, has been optimized for screen readability. Letters that look similar in faces such as Gill Sans are given distinguishing features and greater clarity, as shown here

ABCDEFGHIJKLMNOPQRSTUVWXYZ
abcdefghijklmnopqrstuvwxyz
1234567890 &@£$?!

**ABCDEFGHIJKLMNOPQRSTUVWXYZ
abcdefghijklmnopqrstuvwxyz
1234567890 &@£$?!**

*ABCDEFGHIJKLMNOPQRSTUVWXYZ
abcdefghijklmnopqrstuvwxyz
1234567890 &@£$?!*

1IJil fifi flfl
Verdana

lIJil fifi flfl
Gill Sans

# How type
# is measured

overlays them to hide the text, pumping in the browser text in as a Flash variable. Then the ActionScript inside each Flash file draws that text in your chosen typeface at a 6 point size and scales it up until it fits snugly inside the Flash movie.

All this happens in a split second. However, this does not mean that you can replace every single word of a website with a fancy font – this method is meant for instances of display type only, so try to use restraint. For further details and updates see www.mikeindustries.com/blog/sifr/. Other ways of introducing more fonts into your designs, which do not use Flash, include typekit.com (subscription-based) and the JavaScript-based Cufón.

The way type is measured dates back to the days of hot metal. In 1737, the Frenchman Pierre Fournier le Jeune invented the point system of measurement, by dividing the French inch into 12 'lines' which were further subdivided into six points. Some half-century later, around 1785, another Parisian, François-Ambroise Didot, settled on a standard – the didot point – which is used in continental Europe to this day.

In the United States, the point was standardized by the American Type Founders' Association in 1886 to be 0·013837in (or 0·3515mm). Recently, the point has been further rationalized to make it exactly $\frac{1}{72}$ in (0·01389in or 0·3528mm).

A pica is 12 points, and so measures $\frac{1}{6}$ in (4.2mm). (The didot equivalent to the pica is the cicero.) Although with computerized systems type can be of any height, its size is still generally measured in points, abbreviated to pt.

The use of points to specify size refers back to metal letterpress type. When a font is described as 6pt or 18pt, what is really being measured is the height of the body of lead that the letter sits on. This is the total height from the lowest extremity of a descender (the long vertical down-stroke of a letter such as p or q) to the top of the tallest ascender (the long vertical up-stroke of a letter such as k or d), with a little extra space top and bottom. This is usually called the k-p height.

A more exact way of defining point size is to say that it is the distance from baseline to baseline when type is set solid (without leading, which we will come to later).

Some typefaces have longer ascenders and descenders than others, so it is quite possible for two typefaces to be the same point size but to appear smaller or larger. A more visually accurate method of describing size is to use the x-height. The lower-case letter x is used because all its terminals (ends) touch a line of measurement. Georgia, for example, has a bigger x-height than Times.

Type below 14pt is called body type, text, or book type. Type above 14pt is called display type. Some display types are so decorative as to be unsuitable for text setting and are available in capitals only.

## Measuring type in CSS

In CSS, size can be absolute or relative. Absolute sizes include inches, millimetres, points and pixels; relative sizes include keywords, ems, exes and percentages. It is not considered good practice to use the font-size property to create headings – the structural heading tags h1, h2 and so on should always be used and defined accordingly.

Most designers seem to favour the more precise pixel measurement for type height (forget inches and centimetres straight away), but in practice this is also a relative measurement, as it depends on the resolution of the end-user's display. A 12px letter on a 1680 x 1050 screen will appear much smaller than the same letter on a 640 x 480 screen. Furthermore, browsers such as Internet Explorer 6 will not allow users with limited eyesight to enlarge text defined by pixel size. Internet Explorer 7 does allow text resizing, so as it gradually takes over from the older browsers, this restriction will become less important.

An em, as we will see below, was originally a measurement of width rather than height (this em is not to be confused with the tag for emphasis). In print, this is the width of a capital M. Half an em is an en, which is the width of a capital N. A complete font provides the graphic designer with two types of dash: an em rule and an en rule. In CSS, an em is simply defined as the size of the default browser font, which is generally 16px, and more specifically the distance from baseline to baseline with no additional interlinear space, or leading.

Another measurement in CSS that may be new to print designers is the ex, which also uses the default size of the font (the size the font is drawn at, not the default size the browser uses), but whereas the em uses the square in which the entire character resides, an ex is the height of a lower-case x – the same as the x-height familiar to graphic designers for print.

To recap, in CSS type can be measured in the following ways:

### Absolute units
in (inches; 1in = 2.54cm)
cm (centimetres; 1cm = 10mm)
mm (millimetres)
pt (points; 1pt = $\frac{1}{72}$ in)
pc (picas; 1pc = 12pt)
px (pixels, effectively 1px = 1pt)

### Relative measurements
keywords: `xx-small, x-small, small, medium, large, x-large, xx-large`
em (width of capital M in default browser font)
ex (width of lc x in default browser font)
percentage

The CSS code to define a `<p>` tag in ems, for example, would be:

```
p { font-size: 0.9em; }
```

Note there should be no space between number and unit.

As with colour (see Chapter 5), CSS allows the use of keywords, in this case ranging from `xx-small` (extra extra small) to `xx-large` (extra extra large). The default browser font is medium, so if that is 16px, then large would be 19px, using a scaling factor of 1.2. There are also two relative-size keywords, `smaller` and `larger`, which bump the size keyword along the scale relative to the parent object.

So far we have not discussed the concept of inheritance, which is a cornerstone of CSS. The `<body>` tag always encloses a `<p>` tag, for example, and is thus its 'parent'. Similarly `<em>` and `<strong>` tags are usually found within a `<p>` tag and are thus its 'children'. Inheritance saves a lot of typing in CSS, because if we define the font family, say, in the `<body>` tag, we do not have to define it again when we style our `<p>` tags – unless you want it to be different. The `<p>` tag inherits the font family for the `<body>` tag. Defining a new font family for the `<p>` would, however, override the original one defined in the `<body>` tag.

The use of ems (basically multiples or fractions of the default size) can result in inconsistencies between browsers and platforms. Users may reset their default font size to something smaller than the usual 16px. Internet Explorer 6 users may be surfing with the text set at Smaller, in which case anything less than 1em will look microscopic. Perhaps using a percentage value could be a reliable method for defining size? Setting the `<ul>` list tag to 80% (of the default browser size) would result in text approximately 13px high. However, if another `<ul>` list was nested within this list, it would inherit the 80% and its text would be 10px high.

**The Owen Briggs method**

A popular compromise is the 'Owen Briggs method', which uses a combination of ems and percentages. First we define the `<body>` as 76%, which brings the overall default size down from an oversize 16px to a more designer-friendly 12px. Then the children – `<p>`, `<h1>`, etc. – are sized in ems, which being absolute units do not accumulate in the way percentages do, for example:

```
body { font-size: 76%; }
p { font-size: 1em; }
h1 { font-size: 1.5em; }
```

Further information, screenshots and tutorials can be found at http://www.thenoodleincident.com/tutorials/box_lesson/font/.

# Font weights, variants and properties

## Bold

Spending so much time on so simple a property as size shows how versatile CSS can be. Another case in point is boldness, covered by the `font-weight` property. As well as the keywords `normal, bold, bolder` and `lighter`, it also provides nine numerical values, from 100 to 900, with 400 corresponding to the keyword `normal` and 700 to regular `bold`. To define a level `h1` heading as bold, the CSS code would be:

```
h1 { font-weight: bold; }
```

or

```
h1 { font-weight: 700; }
```

The `bolder` and `lighter` values are relative to the weight inherited from the parent:

```
strong { font-weight: bolder; }
```

Of course, not every font is as rational as Univers, with its five weights and four widths. The weights of fonts are described using all kinds of terms, including Regular, Roman, Book, Medium, Semi- or DemiBold, Bold, Heavy, Black and ExtraBlack, so that mapping a number to a specific weight of a font is not easy. While some fonts may come only in normal and bold, and others could have as many as eight weights, the only real guarantee is that a face of a given value will be no less dark than the faces of lighter values. And your end-user may not even have the fonts installed. So for now, it is perhaps best to stick to normal and bold.

## Italics

The `font-style` property has fewer options: normal, italic and oblique. An oblique font is an upright roman font that has been slanted, as opposed to a true italic font, which has distinct design differences in the letterforms, particularly in the lower-case *a* and *f*. In this example any emphasized text within `h1` will appear in a normal face:

```
h1 { font-style: italic; }
h1 em { font-style: normal; }
```

Note that the `em` in the selector (after `h1`) is the tag for emphasis (usually rendered as italic) *not* the em unit of measurement.

## Small caps

Small caps are catered for by the `font-variant` property. Small caps are capital letters the same height as the lower-case letters. They are often used for acronyms in body text so they do not stand out too much. In print they would have slightly different design characteristics to proper caps. In CSS this transforms lower-case letters and words into scaled-down caps:

```
h2 { font-variant: small-caps; }
```

There is also a `text-transform` property that will automatically capitalize lower-case text it comes across, useful for changing the look of headings, for example.

## Leading

Spacing between lines of type is called leading, named after the strips of lead that were placed between lines of type in hot-metal setting (Fig **4.11**). 'Set solid' means without leading, for example 10/10pt. To write 10/11pt means to ask for 10pt type with a 1pt space (leading) between the lines.

Desktop publishing systems often add 1.5pt leading by default. Always take into account the x-height of a typeface when deciding on a leading value. A good rule of thumb is: the larger the x-height, the more the leading; the smaller the x-height, the less the leading.

In CSS, leading is adjusted using the `line-height` property. As in `font-size`, you can use px, em or percentages. The default browser line-height is 120%: so to tighten up the spacing, use a lower percentage value; or to spread the lines apart, use a higher value. Using a percentage value, rather than an absolute px or pt, means that the leading will adjust itself proportionally if the font size is changed. If, for example, the `font-size` is 12px and the `line-height` is set at 150% (equivalent to 18px) then the leading will be 18 – 12 = 6px.

You are also allowed to use a simple number, without units, for example:

```
p { line-height: 1.5; }
```

Why use 1.5 instead of 150%? If you used a percentage, then the calculated value would be inherited, so that, for example, if there was a paragraph of text on the page defined by a class as 24px, then the `line-height` would remain at 18px, meaning the lines of text would be all squashed up.

Using the number 1.5 would simply multiply each font height by 1.5, so the line height for the 24px text would be 24 x 1.5 = 36px.

**All together now**

Do you have to type out all those properties every time you give a tag the above font properties? No, the font property is a shorthand way of including all the font information in one line, ideally in the order:

```
font-style | font-variant | font-weight | font-size /
line-height | font-family
```

For example:

```
h1 { font:  italic small-caps bold 1.75em/2 Verdana,
Arial, sans-serif; }
```

The list must always include font-size and font-family, in that order, as the last two properties. Other properties can be omitted, and their value will be taken as being the default 'normal'.

**4.11** Leading is achieved in CSS by the `line-height` property: here we see text set solid (top) with no added leading, with positive leading (centre), and negative leading where lines of text begin to overlap (bottom)

It was the best of times, it was the worst of times, it was the age of wisdom, it was the age of foolishness, it was the epoch of belief, it was the epoch of incredulity, it was the season of Light, it was the season of Darkness, it was the spring of hope, it was the winter of despair, we had everything before us, we had nothing before us, we were all going direct to Heaven, we were all going direct the other way...

It was the best of times, it was the worst of times, it was the age of wisdom, it was the age of foolishness, it was the epoch of belief, it was the epoch of incredulity, it was the season of Light, it was the season of Darkness, it was the spring of hope, it was the winter of despair, we had everything before us, we had nothing before us, we were all going direct to Heaven, we were all going direct the other way...

It was the best of times, it was the worst of times, it was the age of wisdom, it was the age of foolishness, it was the epoch of belief, it was the epoch of incredulity, it was the season of Light, it was the season of Darkness, it was the spring of hope, it was the winter of despair, we had everything before us, we had nothing before us, we were all going direct to Heaven, we were all going direct the other way...

Català   Nota Legal

DÍAS CONTADOS

Editorial   Colección   Librerías   Contacto

La Central
Barcelona, Madrid
lacentral.com

Laie
Barcelona. Madrid
laie.es

Paradox
Madrid
paradox.es

Librería Antonio Machado
Madrid
machadolibros.com

Librería Platón
Barcelona

**4.12** Barcelona-based Días Contados, a company translating books into Castilian Spanish and Catalan, uses centred text on its home page and on inside pages to great effect

# Other typographic facilities

## Width and spacing

In graphic design, the space around letters and words is often as important as the letterform itself. When characters are designed, they are also given space either side to prevent consecutive sorts from touching. These are called side bearings, and the information about horizontal spacing built into a typeface by its designer is known as its font metrics.

The width of a line of setting, or the column width of a publication, is called the measure, and is sometimes measured in picas, but more usually nowadays in millimetres. As we have seen, another convenient method of measurement is the em. The em is not an absolute measurement. Its size will vary depending on the typeface and its point size. A 1em indent in 10pt type is 10pt, as a 1em indent in 18pt type is 18pt, so that it will always be in proportion with the rest of the setting.

**Reversing out**
Some websites have reversed-out text – light-coloured text on a dark background, most often white on black. White on black is harder on the eyes than black on white: the letters need to be wider apart, lighter in weight and with more space between the lines, so make sure you increase the leading and tracking and decrease the font weight.

## Kerning and tracking

By adjusting pairs of certain letters containing extremities that might invade the space of other letters, such as Y, W, L and T, it is possible to bring them closer together and improve the visual appearance of a word. This is called kerning (Fig **4.13**). In hot metal, kerning was only possible by physically cutting away the metal body of the type. With computer systems, there are no restrictions on the extent of kerning possible. Adjusting the spacing between all the letters is called tracking (Fig **4.14**). Tracking should not be confused with kerning, which takes place only between pairs of letters. Negative tracking can be used to tighten up the spacing of text, particularly with sans serif faces.

Tracking is covered by the `letter-spacing` property. The default `normal` is equivalent to zero. All the usual measurements are allowed, as are negative amounts, though these could result in letters overlapping.

There is no specific property for kerning, but you could set up a rule using a class selector, for example:

```
.kerning { letter-spacing: -0.1em; }
```

# Yo! World.
# Yo! World.

**4.13** Kerning is used to fine-tune the visual spacing between pairs of letters, achieved in CSS by using negative letter-spacing

## Wild birds of Texas
## Wild birds of Texas
## Wild birds of Texas

**4.14** Letter spacing and word spacing can be achieved in CSS but should be used sparingly – in headings for example

And then use a `<span>` tag to enclose the pair of letters you wish to adjust, as in this `h2` heading:

```
<h2><span class="kerning">Yo</span>! World.</h2>
```

The same could be done to the W and o in 'World'.

The property `word-space` adds space between words. Normally any string of spaces in HTML code will be ignored and collapsed down to one, but the property `white-space` preserves them – probably only ever useful for the layout of poetry.

## Text alignment and spacing

A regular typewriter produces rows of type that line up on the left-hand side but give a ragged appearance on the right. In typesetting, this is called ranged left, flush left or ragged right. Type can also be set ranged right (ragged left); centred (Fig **4.12**); or asymmetrical. In books and magazines, it is usual to see columns of type with neat edges on both sides. This is called justified setting, and it is achieved by introducing variable amounts of space between the words. See Fig **4.15** for examples of each of these variations. More often than not, especially with the narrow columns used in newspapers and magazines, it is not possible to justify a line just by increasing the spaces, so words must be hyphenated. Compositors were taught to break words according to certain rules, but rules for hyphenation are now programmed into computer systems.

In CSS, `text-align` will adjust the horizontal alignment of text. Its values are `left`, `right`, `center` and `justify`. A better way to align elements is through manipulating their left and right margins (see Chapter 3).

```
p { text-align: center; }
```

A widow is the final single word of a paragraph that is carried over to the top of a column, while an orphan is a single word, or few words, left on the last line at the end of a paragraph. Widows and orphans are best avoided, generally by asking the writer to delete a word or two from earlier in the paragraph.

We are now used to paragraphs on the web being full-width throughout with a horizontal space (line space) separating each paragraph. In books, however, the paragraphs may be flush with each other, a new paragraph being identified by the first line being indented. This can be replicated in CSS with an indent of blank space (Fig **4.16**).

```
p { text-indent: 3em }
```

Note that a negative value will produce an overhang, which could disappear off the screen in some browsers unless left padding is used to compensate. The space between paragraphs is adjusted using `margin-top` and `margin-bottom` properties (see Chapter 3). Because different browsers have different defaults for the margins of headlines and blocks of text it is best to 'zero-out' all margins at the beginning of the style sheet:

```
body, h1, h2, p, ul {
  padding: 0;
  margin: 0;;
}
```

Text (and other elements) can also be aligned vertically, relative to the baseline, for example, to produce subscripts ($H_2O$) and superscripts ($E=mc^2$):

```
.superscript { font-size:xx-small; vertical-align:sup; }
.subscript { font-size:xx-small; vertical-align:sub; }
```

Or you can also use the HTML tags `<sup>` and `<sub>`

```
E=MC<sup>2</sup>
```

A revival from medieval manuscripts is the drop cap (Fig **4.17**): an initial letter signalling the beginning of the text. It is usually enlarged to a size equivalent to three or more lines of type, with the type adjacent to it indented to make room. Drop caps work best when the first word comprises a single letter, such as A or I. Failing that, avoid short words, especially ones with only two letters. And take care with those words that form different words when the initial letter is removed, such as 'T-he' or 'E-very'. The pseudo-element `:first-letter` is not really a CSS property but a selector that identifies which part of the text CSS should apply to. For example:

```
p:first-letter {
  font-weight: bold;
  color: red;
  font-size: xx-large;
}
```

will result in a big, bold drop cap at the beginning of *every* paragraph. It may be better to use a `<span>` class if you want only the very first letter of the whole page to be a drop cap.

There is another pseudo-element, `:first-line`, that styles the initial line of a paragraph, for example to make it small caps. The `text-decoration` property of `none`, `underline`, `overline`, `line-through` and `blink` is also probably best left alone. Its only real practical use is to remove the default underlining from a link.

And finally, we must not forget that our letters can be given colour at no extra cost. More on this in the next chapter.

**4.15** Text set ranged left, ranged right, centred and justified. In CSS, this is achieved with the `text-align` property

Call me Ishmael. Some years ago - never mind how long precisely - having little or no money in my purse, and nothing particular to interest me on shore, I thought I would sail about a little and see the watery part of the world.

Call me Ishmael. Some years ago - never mind how long precisely - having little or no money in my purse, and nothing particular to interest me on shore, I thought I would sail about a little and see the watery part of the world.

Call me Ishmael. Some years ago - never mind how long precisely - having little or no money in my purse, and nothing particular to interest me on shore, I thought I would sail about a little and see the watery part of the world.

Call me Ishmael. Some years ago - never mind how long precisely - having little or no money in my purse, and nothing particular to interest me on shore, I thought I would sail about a little and see the watery part of the world.

**4.16** If you want the first line of a paragraph to indent, use the CSS `text-indent` property. A negative value will result in an overhang

Call me Ishmael. Some years ago - never mind how long precisely - having little or no money in my purse, and nothing particular to interest me on shore, I thought I would sail about a little and see the watery part of the world.

Call me Ishmael. Some years ago - never mind how long precisely - having little or no money in my purse, and nothing particular to interest me on shore, I thought I would sail about a little and see the watery part of the world.

**4.17** Drop caps emphasize the first letter of a page or article. To the right is a cap equivalent to two lines of type standing proud; below is a three-line cap with text flowing around it

Call me Ishmael. Some years ago - never mind how long precisely - having little or no money in my purse, and nothing particular to interest me on shore, I thought I would sail about a little and see the watery part of the world.

Call me Ishmael. Some years ago - never mind how long precisely - having little or no money in my purse, and nothing particular to interest me on shore, I thought I would sail about a little and see the watery part of the world.

# Step-by-step 3
## A basic portfolio website

## Step 1.

First prepare your images using Photoshop. For each image, we will require a thumbnail. As the images in this example can be either portrait or landscape, we will opt for square thumbnails 180 x 180px, which will entail some cropping. For aesthetic reasons, make all the large versions the same width, e.g. 550px. An easy way to create thumbnails is to reduce the shortest dimension (the width if the image is portrait; the height if it is landscape) to 180px, then use Photoshop's rectangular marquee tool, set at fixed size, to make your selection, then Image>Crop and File>Save for Web & Devices. Give your images meaningful names, with no spaces, and all lower case. It is good practice when naming thumbnails to add -t to the end of the filename, for example littlehampton.jpg for the large version; littlehampton-t.jpg for the thumbnail.

## Step 2.

Open the index.html page from Step-by-step 2, use 'Save as' to create portfolio.html, and delete the content from the right column. We will create an array of thumbnails in three rows of three to fit neatly on the page. Each thumbnail will have its own caption, and so that the caption will be positioned immediately under the thumbnail, we must create an image/caption combo `<div>`. And because there should only be one instance of a main `#<div>` ID per page and there will be many thumbnails on the page, we define it as a class, called `.thumbnail`:

```
.thumbnail {
  float: left;
  width: 180px;
  margin: 10px 30px 0px 0px;
}
```

and another class for the smaller caption text, thus:

```
.thumbnail p {
text-align: center;
font-size: .9em;
}
```

The HTML will look like:

```
<div class="thumbnail">
<a href="littlehampton.
html"><img src="images/
littlehampton-t.jpg"
width="180" height="180"
border="0" alt="The East Beach
Cafe, Littlehampton"></a>
```

```
<p>The East Beach Cafe,
Littlehampton</p>
</div>
```

If you think the captions will be of differing lengths, it may be prudent to add a height to `.thumbnail` so they will all align neatly.

## Step 3.

To make the new page littlehampton.html open in its own window, leaving portfolio.html still available, add `target="_blank"` to the `<a>` tag. The margins (top, right, bottom, left) defined in `.thumbnail` will keep the thumbnails spaced apart, and if we want to start another row after, say, the third thumbnail, we should add a `clear`:

```
.clearboth { clear: both; }
```

adding to the HTML

```
<br class="clearboth" />
```

Carry on adding thumbnails in rows of three, until all nine are in place (**top**).

## Step 4.

To create the page for the large image, open index.html again and 'Save as' littlehampton.html (you could name these pages gallery1.html, gallery2.html and so on if you prefer, or if you have a large portfolio). Replace the content with the larger image and its caption, leaving the copyright notice in place (**middle**). Repeat the process, making a new page for each of the photographs. You could also add a 'Back' button to these pages to take the viewer back to the main thumbnail page, or buttons taking them on to the next image. So that the links in the main content do not inherit the look of the menu, all the original `<a>` tags are made specific to the `#leftcolumn`, thus:

```
#leftcolumn a:link {
  color: #639194;
  font-size: 1.2em;
  text-decoration: none;
  font-weight: bold;
}
```

and so on. And new links are made for the `#rightcolumn`.

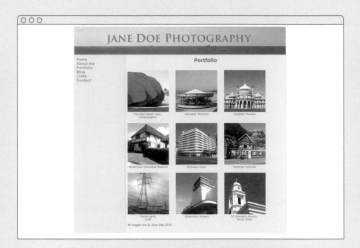

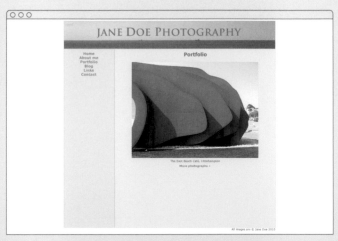

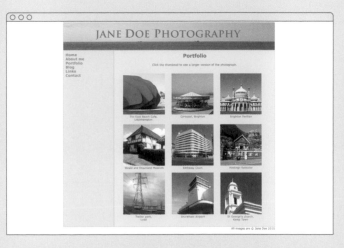

Whether you are a designer, an artist, an illustrator or a photographer, you will need a portfolio, or gallery, site to showcase your work to potential clients. The most basic of these has an array of thumbnails, each of which with a click of the mouse takes you to a larger version, with either a pop-up window, or as here, a new HTML page. This tutorial builds on the website created in Step-by-step 2 (pages 76–79), so we will not be making many changes to the colour scheme or type formatting.

## Step 5.

Back on the portfolio page, you will notice that the copyright line does not look quite right, so we create another `<div>` called `#footer` and float it right. You could enclose the entire gallery of portfolio `<div>`s in yet another `<div>` called `#gallery` to position it on the page and keep it all together as a module:

```
#gallery {
  display: block;
  text-align: center;
  margin-left: 50px;
}
```

It may also be useful to add an instruction line so that viewers will know to click the thumbnail to reveal a larger version (**opposite below**). If you have more photos, simply make a page called portfolio2.html, and link to it from the page we just made. The HTML in PageSpinner is shown **right** and the CSS **below right**.

## Step 6.

There are many other ways to design a portfolio site, and you can adjust the CSS to your heart's content until it is finally all working and can be uploaded to your host for the world to see.

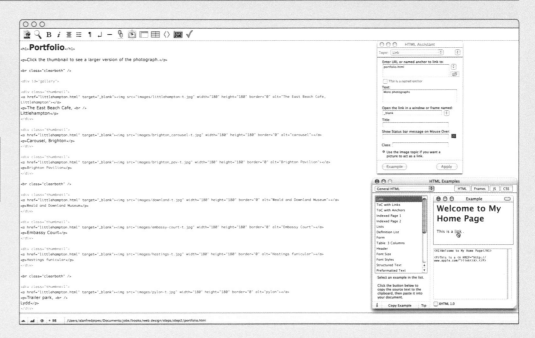

Dutch graphic designer Mike Giesser uses
CSS with just a touch of JavaScript to
create this easy-to-navigate 'indexed'
portfolio site

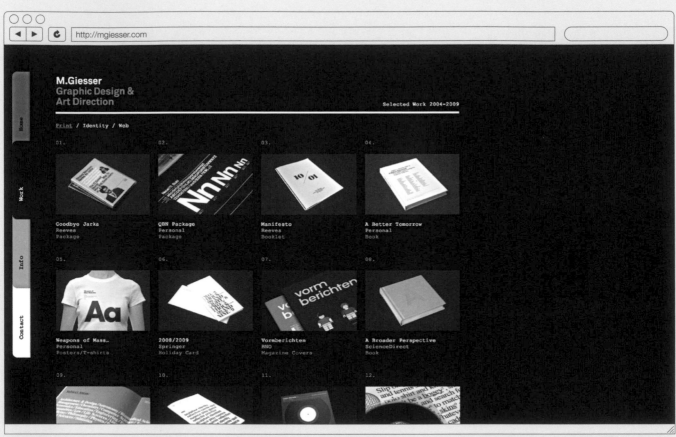

Influential author and book designer
Richard Hollis has a portfolio site that
appears to break free from the grid,
demonstrating the power of CSS

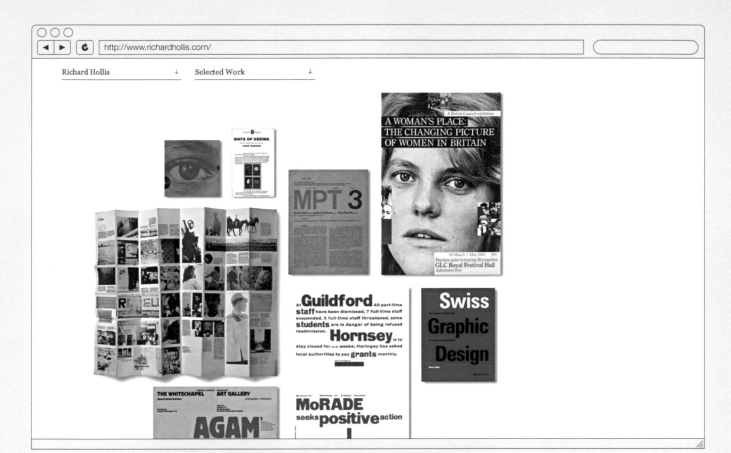

## I, Eye

*Albion Broadsheet no.2*

A self-published broadsheet based on
Hollis's travels in post-revolutionary
Cuba.

Printed litho in an edition of about 100,
each copy was furnished with a
handwritten felt-pen title and facsimiles
of Cuban entry and exit passport stamps.
The designer did much of the printer's
work: positive films of the half-tones and
typewritten text were assembled ready
for platemaking. Although this was
described as Albion Broadsheet no.2,
there was no no.1. It was sold for one
penny.

Client: --
Date: 1962
Category:  Miscellaneous & personal work

# Trailblazer 3
## Grïngo

Brazilian design studio Grïngo was founded in 2006 by childhood friends, and now partners, from São Paulo: André Matarazzo (taking on the strategic thinking and creative side) and Fernanda Jesus (who looks after client relations). After studying hotel management, which he believed would yield adventures around the world, Matarazzo abandoned the hospitality sector in 1997 to join McCann-Erickson in São Paulo to work on a new form of advertising, just nascent in Brazil, called 'digital'. He'd always been a very visual person, and loved graphic design before he knew what it really represented. He also loved computers: join the two passions together and you have digital design. He designed his first website in 1996 – a small project for a vending machine business his father ran, based on a Microsoft FrontPage template. Matarazzo describes it now as 'hideous'.

After three years as art director at web-design company Blast Radius, Vancouver, and another two at Blast Radius, Amsterdam, plus almost two years as Creative Director at Farfar, Stockholm, and a quick dab at TYO-ID, Tokyo, Matarazzo became homesick. With the experience gained at these international agencies he moved back to Brazil to start Grïngo. Jesus followed a more conventional route, taking an MBA at the University of São Paulo.

Grïngo has grown over the years from production to a full-service digital strategy and creative agency that employs over 60 staff and freelancers with offices in São Paulo and Rio de Janeiro, juggling 20 to 30 projects at any time. It holds several multinational accounts, including Coca-Cola, Windows Live, Absolut Vodka, Levi's and São Paulo FC. In the past three years Grïngo has won three Cyber Lions at The Cannes Lions International Advertising Festival: in 2007 a Bronze for Still Alive (creative and production); in 2007 a Bronze for Africa Auditorium (creative and production) and in 2008 a Silver for Grïngo's Swear Words Dictionary. At the time of writing they had also achieved 23 FWA (Favourite Website Awards) website of the day awards, a silver from the One Show Interactive and 14 accolades from the Wave Festival (Festival Latino-Americano de Communicação).

Grïngo, according to Matarazzo, has evolved from a focus on impactful mini-sites, usually some form of advertainment, to become a creative agency that is digital-centric, but media agnostic. They believe that the centre of all communication must be digital, the top medium for engagement and effective exchange and learning. Advertising, he says, is no longer merely about communicating a message, but participating in and bettering people's lives. Despite their 'chilled boyish good looks', they do research, analysis, strategy, concept creation, production, media buy and business intelligence – and actually find it fun.

A Grïngo is 'a foreigner' in Brazilian Portuguese. Matarazzo insists it's not pejorative. 'I guess the name Grïngo personifies our work methodology and structure. I've taken a few of the best practices I've seen while working around the world: extreme care for poetry and design from Japan; the nonsense humour and horizontal working processes of Sweden; the total professionalism and metrics of success and how to conduct business I found in Canada, and so on. I guess Grïngo is a little of all this.'

Like many web designers, he is largely self-taught. He says: 'I think going to a great design school must be fantastic but you can certainly do without if you dedicate yourself enough to reading what's available, looking for your references online, chatting to good people, becoming an intern at a good studio. And let's face it, some people just have the gift and others spend years attending a good school but pump out mediocre work. I think about 70 per cent of our designers never went to design school. I am very excited about folks coming out of Hyper Island (an industry-based learning programme based in Sweden) and their knowledge of projects and hands-on experimentation. I guess in some decades the business will be more mature and we can just pull from a great school someone who already knows a lot. Right now I find almost everyone needs to be taught the basics again when they come to Grïngo.'

While many of Grïngo's websites are Flash-based, Matarazzo is not a Flash programmer – he has a team of specialists to do that. And he is confident of Flash's future: 'I imagine it will continue developing fast and adding many functionalities out-of-the-box.' But it should be used appropriately: 'When I check my webmail, please give me something simple and clean. When I want to kill some time and get entertained, please give me an awesome site with amazing graphics and a storyline that intrigues me.' But, 'I am tired of the extra baroque stuff. Just don't make me think too hard, it gets in the way of beauty. Disruptive is fine, it makes you laugh and you may send it to a friend, but then what? I am interested in deeper engagement nowadays.'

www.gringo.nu
http://blog.gringo.nu/
twitter.com/gringo_nu
www.thefwa.com/profile/gringo-rib

**Fig 1** Absolut Brasil (2007): 12 artists were invited to design new labels for vodka bottles that brought their visions of Brazil to life

**Fig 2** Absolut Mango (2008): how to put some samba into your drink

**Fig 3** Coca-Cola Football (2008): who is better – Maradonna or Biro-Biro? Let them slug it out in this 3D game

**Fig 4** Coca-Cola Light (2008): discover the best eateries around the world

**Figs 5 and 6** Two screenshots from the Essa eu banco (I can bank it) website for Banco Itaú (2009): a day in the life of a character of your choice, and ways you can save for the future

Fig 1

Fig 2

Fig 3

Fig 4

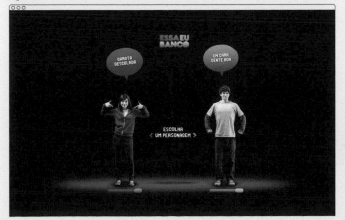

Fig 5

Fig 6

# Images and colour schemes

**5**

Graphic designers coming from a mainly print background will be used to working in CMYK colour. Cyan, magenta, yellow and black (key) are mixed to produce all the colours of the rainbow – at least in theory. In practice, CMYK is a compromise and has trouble reproducing many of the colours that we can see with our eyes. If the budget allows, you may be able to add an extra Pantone spot colour, or use six-colour 'hifi' that adds orange and green inks to increase the colour gamut.

The good news for designers of websites is that they get to work with RGB (red, green, blue) colour, which has a bigger gamut than the above. Not only that, but using a resolution of 72dpi, rather than the print norm of 300dpi, means smaller, more manageable files. But before we discuss colour in greater detail, let's look at images and graphic formats.

**5.1** Newsmap uses colour coding to overview the constantly changing shape of Google News. It groups news stories with similar content and places them into clusters, the size of each cell determined by the amount of related articles. It also allows you to compare the emphasis given to news in different countries

# Graphics Formats: GIFs, JPEGs and PNGs

As we learned in Chapter 2, images are added to the HTML using the code:

```
<img src="jane-doe.jpg" width="250" height="280" border="0"
alt="Self-portrait">
```

The abbreviation `src` stands for 'source' and tells the browser the location of the image, in this case the root folder (the same one as the HTML pages); `alt` stands for 'alternative text', necessary for browsers that do not display images and for screen-reading devices. Adding the dimensions of the image means that the browser will make space for the picture before it loads. If missed out, the page content and layout will jump about as various images are loaded. Because the `<img>` tag is one of those few exceptions that does not come in pairs, to comply with strict XHTML, we need to add a space and slash to the end:

```
<img src="jane-doe.jpg" width="250" height="280" border="0"
alt="Self-portrait" />
```

It is always good practice to put all the images into a separate subfolder, here called images, which would make the code:

```
<img src="images/jane-doe.jpg" width="250" height="280"
border="0" alt="Self-portrait" />
```

Always ensure that the structure of the website on the server is identical to the structure on your computer or else the browser will not be able to locate the images.

Images should be first prepared in a program such as Photoshop, to crop them to the right size and resolution. Generally, images with areas of flat colour, such as logos and buttons, are best saved as GIFs, and continuous-tone photographic-type images as JPEGs. The GIF (Graphics Interchange Format) was originally developed for CompuServe (it is still called CompuServe GIF on the Photoshop menu). It can only handle a palette of 256 colours, also known as 8-bit indexed colour. A later version, called GIF89a, also supports transparency (so that images with irregular outlines can appear to blend into the background), and interlacing, so that the image first appears as a pixellated picture that gradually sharpens up as it downloads. GIF89a also allows animated GIFs to be assembled from a series of still frames. All browsers (except completely non-graphical ones like Lynx) support GIFs.

Most also support JPEG (Joint Photographic Experts Group) files. JPEGs (files with the suffix .jpeg, or more commonly .jpg)

can display 24-bit colour. Photoshop has a 'Save for Web & Devices' feature (Fig **5.3**) that does wonders to compress JPEG and GIF images, trading off file size against image quality. Too much compression can result in unwanted visual 'artefacts' appearing along contrasty edges, such as around text and where the sky meets a face or tree. JPEGs also suffer from generation loss – the more they are edited and copied, the worse they can look (Fig **5.2**).

PNG (Portable Network Graphics) is a lossless, portable format that provides a patent-free replacement for GIFs and print-based TIFFs (Tagged Image File Format). It can work with indexed colour, like GIFs, or with RGB. PNG is a better choice than JPEG for storing images containing text, line art or sharp transitions, although it will have a larger file size. Another advantage of using a PNG is that it has a wider range of transparency options than a GIF. Either a single pixel value can be declared as transparent or an alpha channel can be added (enabling any percentage of partial transparency to be used). Older browsers do not support PNGs, but as they are phased out, it will become a more widespread format.

**Thumbnails made simple**

If you are making a portfolio or gallery page (see Step-by-step 3), you will need to prepare thumbnails (small versions of images). These will often be a different shape from the bigger image, e.g. square, so some creative cropping is usually necessary to select the most important portion of the image. In Photoshop, first reduce the shortest dimension to the size of the thumbnail, e.g. 180px, then use Photoshop's rectangular marquee tool, set at 'fixed size' (180 x 180px) to make your selection, then Image>Crop and File>Save for Web & Devices. Give your images meaningful names, no spaces, all lower case. It is good practice when naming the thumbnails to add a -t to the end of the filename, for example 'big-image.jpg' for the large version, 'big-image-t.jpg' for the thumbnail.

**5.2** JPEG is a lossy file format, which means that the quality of the image deteriorates each time the file is copied, resulting in artefacts around contrasting edges, such as around sharp text or buildings silhouetted against the sky

**5.3** Photoshop has a useful 'Save for Web & Devices' tool that lets you compare your original image with various compressions of JPEGs and GIFs

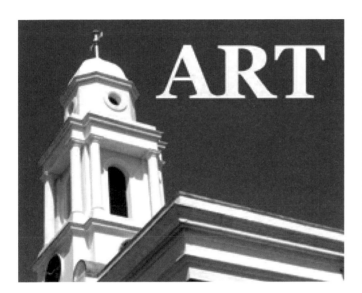

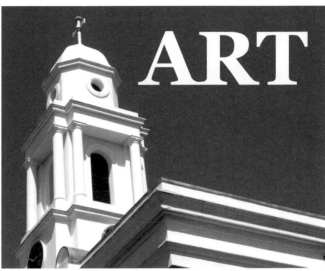

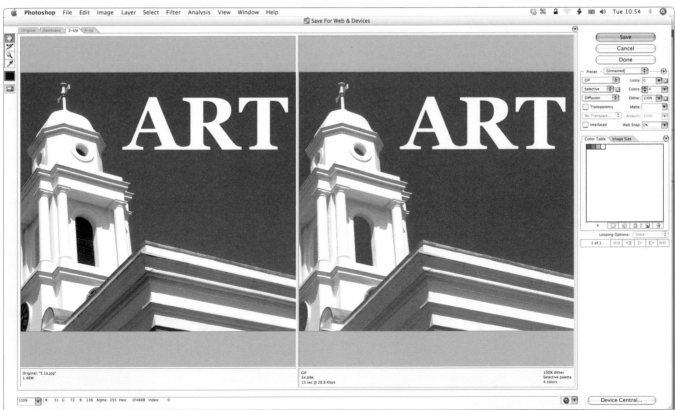

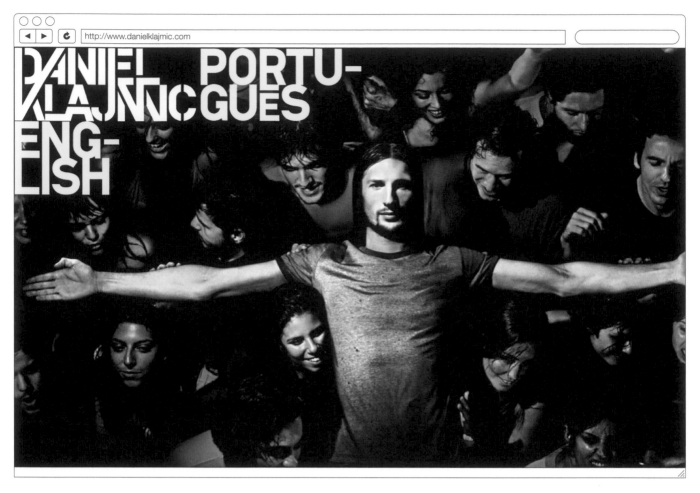

**5.4** Brazilian photographer Daniel Klajmic uses big, bold, primary yellow capital letters to give impact to his portfolio site. Design was by Quinta-feira: Art Direction & Graphic Design

**5.5** The JavaScript and Flash-based website of Tokyo-based graphic designer Kashiwa Sato, renowned for his work for fashion label Uniqlo (see page 20), uses moving flags of colour instead of thumbnails to direct users to slideshows of projects

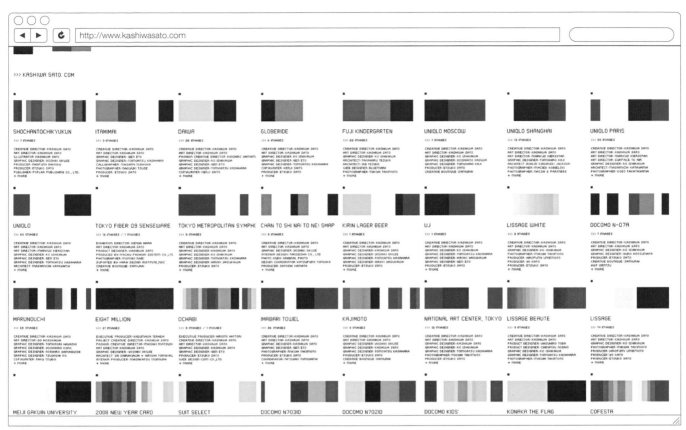

# Colour

Website designers get to work in RGB all the time, and at screen resolution of 72dpi (dots per inch), so what they see on the screen will be the same as in the finished product. There are slight differences, however, in the way Macs and PCs display colours, and how different browsers parse the colour information. Most people are assumed to have at least a 256-colour monitor, and taking into account the above constraints, we arrive at 216 'web-safe' colours, which will be displayed without resorting to dithering (optically mixing two or more colours). As computers have improved, this is not such a big issue as it used to be, but as new devices come on to the market, such as mobile phones and netbooks, it may still be worth bearing in mind. Charts of web-safe colours can be found on the internet, for example www.lynda.com/hex.html.

## Hexadecimal numbering

Web colours are generally described using a six-digit number comprising three sets of hexadecimal (hex) numbers, one each for the red, green and blue components of the colour. Hexadecimal numbers (numbers to base 16) are, as mentioned in Chapter 4, a legacy from computer science and are used because they directly translate to binary, the number system (base 2, i.e. just 0s and 1s) that computers use internally.

Each hex component ranges from 00 to ff, equivalent to 0 to 255 in decimal notation: 00 (0 in decimal) represents the lowest intensity; ff (255), the highest intensity of each of the colour components. This results in 16 million possible colours. So, 000000 is the complete absence of colour – i.e. black – and ffffff is the most intense colour, white. An intermediate colour, for example, with components: red = 50, green = 100, blue = 10 in decimal will convert to the hex 32 64 0a – note that a leading zero is added to the third number to make it up to six digits in all. These are then concatenated to #32640a and the hash mark added. A program such as Photoshop will take care of the conversions automatically, but there are also online calculators available, for example <www.telacommunications.com/nutshell/rgbform.htm>. Web-safe colours only use hex values of double numbers, 6699ff, for example, which as a shortcut can be shortened to just three digits: 69f.

Some web creators prefer to specify colours by name rather than by hexadecimal value, but as the specifications are constantly being updated, it's best to stick with the hex equivalents. There are 16 standard colours in HTML 4.01 with names that are recognized by all browsers. They include teal #008080, red #ff0000 and lime #00ff00. CSS 2.1 has added orange #ffa500 to the list. There is also a more extensive, but non-standard list of colours called X11 supported by many browsers, but these are not recommended. These include such exotic names as Blanched Almond (#ffebcd), Chocolate (#d2691e), Dodger Blue (#1e90ff), Old Lace (#fdf5e6) and Tomato (#ff6347).

In addition, CSS allows for colours to be defined by RGB value (in decimal numbers or percentage), for example, a <p> tag can be coloured red in any of the following ways:

```
p { color: red; }
p { color: #ff0000; }
p { color: #f00; }
p { color: rgb(255,0,0); }
p { color: rgb(100%, 0%, 0%); }
```

Colours can also be defined by HSL (hue, saturation and lightness) values (see below). In addition

```
p { color: hsl(0, 100%, 50%); }
```

also produces red. These colours can be used to define text and backgrounds.

But which colours to choose? Which colours best go with other colours? We will discuss colour schemes, but first a little colour theory.

# Colour theory

In transmitted light (including computer screens), the three primary colours are red, green and blue. In colours reflected from pigments, the three primary colours are red, yellow and blue. Mix any two, and you have the secondary colours: orange, green and purple for pigments; cyan, yellow and magenta for transmitted colours – colours that designers for print know well. Here we are more interested in how colours interact in colour schemes. No matter how they were created, placing red next to green, say, will have the same effect on the brain whether seen on screen or on the printed page. We know from colour psychology that the brain accepts four colours – red, yellow, green and blue – as primaries, and this is reflected in the composition of modern colour wheels (Fig **5.6**).

Our eyes can detect visible light from violet, with a wavelength of around 400 nanometres, to red, at about 700 nanometres. Isaac Newton (1643–1727) discovered that by refracting white light through a prism it breaks down into the visible spectrum, which the human eye perceives as a smoothly varying rainbow.

Transmitted colour (Fig **5.7**) is light that comes direct from an energy source, or shining through coloured filters in the theatre or displayed on a computer screen. The primary colours of light are red, green and blue (RGB), and other colours are made by combining different intensities of these three colours.

Pigment colours (Fig **5.8**) are created because the materials in pigments and dyes absorb different wavelengths of light, and reflect or re-transmit others. We say that colour is a property of light, not of the material itself, although the molecular structure of an object does affect the way some wavelengths of light are absorbed and others re-transmitted. Green grass absorbs (subtracts) all the colours except green, so that is how we see it. With pigment, the colour produced depends on the characteristics of that particular pigment: that is why there are so many colours available in art stores – it is usually impossible to achieve the same vibrant orange or green of a pigment of that colour by mixing the primary colours of pigments (red, yellow and blue).

**5.6** A 12-hue colour wheel, attributed to Johannes Itten, comprising the three subtractive primary colours of yellow, red and blue, their secondaries of orange, green and purple and their tertiaries, arranged in order of the spectrum

**5.7** The additive primary colours, as found in transmitted light such as a computer screen, are red, green and blue. Added together they make white

**5.8** The subtractive primary colours, as found in reflected light from pigments in a painting or printed page, are red, yellow and blue. Added together they make black

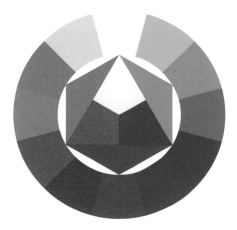

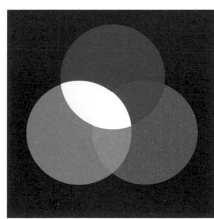

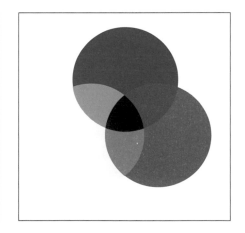

Light colour is inherently additive; pigment colour is inherently subtractive. A colour display on a monitor starts out black, and light is added to the screen to create colour. The more of the primary colours red, green and blue are added, the brighter and lighter the screen becomes. At 100% intensity of red, green and blue, the screen is white.

Regardless of the physics of how colour is created, whether it is transmitted or reflected light, most designers and illustrators will use colour on screen as if it were paint, i.e. pigment. It thus makes more sense to talk about red and green being complementary colours than red and cyan. The relationships between colours that you see on screen are exactly the same as what you see in print. The primary colours of pigments are red, yellow and blue. The secondary colours are made from a mixture of two primaries: red and yellow make orange; red and blue make purple; yellow and blue make green. The tertiary colours are made from a mixture of two secondaries, or two complementary colours, such as red and green. Examples are olive green, maroon, and various browns. An intermediate

colour is any mixture of a primary with a secondary neighbour, for example yellow-green. An equilateral triangle with vertices at the primaries is called the primary triad (see Fig **5.16**). Similar triads can join up the secondaries and tertiaries.

Saturation, also known as intensity or chroma, is the strength or purity of a colour. A saturated colour is bright and intense, almost a pure hue, whereas a desaturated colour has no hue and is called achromatic. Shocking pink and rose are two saturations of the hue red (Fig **5.9**). Different saturations can be achieved by mixing a pure hue with a neutral grey or with its complementary colour. The complementary colour of red, for example, is green. A tone is a low-intensity colour produced by mixing a hue with a shade of grey.

Brightness, also known as luminance or value, is the relative lightness or darkness of a colour. Zero brightness is black and 100% is white, intermediate values are light or dark colours. A shade is a dark colour made by mixing a hue with black. A tint is a light colour made by mixing a hue with white (Fig **5.10**).

In 1872, the Scottish physicist James Clerk Maxwell

**5.9** Pink and rose are two saturations of the hue red (top)

**5.10** A shade (middle) is a dark colour created by mixing a pure hue with black; a tint (bottom) is a light colour produced by mixing a hue with white

**5.11** A 3D colour tree, designed by Albert Munsell, has hues on the outside edge, but because some are lighter than others the branches are of unequal length

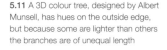

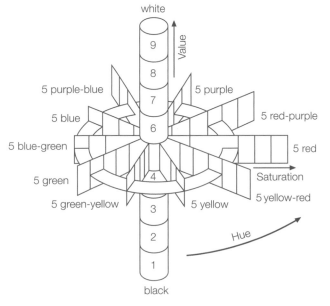

(1831–1879) developed a colour chart, in the form of a triangle, from his studies of the electromagnetic theory of light. Newton had said that the seven basic colours made visible by a prism were elementary and unmixable; Maxwell proved that only three colours – red, green and blue – were necessary to create all the others. His work became the basis for colour photography, colour printing and computer screens.

The simplest way of arranging colours is in a colour wheel or triangle, the most familiar being the 12-step colour wheel of Johannes Itten (1888–1967), a teacher at the Bauhaus school in Germany (see Fig **5.6**). A colour wheel such as this shows only the hues, however. To show darker and lighter colours, we need a 3D colour space, the best known of which is the tree, developed by the American painter Albert Henry Munsell (1858–1918) in which the 'trunk' goes from black (0) to white (10) and the branches radiate out with the neutrals next to the trunk and the brightest colours at the extremities (Fig **5.11**).

In 1931, a world standard for measuring colour was established by the Commission Internationale de l'Eclairage

(CIE) known as the CIE chromaticity chart, a 1976 version of which – the L*a*b model – is used to measure and quantify the colours produced by computer screens (Fig **5.12**). L stands for luminance; a and b are chromatic components covering the four primaries – a is for green to red, and b for blue to yellow. Programs such as Adobe Photoshop use the L*a*b model internally when converting from RGB to CMYK. Although RGB has a bigger gamut than CMYK (Fig **5.13**) it can still display only around 70% of the colours that can be perceived by the human eye; CMYK can manage only about 20% of all possible colours.

**5.12** The CEI chromaticity sail has hues around the edge with white near the middle – it defines the gamut of the visible spectrum. The L*a*b colour model is based on this colour map

**5.13** The gamuts of RGB and CMYK can be mapped onto a CIE sail to show what colours can be reproduced. RGB can display only 70% of the colours that can be perceived by the human eye; CMYK only about 20% of all colours

▬ Spectral colour gamut

▬ Hexachrome gamut

▬ CMYK gamut

▬ RGB gamut

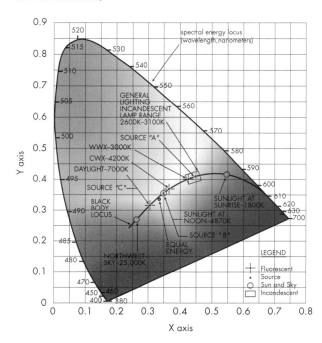

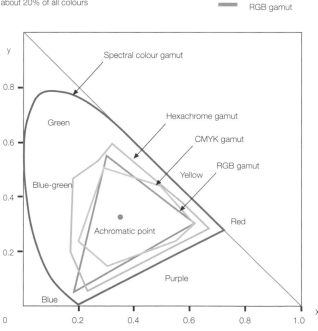

# Colour schemes

Colour theorists are interested not only in classifying colour, but also in how colours work with each other. Colour schemes have connotations of interior design – matching the colour of the walls with woodwork and furnishings – but also have a place in web design. They are like music, with colours as notes working with or against each other to form harmonies and chords – or jarring discords. Many such schemes were devised by Johannes Itten and his pupil Josef Albers (1888–1976). We use Itten's 12-step colour wheel here for simplicity (see page 115); regardless of whether colours are pigments or light they produce the same psychological response when placed close to each other.

An achromatic colour scheme comprises black, white and the greys in between; there are no possible colour contrasts. Black with white provides the strongest contrast available. A chromatic grey or neutral relief colour scheme means just dull colours, sometimes with a hint of brightness. Colours near the centre of a 3D colour wheel such as the Munsell tree (Fig **5.11**) are neutral, and this scheme will be harmonious since strong hue contrasts are not possible.

The monochromatic colour scheme is the next simplest type, consisting of one hue and its various brightnesses, and sometimes variations in saturation. It looks clean and elegant, producing a soothing effect, especially with cool blue or green hues. The analogous colour scheme (Fig **5.14**) is based on a pie-shaped slice of three or more hues located next to each other on the colour wheel, usually with one hue in common: yellow-orange, yellow and yellow-green, for example. They are at their most harmonious when the middle colour is a primary. These subtle schemes dominate the web at present.

A complementary colour scheme (Figs **5.15, 5.18**) is built around two hues that are opposite one another on the colour wheel. This scheme is high-contrast and intense, to the point of creating vibrating colours, and so is not recommended for text on a background colour. A double complementary scheme uses two sets of complementaries, and if they come from equidistant places on the wheel, this is termed a quadrad. This scheme is hard to harmonize; if all four hues are used in equal amounts, the scheme may look unbalanced. A split

**5.14** An analogous colour scheme uses colours close to one another on the colour wheel

**5.15** A complementary colour scheme uses colours opposite one another on the colour wheel; a split complementary scheme used a colour one step along from the complementary (dotted line)

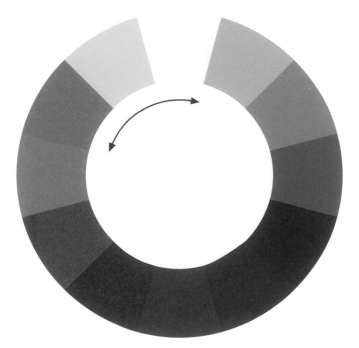

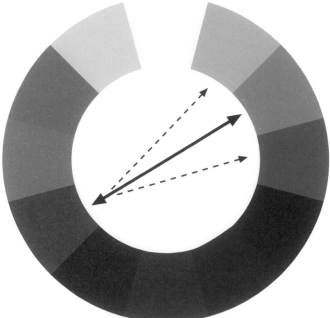

complementary colour scheme comprises any hue plus the two colours either side of its complementary. Contrast is less marked than with a pure complementary scheme, but more intense than the double complementary, and much more interesting.

A triad colour scheme is any set of three hues that are equidistant on the colour wheel, forming the vertices of an equilateral triangle (Fig **5.16**). A primary triad provides the liveliest set of colours (Fig **5.19**); a secondary triad is softer, because, while the interval between the hues is the same, any two secondaries will be related, sharing a common primary: orange and green, for example, both contain yellow. A scheme based on the rectangle is called a quadrad, which could also be a double complementary. A tetrad is also based on a square, but comprises a primary, its complement, and a complementary pair of tertiaries.

A neutral colour scheme includes colours not found on the colour wheel, such as beige, brown, white, black and grey. An accented neutral colour scheme is mainly neutral colours plus highlights of a brighter colour such as red.

## Choosing a scheme

Choosing a colour scheme is a highly subjective process. Your clients may have colours they prefer, in their logos or corporate identity branding for example, so you may be constrained and guided by these. You may want to use colours sampled from an image on your home page.

You should be clear about your site's brand message and choose colours that reinforce it. For a financial institution, for example, use cool, muted colours such as blues, greys and greens, which convey stability and trust. On the other hand, a site aimed at a younger audience could make use of brighter, brasher, more saturated colours. Don't overdo the number of colours in your palette: three or four colours, plus white and black, should be enough. Too many colours can distract and confuse the user.

Black text on a white background provides the highest degree of contrast, but a white background may be seen as cold and clinical and black text too boring. Try more subtle shades, as

**5.16** A triadic scheme uses three colours equally spaced on the colour wheel, such as the three primaries; a quadrad colour scheme uses four colours at the corners of a square placed on the colour wheel

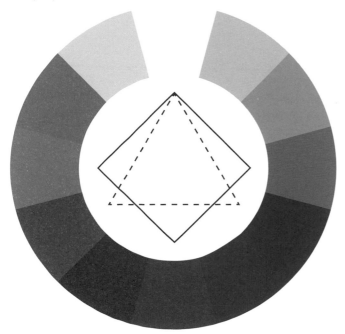

**5.17** US designer Duane King's Thinking
for a Living website was developed by
Ian Coyle and is delivered by WordPress.
It focuses on typography and legibility,
creating a quiet place for contemplation
and thought. The site is designed around
a 12-column grid system and is set in
Georgia, in both regular and italic faces
at 14, 21 and 48 points on a background
of TFAL Pink (#f8e7e1). Grid columns are
60 pixels wide with 20 pixel gutters and
a baseline grid spaced at 20 pixels

you would when painting a room – say, off-white for the walls and dark greys for the details. To test for contrast and legibility, convert your colour scheme to greyscale: can it still be read? Fig **5.17** is a good example of a website that uses subtle shades and is still very legible. Be aware that colour trends can quickly go out of fashion – but you can use retro colour palettes to evoke feelings of nostalgia.

The art of using one of these colour schemes is to vary the proportions of the colours, rather than distributing them in equal measures. A designer can never be tied to a rigid set of colours, but taking a colour scheme based on a dominant hue as a starting point and adapting it will result in a composition with a degree of 'tonality'. Various colour-scheme planners can be found on the web, such as http://kuler.adobe.com, http://www.colourspire.com/ and http://ColourSchemeDesigner.com/. If you start with a particular colour, perhaps one in the client's logo, these planners will suggest harmonious and/or contrasting colours for you to incorporate into your scheme. The last website listed also shows how a particular colour scheme will look to a person with colour blindness.

## Additional considerations

Around one person in twelve has some sort of colour deficiency: 8% of men and 0.4% of women in the United States suffer from it. Deuteranomaly is the most common colour deficiency, occurring in about 6% of American men. This results in a reduction in sensitivity to the green area of the spectrum. For example, in the evening, green cars can appear to be black, although the intensity of the colour is unchanged. At worst a colour-blind person may see only shades of grey. It is important therefore to consider adding contrast to your colour schemes. Almost all colour-blind people retain some blue-yellow discrimination, even if they mix up red and green.

Architects and designers use colour psychology to modify our behaviour. Fast-food restaurants are painted orange or pink to induce excitement. They excite you to come in, eat quickly, then vacate the table for the next set of excited customers. Pink can be energizing or calming. Prisons are often painted pink to cheer up those who work there and subdue the inmates. Blue is rarely used in restaurants, because it is a relaxing colour – the customers won't want to leave. Hospitals used to be painted pale green to soothe patients.

Remember too that colours can have multiple cultural connotations and both positive and negative associations. White in western countries is the colour of weddings; in China, India and Vietnam wedding dresses are red, their traditional colour of good luck and happiness, although this is changing. In Jan van Eyck's 1434 Arnolfini double portrait, the woman's wedding dress is green, symbolizing hope that she may soon become a mother. In the west, people wear black to funerals, but in many south and east Asian cultures, white is symbolic of death. Green used to be associated with poison, but is now more positively associated with ecology and saving the planet.

Once your colour scheme is decided, write down the colours so you can refer to them later and allocate them to areas of your website, to headings and text, and build them into the CSS. If you don't like what you see in the browser, they can always be fine-tuned later without affecting the HTML pages. In the next chapter we look at all the add-ons, bells and whistles that can bring your website alive.

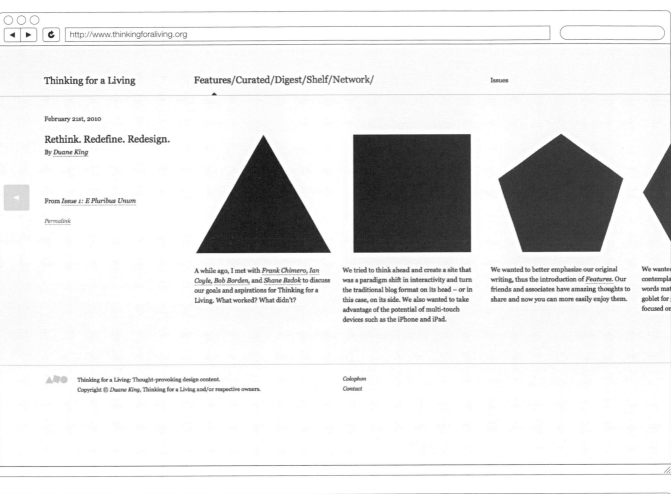

http://www.thinkingforaliving.org

**Thinking for a Living**          Features/Curated/Digest/Shelf/Network/                    Issues

February 21st, 2010

### Rethink. Redefine. Redesign.
By *Duane King*

From *Issue 1: E Pluribus Unum*

*Permalink*

A while ago, I met with *Frank Chimero, Ian Coyle, Bob Borden,* and *Shane Bzdok* to discuss our goals and aspirations for Thinking for a Living. What worked? What didn't?

We tried to think ahead and create a site that was a paradigm shift in interactivity and turn the traditional blog format on its head – or in this case, on its side. We also wanted to take advantage of the potential of multi-touch devices such as the iPhone and iPad.

We wanted to better emphasize our original writing, thus the introduction of *Features.* Our friends and associates have amazing thoughts to share and now you can more easily enjoy them.

We wanted contempla words mat goblet for focused or

Thinking for a Living: Thought-provoking design content.
Copyright © *Duane King*, Thinking for a Living and/or respective owners.

Colophon
Contact

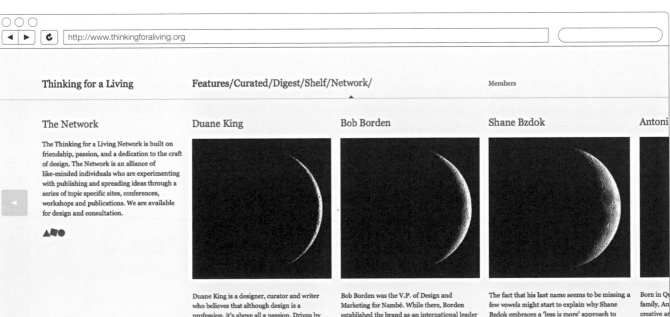

http://www.thinkingforaliving.org

**Thinking for a Living**          Features/Curated/Digest/Shelf/Network/                    Members

### The Network

The Thinking for a Living Network is built on friendship, passion, and a dedication to the craft of design. The Network is an alliance of like-minded individuals who are experimenting with publishing and spreading ideas through a series of topic specific sites, conferences, workshops and publications. We are available for design and consultation.

**Duane King**

Duane King is a designer, curator and writer who believes that although design is a profession, it's above all a passion. Driven by curiosity, his work has been recognized by Graphis, The 100 Show, The Art Directors Club, I.D. Magazine, Communications Arts, Creative Review, IdN, Print and HOW Magazine. Among his clients: MoMA, Bloomingdale's, Luigi Bormioli, Nambé, Orrefors, Kosta Boda, Neiman Marcus, Herman Miller, Northrop Grumman, Activision, Sega, id Software and FootAction USA. Duane is the founder of Thinking for a Living.

*King, Duane*
*Twitter*
*Flickr*

**Bob Borden**

Bob Borden was the V.P. of Design and Marketing for Nambé. While there, Borden established the brand as an international leader in product design, sophisticated marketing, and merchandising. Under Borden's creative direction and eye for quality design, Nambé's products were accepted into the permanent collections of some 25 museums around the world. Included: the Museum of Modern Art in both New York and San Francisco, the International Museum of Design in London, and the Living Design Museum in Tokyo.

*Twitter*

*Permalink*

**Shane Bzdok**

The fact that his last name seems to be missing a few vowels might start to explain why Shane Bzdok embraces a 'less is more' approach to design. His love for clean, honest design and typography guides his award-winning print and interactive work for clients such as: Luigi Bormioli, Nambé, Northrop Grumman, Orrefors, Kosta Boda, The Museum of Modern Art and The Ritz-Carlton. Shane also runs the graphic design trivia feed, Design Facts and is a managing partner and contributor at Thinking for a Living.

*Shane Bzdok*
*Design Facts*
*Twitter*

*Permalink*

**Antoni**

Born in Q family, An creative a resides in Art Directo which have Cable, Lay Gillette, C America. for his wor is also the ever-grow

*AisleOne*
*The Grid S*
*Twitter*

*Permalink*

**5.18** The website for Innocent drinks and smoothies uses complementaries for its colour scheme

**5.19** New York band Au Revoir Simone's Flash-based site uses the primary triadic colour scheme of red, green and blue, with touches of orange

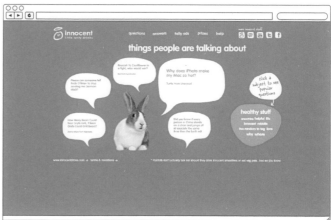

# Step-by-step 4
## Developing a website using background colours and faux columns

## Step 1.

These two-column CSS layouts from www.code-sucks.com (from a method developed by Dan Cederholm) use a neat trick to make the left and right columns lock equal in height and independent of each other. A parent column called faux is created and a long thin GIF, the width of the website, at 922px wide and 22px high, is created that contains both the left and right child columns as different-coloured areas. This is tiled vertically to produce the background image that grows as content is added (**below**). Note the fix to allow older browsers such as Internet Explorer 6. The CSS will look as below:
The background GIF (note how it is the full width of the layout, but only a nominal height) is changed in Photoshop to reflect the new colour scheme and saved to the images folder (**bottom left**).

## Step 2.

A header banner is made in Photoshop at 922px x 122px and added as a background image to the CSS (**below**) rather than to the HTML, so that it can always be changed in future without having to change all the pages.
In addition, some text is added to the HTML page so it now appears as shown here (**bottom right**).

```
#faux {
  background: url(images/faux-3-2-col.gif);
  margin-bottom: 0px;
  overflow: auto; /* Paul O Brien Fix for IE www.pmob.co.uk */
  width: 100%;
}
```

```
#header {
  width: 922px;
  padding: 0px;
  height: 110px;
  margin: 10px 0px 0px 0px;
  background: url(images/banner.jpg);
}
```

One problem that can occur when using the CSS box model of layout is that the height of a column is determined by the amount of content contained in it. Thus, a menu column, say, would appear shorter than the main body that contains lots of text and images. One way to get round this (used in Step-by-step 3 on pages 102–5) is to add an equal height property to both columns, but the layout could still break down if the content you add exceeds the fixed height of the container. The faux column method creates invisible (unequal) column containers while a background GIF, which tiles automatically downwards as the content increases, gives the impression of neat and tidy columns.

## Step 3.

Next the text is styled to a sans serif font and the Owen Briggs method (see tip on page 95) is applied to the type size. Leading is added by adjusting the `<line-height>` property and space between the paragraphs and headings increased by adding space to the bottom padding.

The image is added and you can see how the background GIF tiles to accommodate the content and give the impression that the columns are increasing in height equally (**right**).

```css
body {
  font-family: Verdana,
  Helvetica, Arial,
  sans-serif;
  font-size: 80%;
}

p {
  font-size: 1em;
  line-height: 1.25em;
  padding-bottom: 1.25em;
}

h1 {
  font-size: 2em;
  padding-bottom: 1.25em;
  text-align: center;
}

h2 { font-size: 1.25em;
  padding-bottom: 1.25em;
  text-align: center;
}
```

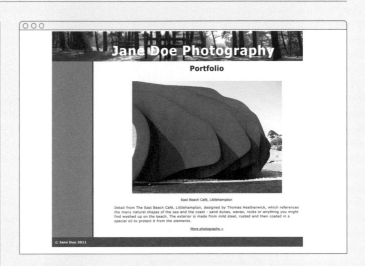

## Step 4.

It's now time to look at the menu, which will occupy the left column. Again, rather than reinvent the wheel we can use a tried-and-tested public-domain template from Listamatic – css.maxdesign.com.au/listamatic – designed by Russ Weakley. This uses the unordered list tag `<ul>`. A div called #navcontainer is nested within the div #leftcolumn, with the menu items listed as per this code (**right**).

In the CSS, #navcontainer and #navlist are defined to style the `<ul>` tag and the `<a>` links. An unordered list has a bullet by default and this is removed using :

```css
list-style-type: none;
```

and the default underlining removed from the links using:

```css
text-decoration: none;
```

The colour scheme was set by the banner image – the blue-grey of a shadow under the trees was sampled and keyed into kuler.adobe.com and the other colours picked by eye from those suggested.

The text colour and links are still defaults but can be changed easily later – because we have used background images, the website is future-proof as we need only change the CSS, not the HTML pages. All that remains is to add a class called `.caption` that defines a smaller size for the caption text, and a 'More photographs' button, and that's about it (**below right**).

```html
<div id="navcontainer">
<ul id="navlist">
<li id="active"><a href="index.html" id="current">Home</a></li>
<li><a href="about.html">About me</a></li>
<li><a href="portfolio.html">Portfolio</a></li>
<li><a href="blog.html">Blog</a></li>
<li><a href="links.html">Links</a></li>
</ul>
</div>
```

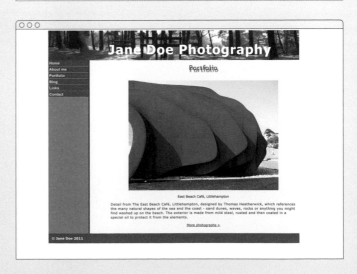

# Step 5.

The **h1** heading 'Portfolio' has been further styled using a link to the Google font library by adding code (**top**) to the very top of the **<head>** section of the HTML, and (**right**) to the CSS.

The property **text-shadow** adds a drop shadow effect.

We need to add some description and keyword meta tags in the **<head>** for the search engines and then we can 'save as' the index.html page to create the other pages in the website.

The finished HTML is shown in PageSpinner (**right**) and the CSS in Style Master (**bottom**).

```
<link href='http://fonts.googleapis.com/css?family=Molengo' rel='stylesheet' type='text/css'>
```

```css
h1 {
  font-family: 'Molengo', arial, sans-serif;
  text-shadow: 4px 4px 4px #aaa;
  font-size: 2em;
  padding-bottom: 1.25em;
  text-align: center;
}
```

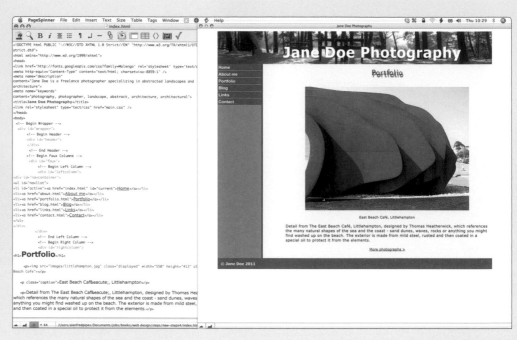

The portfolio website of German eco-product designer Daniel Angermann may be more sophisticated than the examples described in the Step-by-steps, but demonstrates what can be done with some imagination

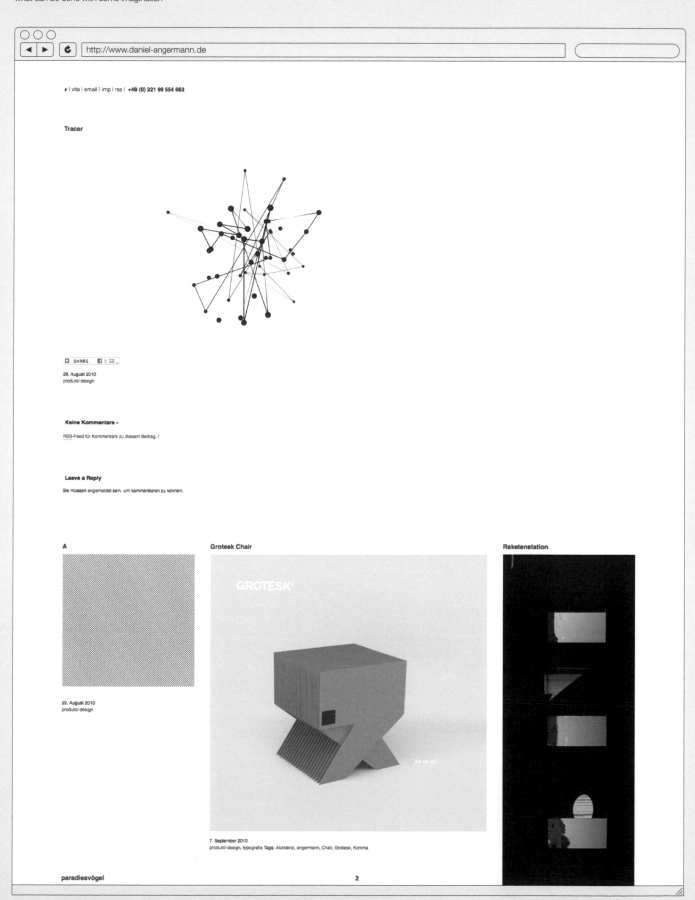

# Trailblazer 4
## Soleil Noir

Benjamin Laugel (president and creative director of Soleil Noir) founded the Paris-based studio in 2000 with Olivier Marchand. After taking a masters degree in digital communication at ISCOM (Institut supérieur de communication et de publicité) in Paris, he started working at French cosmetic company Orlane. He soon realized that he preferred the packaging and its design to the product itself, so set up Soleil Noir, a 'human-sized studio', to create mostly Flash-based immersive and interactive experiences for 50 or so global clients, including Disney Television, Nespresso, Samsung, EMI and Alfa Romeo. The studio employs 22 staff, and has received numerous prizes, among them 25 FWA Sites of the Day awards.

Laugel is European representative of SoDA (Society of Digital Agencies), Board Member of the Club des Directeurs Artistiques, and jury member of several international competitions. Olivier Marchand (vice president and production director) also studied at ISCOM, and graduated with a masters degree in digital communication. He created many sites as a freelancer while at college, before bringing his creativity and experience to Soleil Noir.

Where did they learn web design? 'Not in school, that's for sure!' says Laugel, 'We really taught ourselves. I was already on the internet in 1995 with CompuServe, bulletin boards and IRC (Internet Relay Chat). They were different times but that's where I learned how to use the web and, especially, to communicate with others online.

'I've always been hooked on TV and animation, so using animation software (because that's all there was then) such as Flash to reproduce what was already around me came naturally. Olivier and I were the first to create a French record label's site (or any music-related site, for that matter), the hostile.fr site, in Flash. That was in 1999. I haven't touched Flash in a while for the simple reason that it's changed a lot and the people I work with are much more skilled than I am! But I try to keep up with the technology and the possibilities that the software we use offers.'

What has been their favourite project? 'Mine was Myst IV Revelation', says Laugel. 'Everything came off so smoothly. We had so much content we didn't know what to do with it, plus time, carte blanche when it came to creation and development … all that has changed so much. Our work is strategic, creative and extremely technical at the same time. Our collaborators are aware of these factors, which is why we manage to create magnificent interactive experiences with and for them.'

Do they always work in Flash? 'Soleil Noir has very strong Flash expertise (we've been an Adobe Partner since 2008), but the market and our curiosity entices us to explore new ways of developing and communicating. For example, right now we're developing two iPhone applications, an iPad application and an HTML5/CSS3 site.'

Do they think there is a future for Flash, with Steve Jobs not supporting it on iPad? 'Of course Flash still has a future! I understand Steve Jobs's position. What he cares about most is wanting his devices to work perfectly. That's why I find it normal that Adobe is optimizing its software and plug-ins to enhance the user's experience as much as possible. Flash is everywhere on the internet. Apple can't do without it, and neither can anybody else. I think Adobe and Apple are doing their utmost to let users quickly benefit from technology, allowing them to see everything on any kind of device.'

What do they think of CSS/XHTML? 'I have the feeling that CSS/HTML seems like a novelty for the most part!' says Laugel. 'HTML has been around since 1991, HTML4 since 1997, CSS since the late 90s. Today HTML5 makes it possible to fully enter the multimedia world. The idea isn't just to wonder whether HTML5 is better than Flash but to adapt the technology to the message and the user's experience. Why use Flash where we don't need it? And why insist on developing in HTML/CSS when Flash takes one-tenth of the time for better quality?'

What do they think of integrating Web 2.0 (Twitter, Flickr, Facebook, blogs, etc.) into their websites? 'There's no way around it! Social platforms are springboards for brands and a highly effective way of spreading messages and creating communities. But they must be used well because, although the benefits might be exponential, employing those media poorly can quickly damage a brand and even cancel out its global communication. Those platforms have their own languages, habits and codes and it's essential for brands to learn how to use them before becoming involved with them.'

How do they see the future of web design? 'Mobile of course! Content is also a part of our future. Today users are browsing, commenting and creating content. It's no longer enough to look beautiful, you also have to be effective, and effectiveness depends on creating original, exclusive content that web users will identify with.'

What are their favourite websites? 'Nowadays I pay more attention to aggregators and apps,' says Laugel. 'I enjoy browsing ffffound.com and fubiz.net, taking my competitors' temperature and feasting my eyes on thefwa.com, spying on Facebook, adding "underground" links on Twitter and publishing my pictures on Flickr and my videos on Vimeo. I dabble in everything and my clients love that!'

**Fig 1** The challenge was to modernize the online presence of the Thierry Mugler brand at www.thierrymugler.com that gathered fashion, make-up, photography and design in one place, while also developing a new content-management system. Using the concept of a live fashion show, Soleil Noir incorporated a strong Web 2.0 component, allowing the brand's fans to stay in touch and provide feedback

**Fig 2** For the launch of a new range of CITIZ coffee machines by Nespresso, with a target audience of 30-year-old urban men, the aim was to enhance the global ad campaign by inviting the user 'behind the scenes' of the print ads. Immersive experiences were created for each of the three machines in the range, starting from the coffee machine placed in the city background, then, placed in an apartment (one room per type of machine), then ending with a detailed view of the machine and a product demo

**Fig 3** For Nespresso's Tanzarú coffee blend, combining Tanzanian and Peruvian beans, Soleil Noir were asked to create a website to be launched simultaneously in 27 countries and 15 languages. Instead of a direct telling of the product's story, they decided to create a dreamlike journey in an imaginary world, recreating the taste of Tanzarú through a visual and audio experience. Visitors can activate animations, sounds and colours in a surreal landscape, bringing the environment to life by interacting with animals, plants and backgrounds

Fig 1

Fig 2

Fig 3

Fig 4

Fig 5

**Fig 4** For the launch of the new music library for the communication sector by French music publisher Red Tracks Publishing, Soleil Noir were asked to re-imagine how to present and search through the tracks, using an innovative concept and intuitive navigation. They created the search engine and visual identity for www.findyourtracks.fr, offering a new approach to exploring the library, using ambiances, targets and styles. This new type of navigation, together with the automatic display of results, made the search faster and more efficient, while also creating a user-friendly interface – music can be located in just a few simple clicks

**Fig 5** When asked to create a website for the launch of Samsung's Player Star smartphone, highlighting its multi-touch functionalities in a new interactive way, Soleil Noir gave users the opportunity to imagine themselves in situations with the product. They conceived three messages and settings that were based on the innovative features of the phone, together with their interactive videos: 'Share your emotions', 'Stay connected' and 'Tools for your business'

Where do they find inspiration? 'Teamwork,' says Laugel. 'We brainstorm a lot with art directors, developers, motion designers, sound designers, etc. Everybody has ideas and the good ones don't always come from the same people. We also keep an eye on other things. I love movie and TV credits that I find ultra creative. That's where my ideas come from sometimes. We have people interested in other things besides the web and they offer us a wide variety of creative views. As I often say, the expertise we've acquired lets us move beyond technology and technical issues, allowing us to fully focus on the idea and concept.'

What advice would you give someone at college wanting to be a web designer? 'Be more interested in the web than students using it on a daily basis. I've noticed that most "young people" today don't have web culture. Digital is starting to have a history and it's important to know the references. I'd also tell them to express their ideas and release the interactive, conceptual originality in their heads. There are two things needed to create successful web design: user-friendliness and the graphics layout. They must be in osmosis and round each other off.

'The last point is, keep it simple. We're swamped by graphics and messages. A simple approach helps to catch people's attention better – above all focus on the navigation pathway and on making content look good. Always keep in mind that what you're doing might be used by your parents, who will often question your work.'

How should web design beginners promote themselves? 'By using online folios like cargocollective.com, learning how to use Twitter as a way to disseminate and share what you're interested in, stressing simplicity, and being as original as you can. We get 10 to 15 CVs a day, and what we look at more than experience is how they are presented. Don't forget that if content is paramount, the container is fundamental because it makes the content look good! Last but not least, be daring! There are no set rules in our occupation, so always let your work and words be surprising!'

www.soleilnoir.net
twitter.com/SN_Studio
www.flickr.com/photos/sn_studio/
www.thefwa.com/profile/soleil-noir-pin

www.thebioagency.com

**BIO.**
**Big Ideas Online.**
That's what we stand for.

We're a digital agency that specialises in having
Big Ideas and bringing them to life online.

Big Ideas build brands and change markets.
Everyone notices a Big Idea. They don't forget
them, either.

So, we insist that every piece of work we do -
websites, advertising, strategy, applications, video,
email campaigns, virals, games and back-end
development - has a Big Idea driving it.

Come and have a look at what we've been up to.
Or get in touch.

menu

Latest views
17/02/'10  BIO's site receives praise from Adobe writer...
17/02/'10  Things are starting to get interesting...
16/02/'10  Whoa - Google Earth demo on TED lectures...

Keep me posted with news  ›

home · work · what we do · bio green · managing partners · careers · news & views · contact
@theBIOagency   info@thebioagency.com   t. +44 (0) 20 7079 2450   f. +44 (0) 20 7079 2455   second floor, 75 wells street, london W1T 3QH, uk

---

www.thebioagency.com

menu

**BIO.**
**Big Ideas Online.**
That's what we stand for.

We're a digital agency that specialises in having
Big Ideas and bringing them to life online.

Big Ideas build brands and change markets.
Everyone notices a Big Idea. They don't forget
them, either.

So, we insist that every piece of work we do -
websites, advertising, strategy, applications, video,
email campaigns, virals, games and back-end
development - has a Big Idea driving it.

Come and have a look at what we've been up to.
Or get in touch.

Latest views
17/02/'10  BIO's site receives praise from Adobe writer...
17/02/'10  Things are starting to get interesting...
16/02/'10  Whoa - Google Earth demo on TED lectures...

Keep me posted with news  ›

home · work · what we do · bio green · managing partners · careers · news & views · contact
@theBIOagency   info@thebioagency.com   t. +44 (0) 20 7079 2450   f. +44 (0) 20 7079 2455   second floor, 75 wells street, london W1T 3QH, uk

# Added extras

# 6

The great attraction of Web 2.0 applications such as Facebook, Flickr and Twitter is their interactivity. With a blog you can elicit comments; with a Facebook or Flickr special interest group you can share experiences or fire up heated debates; with Twitter, an idea can be published instantly, and rapidly disseminated. The traditional HTML/CSS websites that we have discussed so far can seem rather static – they only ever change when the designer decides to update them, so remember to update your website regularly with new content. These kinds of websites resemble traditional publishing: you put a book or magazine out into the wide world and the only feedback you can expect are the sales figures and maybe the odd review in a specialist journal.

Ways of enlivening your site range from adding an animated GIF or embedding content from Twitter, images from Flickr or news from a blog, to making your site dynamic with Flash or JavaScript. This takes us into another area altogether – into the world of programming, a thought that many designers may regard with horror. Most graphic designers will delegate this work to a programming professional (who might enjoy it). Some designers specialize only in Flash-based websites (Fig **6.1**). Shopping sites such as Amazon and eBay have websites that are compiled 'on the fly' from a constantly updated database using a scripting language such as PHP (Hypertext Preprocessor) or ASP (Active Server Pages) – you may have noticed the .php or .asp acronym at the end of a URL instead of .html. Programming is beyond the scope of this book, but we shall briefly look at each technology later.

**6.1** London-based BIO Agency's Flash-based website uses the graphic device of a 'good idea' lightbulb, which changes appropriately as your mouse explores their client list below. BIO stands for Big Ideas Online

**6.2** Warp is an independent record label, founded in Sheffield in 1989, notable for electronic music. Their dynamic website almost certainly uses SSI, but it cannot be discerned just by looking at the source – on the server, all the changing content will have been called in

# SSI (Server Side Includes)

We start with a technique that will not make your site look any different, but will make your job a great deal easier, particularly if the site is frequently being updated manually. Imagine that you have created a website with a large menu running down the left-hand column. The site now contains many hundreds of pages, but the client wishes to add another item to the menu, and remove one. What do you do? In the days of framesets, this was easy – you just amended the frame containing the menu and the whole website was updated. With an HTML/CSS website, however, you would have to make each change individually to each and every page. And what about the copyright notice at the bottom of the page in the footer? It says © 2011 at present, but what about when it's 2012? Same problem. If you used a Dreamweaver template to design the site, you may have to make the change only once, but you would still have to upload all the revised pages to the server.

With SSI (Server Side Includes) you simply extract the block of menu code from your home page and place it into a new text document called `menu.html` – that is, a page stripped of the usual `DOCTYPE`, `head` and `body` HTML tags (it could also be called `menu.txt`). Back in the home page, and in all the others, you replace the menu code with the statement:

```
<!--#include file="menu.html"-->
```

when the included file is within the same directory folder as the page that wants it, otherwise:

```
<!--#include virtual="/includes/menu.html"-->
```

if the file is in a folder/directory called includes.

This calls in the code for the menu and fits it into the right place. As the term SSI implies, this is done at the server, so it is essential to check first that your server supports SSI – not all hosting services do. Check your ISP's FAQ pages and search for htaccess (hypertext access). If this is not permitted, then you won't be able to use SSI.

Now if the menu needs to be changed, you simply update the `menu.html` text document and upload to the server and all the menus will update automatically. Any common piece of text throughout the site that you think might be updated or changed at some point can be made into an SSI. To enable a web server to recognize an SSI-enabled HTML file, it is usual to end the URL with `.shtml`, so that the home page, for example, would become `index.shtml`. You would also have to add the `s` to any internal links too, particularly in the menu

(but the SSI file remains as `menu.html`). You can, however, fool the server into thinking a `.html` file is a `.shtml` file using `.htaccess` – sites such as http://www.andreas.com/faq-ssi. html tell you how.

Obviously it is best to develop an SSI site from scratch, but it is a relatively simple matter to convert a small site, and it only has to be done once. A disadvantage is that you cannot preview your website on your computer: it will only come together once uploaded by FTP to the server and viewed in a browser.

Believe it or not, you have just done some programming.

**6.3** In the Layers palette of Photoshop, start with the first frame, duplicate the layer and then change the image incrementally – in this case changing the transparency of the text. Duplicate this new layer – and so on to create the number of steps you need **(top left)**

**6.4** In the Animation (Frames) window, change 'forever' to 'once' at bottom left, otherwise the animation will loop indefinitely **(top right)**

**6.5** All five frames used in the animation are shown in order in this simulated screenshot **(bottom)**

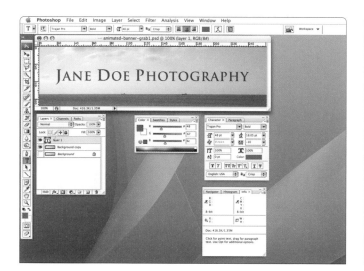

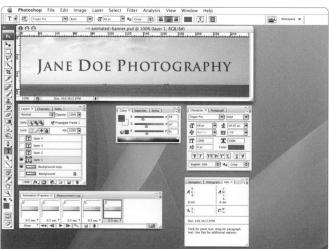

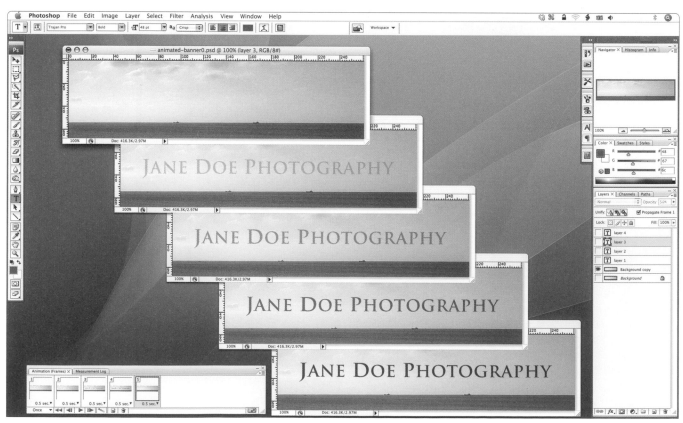

# Animated GIFs

One thing that a GIF can do that a JPEG cannot is become animated. An animated GIF is the simplest form of animation; it is recognized by all browsers and rarely causes problems. Animated GIFs are usually encountered as banner advertisements and can be annoying. But a subtle piece of animation can add interest to an otherwise lifeless site. How does it work? The browser simply replaces one GIF after another into the same space on the page and the eye perceives it as a fluid movement, like a flip-book animation. There are various programs available to construct animated GIFs, such as GIF Construction Set Professional from Alchemy Mindworks, and Easy GIF Animator from Blumentals Software, but the most common method until recently was to use Adobe Photoshop with its co-worker ImageReady. However, with the release of Adobe's Creative Suite 3 in 2007, ImageReady was officially retired and its functionality integrated into Photoshop.

In Photoshop, the first step is to load up all the separate images as layers, in order, with the first image in the animation preferably at the bottom. Or if you are creating the animation from scratch, start with the first frame, duplicate the layer and change the image incrementally, duplicate this new layer and so on (Fig **6.3**). In this example we start with a background layer containing a photo of the sea plus a text layer containing the title of the website. We aim to create a simple fade-in from the background photo with no text, to text at 100% opacity (layer 1), in three stages: 25% (layer 4), 50% (layer 3) and 75% (layer 2).

In the Layers palette, uncheck the eye icons of all the layers except the one that you'd like to become the first frame of the sequence. In the Window menu, select Animation, and you should see your first layer loaded as the first frame in the animation window that appears. To set the time for each frame, click the bottom of frame 1 in the animation window: this will pop up a menu showing times in seconds. Next create a new frame using the button next to the Trash and select the layers you need from the layers palette: in this example that is the background plus layer 4, the 25% text.

In the Layers palette, deselect the layer we just used for frame 1, by clicking on the eye, then select the next layer in the sequence for frame 2, in this case layer 3, the 50% text. This will put the contents of the second layer in the sequence into frame 2. And so on until we have five frames. We want our fade-in to happen once only, so change 'forever' to 'once', bottom left, otherwise it will loop indefinitely (Fig **6.4**).

You can test the animation by hitting the play button at any time, and the transitions between frames can be made even smoother by adding Tween frames, using the Tween button

(the 'chain' icon at the bottom of the Animation palette). When you are happy with the order and time settings of the frames, go to 'Save for Web & Devices', and choose to save as a GIF. Because GIFs are better at flat colours than JPEGs, we will need quite a large indexed colour palette to reproduce all the subtle tones in the image, so be aware this will consequentially bump up the file size. The five frames used in the animation are simulated in Fig **6.5**. For an example of the successful use of animated GIFs see Figs **6.6** and **6.7**.

**Add a favicon**

A favicon (short for favourites icon) is the tiny icon you sometimes see when you add a web address to a bookmark list or see the URL in your browser's toolbar. They were introduced by Microsoft in Internet Explorer 4 and are generally 16 x 16px. Having one can help make your website memorable. A file called favicon.ico is placed in the root directory of your website and accessed by code in the `<head>` section of the HTML:

```
<link rel="icon" type="image/vnd.microsoft.icon"
href="favicon.ico" />
```

The icon is best designed as a .png and then converted to .ico using a Photoshop plug-in or a website generator such as www.genfavicon.com or www.favicon.co.uk.

**6.6** Bryan Dalton is a multifaceted artist form Portland, Oregon, best known for Sweet Gifs, a website devoted entirely to animated pop-art GIFs by himself and other contributors

**6.7** I'm Not An Artist is a non-stop 'paranoia' about non-stop design workers. It's a project commissioned by Elisava School of Design, Barcelona, with concept, creative direction and design by Soon in Tokyo, a communications agency made up of former Elisava students and teachers. It starts with 56 animated GIFs directed by Johnny Kelly and Matthew Cooper and aims to grow with the participation of young designers and creatives from all over the world

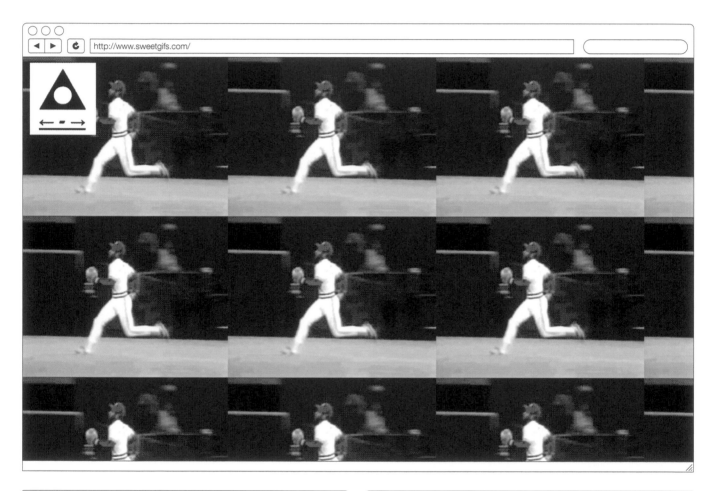

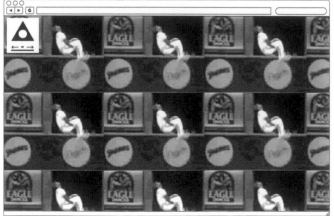

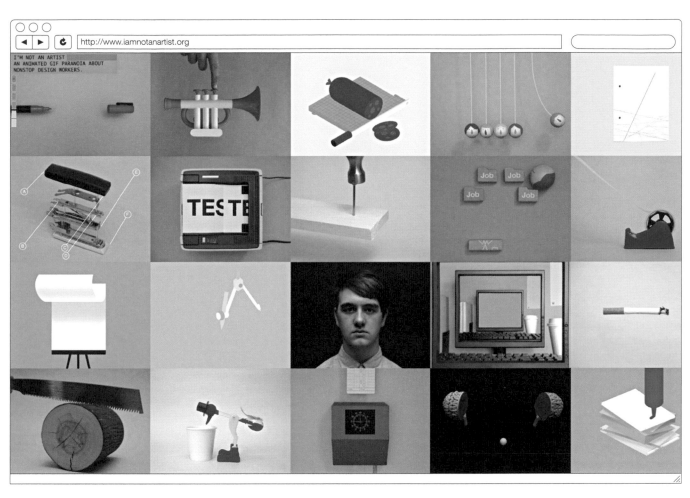

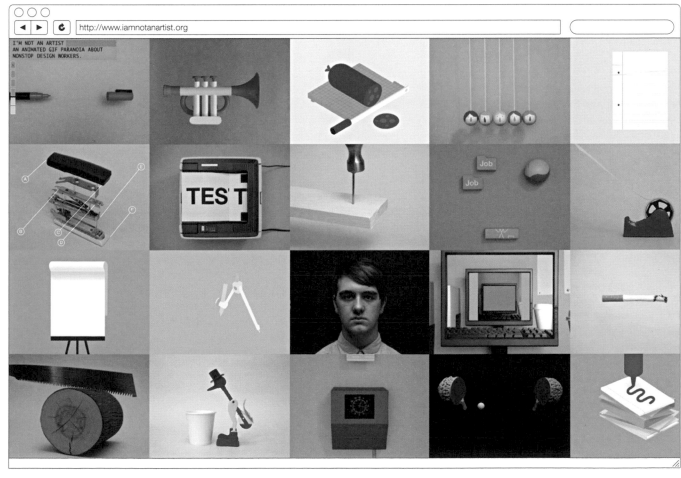

# Flash

One thing an animated GIF does not have is sound: for animations with music and sound effects, you need Flash. Back in the days before CSS, graphic designers would go to great lengths to make the web reproduce their typography and layouts; they would convert type into images and even construct entire websites using the multimedia program Adobe Director (formerly Macromedia Director). Visually these might have looked fine, but the trade-off was a near invisibility to the search engines and a snub to accessibility aids; they required the user to download Shockwave plug-ins, represented huge files and hence download time, and were notoriously difficult to print out. Flash too has suffered from these drawbacks, but has evolved to address them in recent years. Using Director or Flash also requires the developer – you – to purchase proprietary software.

Adobe Flash (formerly Macromedia Flash) began life as FutureSplash, launched in 1996 and based on a drawing application called SmartSketch. It started off as a vector-based web animation program, using some novel drawing and painting tools, based around key frames and a timeline (Fig **6.8**). Animation is object-based, which means you can incorporate simple animations into more complex ones. It also means you have to be methodical: for example, to animate a walking person, first animate the legs on their own then reuse that 'object' in a whole person assemblage. Flash programming really requires a whole book of its own, so can only be outlined here.

Output file format is .swf (ShockWave Flash) and these movies can be 'played' in a standalone Flash Player or embedded into a web page using code such as:

```
<object width="500" height="400">
<param name="movie" value="flash-movie.swf">
<embed src="flash-movie.swf" width="500" height="400">
</embed>
</object>
```

This uses both the `<embed>` tag and the `<object>` tag. This is because while the `<object>` tag is recognized by Internet Explorer, it is ignored by Netscape, which recognizes the `<embed>` tag.

You do not have to use Flash only for animation. Its built-in scripting language is called ActionScript, and allows you to allocate actions to buttons, menus and events, such as mouse clicks, so that entire websites can be built using only Flash. An advantage of Flash is that transitions between pages can be smoother using Flash (Fig **6.9**). An abrupt jump from one page to another in a CSS/XHTML site can be disorienting. However, a very slow transition, or fade, can be frustrating to watch.

Another plus point is that any fonts used in the Flash animation will reproduce on the user's computer, whether they have them installed or not. It has become a favourite for graphic designers' websites, and many designers use nothing else.

ActionScript 3.0 is an object-oriented programming language, which means that chunks of code can be reused to build quite complex Flash applications, including games. Because of Flash's ubiquity, video sites on the web, such as YouTube and Google Video, use Flash to embed streaming video clips into their 'players'. Websites often have an intro animation made using Flash, though these can be annoying if you have to wait too long for them to load, and if they serve no real purpose can become an irritation to watch more than once – so always include a 'skip intro' button so that the user can jump straight to the website proper.

If you must use Flash – if you are a Flash animator showing your skills, for example – make sure you put keywords in the `<meta>` tags and *also* as plain text below the intro, install a 'mute' button to turn off any music, provide a 'loading bar' that indicates the time or percentage left for the Flash to load completely, and always provide a link to where the user can download the latest plug-in.

Despite upgrades, usability remains an issue. Flash does not behave in the same way as normal HTML pages: the ability to select text, scrolling, using forms and right-clicking are not the same as on a regular web page. Unexpected actions can confuse users and should be borne in mind by the designer. Recent improvements include the ability to control text size using full-page zoom, and to include alternative text.

Steve Jobs of Apple has openly criticized the stability of Flash, claiming that when a Macintosh crashes, 'more often than not' the cause is Flash. As a consequence, at the time of writing, Flash has not been supported on the iPhone or iPad.

Jobs is backing HTML5, the proposed next standard for HTML 4.01 and XHTML 1.0, which aims to replace proprietary plug-in-based rich internet application (RIA) technologies such as Flash, using new `<audio>` and `<video>` elements and APIs (application programming interfaces). YouTube and Vimeo are experimenting with HTML5 but, at the time of writing, there is still a long way to go.

**6.8** Flash uses a timeline for events and
animations, as seen in this screenshot
for a website design by Phil Weyman
of kralinator.com for jewellery designer
Andrea Eserin

**6.9** The finished website, viewed in Safari,
incorporates fade effects when moving
from page to page

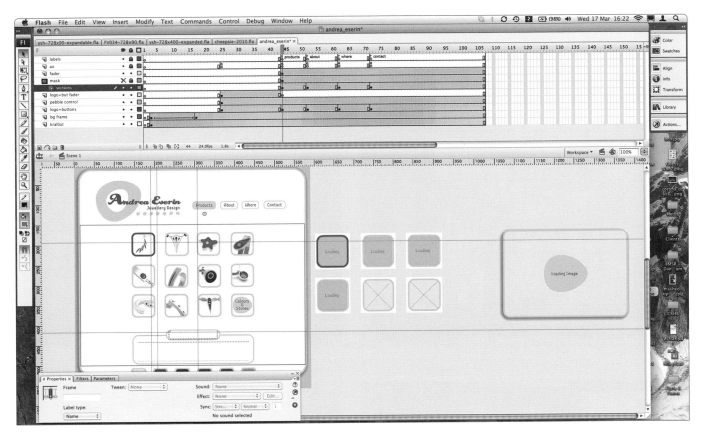

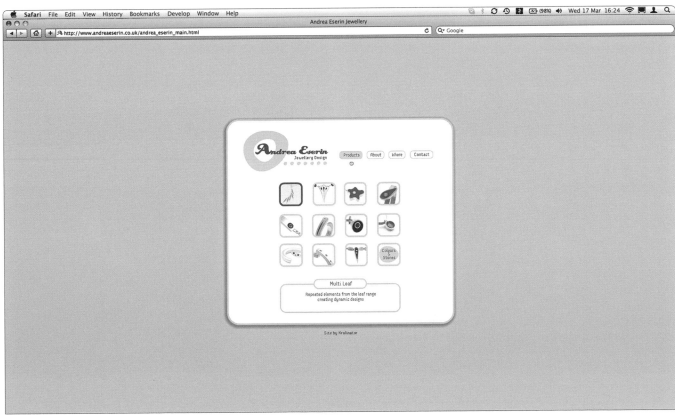

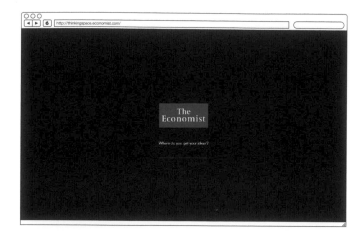

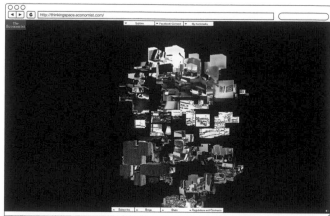

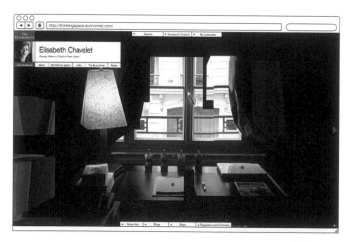

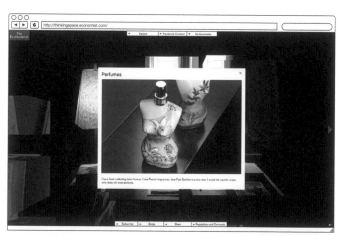

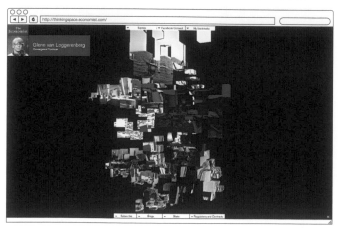

**6.10** The 'thinkingspace' website of UK magazine *The Economist* uses Flash to give a dramatic 3D interface with red dots leading to pop-up audio interviews. The site was built in Papervision3D by London designers Hi-ReS

**6.11** Italian organic fruit growers Mura Mura use Flash on their website to create animations of bees as well as changing images

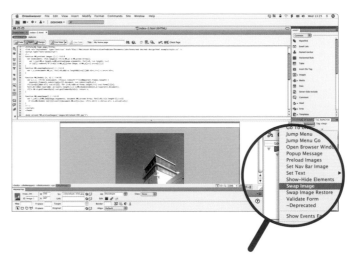

# JavaScript

Many of the effects that make a website more interactive, such as an image changing when your mouse rolls over a menu or pop-up windows, are created using JavaScript. It was originally developed by Brendan Eich of Netscape under the name Mocha, which was later renamed to LiveScript, and is unrelated to the programming language Java, although it was developed to look like Java, albeit easier for non-programmers to work with. JavaScript is a trademark of Sun Microsystems used under licence for technology invented and implemented by Netscape and its replacements such as Mozilla. It is officially now named ECMAScript, ECMA standing for European Computer Manufacturers Association, though the term JavaScript is still preferred by programmers. ActionScript, the programming language used in Adobe Flash, is another implementation of the ECMAScript standard.

As a client-side language – that is, run locally in a user's browser (rather than on a remote server) – it responds quickly to user actions, making an action seem more responsive. A rather trivial example of JavaScript code would be:

```
<script type="text/javascript">
    document.write('Yo! World');
</script>
<noscript>
Your browser either does not support JavaScript, or you have
JavaScript turned off.
</noscript>
```

which writes the phrase 'Yo! World' to the screen. Of course, HTML is much better at doing that, and JavaScript actions are usually more complex. As a client-side language, Java Script must be installed (and switched on) on the user's computer. The `<noscript>` is a courtesy to users without JavaScript – as with CSS you should aim for your design to degrade gracefully if things go wrong.

A script placed in the `<body>` of a page, like the one above, will be executed immediately the page loads into the browser. Scripts to be executed when they are called, or when an event is triggered, go into the `<head>` section. This will ensure that the script is loaded and ready before it is needed. As with CSS and SSI, longer scripts – and scripts used over and over on multiple pages – can be put into a separate external document with the suffix .js and brought in by a statement in the `<head>` section, thus:

```
<script type="text/javascript" src="external-file.js"></script>
```

**6.12** Dreamweaver's Swap Image behaviour will write JavaScript that replaces an image with another of the same size when the mouse rolls over it, and will restore the original image when the mouse moves away. It also automatically preloads the images so that they are ready for action. This is useful for rollover effects with menus or thumbnails

A complete description of JavaScript is not possible here, but there are many tutorials on the web, for example at www.w3schools.com/js/default.asp, and there are JavaScript 'libraries' on the web, such as jquery.com and script.aculo.us, where you can obtain ready-made scripts to cut and paste into your code to add functionality.

If you are using Dreamweaver, it will create 'behaviours' without your needing to do any scripting, and place them in the HTML (Fig **6.12**). A behaviour, in Dreamweaver, is a combination of an event and the action triggered by that event. In the Behaviours panel, you add a behaviour to a page by specifying an action and then specifying the event that triggers that action. For example, when a user moves the pointer over a link, the browser generates an `onMouseOver` event for that link and the browser checks whether it should call some JavaScript code in response.

Different events are defined for different page elements; for example, in most browsers `onMouseOver` and `onClick` are events associated with links; `onLoad` is an event associated with images. The Swap Image behaviour, for example, swaps one image for another of the same size by changing the `src` attribute of the `<img>` tag. It is used to create button rollovers and other image effects. This behaviour will automatically preload the images, so they are cached and ready to appear.

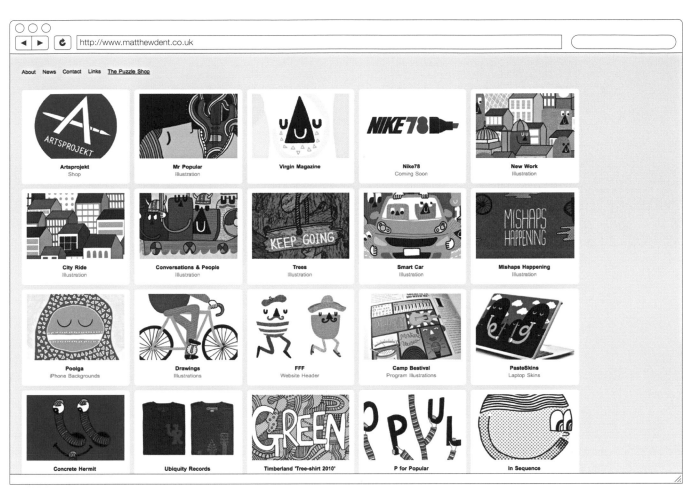

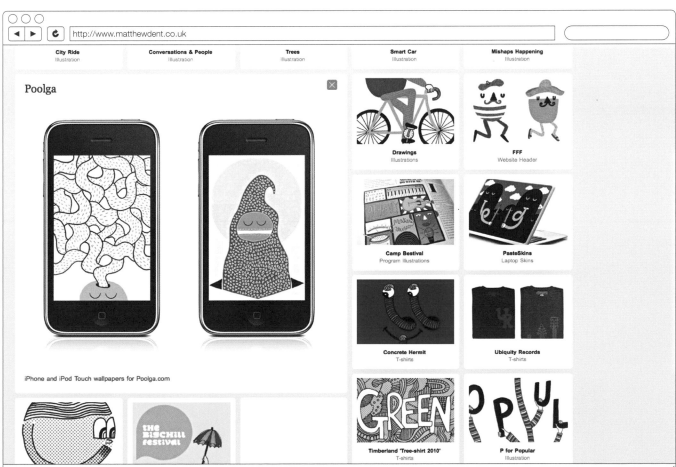

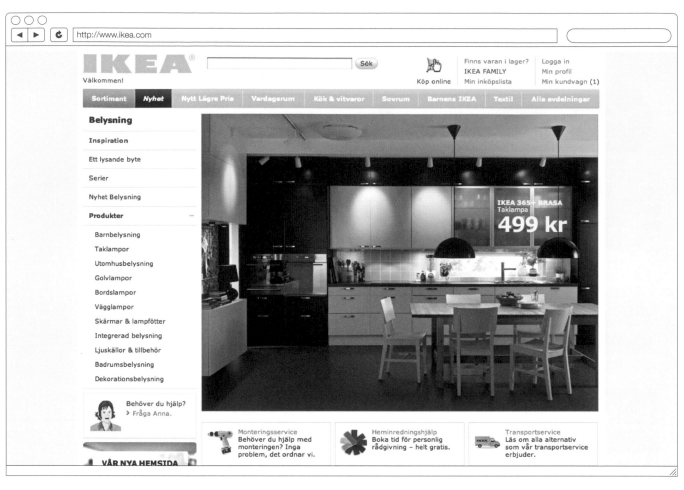

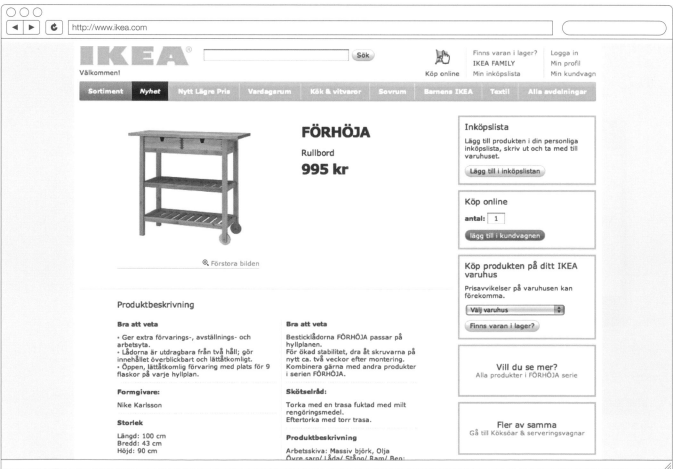

**6.14** Swedish furniture retailer IKEA's e-commerce website comprises all the necessary features to search for and buy items for home interiors. The main site takes you to localized sites around the world, in many different languages. Not all IKEA's products are delivered, so you can print out a shopping list to take to your nearest store.

# E-commerce

When browsing the web, you may have noticed that not every page address ends in .html (or even .shtml). A page that ends .asp means it is a text file that contains both HTML and scripts configured to interact with ASP (Active Server Pages) on the server – a server-side program, such as SSI. ASP was introduced by Microsoft in 1996 and uses as a default VBScript (Visual Basic Scripting), a language similar in function to JavaScript, although other languages can be used. An example of the syntax would be:

```
<% Response.Write "Yo! World." %>
```

PHP, which originally stood for Personal Home Page but now means the recursive acronym PHP: Hypertext Preprocessor, is another server-side language: code is embedded into the HTML source document and interpreted by a server with a PHP processor module, to generate the web page. It started off in 1994 as a set of CGI (Common Gateway Interface) scripts written in the C programming language by Rasmus Lerdorf to perform tasks such as displaying his résumé and recording how much traffic his page was receiving. It is free software released under licence by www.php.net. As well as for e-commerce sites, PHP is used by many social networking and blogging sites, such as Facebook and WordPress. Syntax is of the form:

```
<?php echo 'Yo! World.'; ?>
```

To keep a large-scale online shopping website up to date and constantly changing would be a mammoth, if not impossible, task to undertake manually (Fig **6.14**). Technologies such as ASP and PHP, working with a database management system such as MySQL (Structured Query Language, named after developer Michael Widenius's daughter My), enable a website to respond 'on the fly' creating unique responsive pages as you browse them.

For small-scale merchandise operations – suppose you wish to sell T-shirts, badges or prints from your website – there are a number of simpler options. The most basic method is to communicate with your customers by email. If you want to be able to process credit card transactions, you will need to set up a PayPal account. PayPal is now a subsidiary of auction site eBay and takes a commission for every transaction. You will need an account, but your customers need not have one. The PayPal website will produce form code that, for example, creates a 'Buy now' button for each of your products, which takes the customer to www.paypal.com for processing; all you

**6.15** Etsy provides artists and makers with a simple-to-use online outlet for their wares, like Emma McCann's Etsy online shop at www.screeningbluemurder.etsy.com

do is paste in the HTML code where they recommend.

A more comprehensive service is provided by selling sites such as Etsy, which has become popular with artist/makers (Fig **6.15**). Sellers have personalized stores where they set out their wares, rather like an online version of a traditional craft fair. Launched in 2005, Etsy makes money by charging a listing fee of 20 cents US for each item and taking a percentage of every sale.

**6.17** Sixpack is a French clothing retailer, based in Avignon, specializing in graffiti-based T-shirts. Their e-commerce website is clear, uncluttered and fast. It builds on the user experience by adding links to RSS, Twitter, Facebook and MySpace

# Content-management systems

One application of PHP is the content-management system (CMS). What do you do if you have created a website and the client wants to be able to update it, but knows nothing about HTML? You configure a CMS so that their adding to or modifying a website becomes a form-filling exercise. If you have used WordPress, you'll get the idea. Adobe's answer is a program called Contribute, designed to integrate with Dreamweaver, which consists of a 'client' for editing, and a 'publishing server'. Users can make updates via a browser. As a commercial product, it does come with a price tag. Other CMSs include Drupal, ExpressionEngine and Joomla, but our old friend WordPress is one of the most popular.

With a CMS, the designer sets up a template and the client logs on to a password-protected form via his or her browser to add or update content (Fig **6.16**). Plug-ins or modules can be installed to extend a site's functionality. Although they claim to be easy to use for the non-coder, as with blogs, a little HTML knowledge can help immensely, especially when troubleshooting. For example, when pasting

in text from a word processor, the type formatting can sometimes be brought in too, overriding the CSS of the site. It's simple enough to go into the HTML and remove any spurious `<span>` tags containing font info if you know what to look for. Conversely, anyone with a modicum of HTML knowledge can find the CMS experience very frustrating, so be aware of your customer's skill base.

Generally speaking, using a CMS has no effect on the look and feel of the site – that is determined by the designer in the CSS. The designer can also provide different levels of access to a CMS: a simple interface for casual users, such as members of a portfolio site, to update their text and images, with more power being allocated to people with admin access. Workflow management can also be set up, so that, say, a content creator could submit a story in draft mode, which would not be published until a copy editor had cleaned it up and the editor-in-chief approved it.

**6.16** The Brighton Illustrators Group website, designed by Tim Jukes, uses the ExpressionEngine content management system so that users can update the content. This is the slightly more complex admin screen for data entry, very similar to WordPress

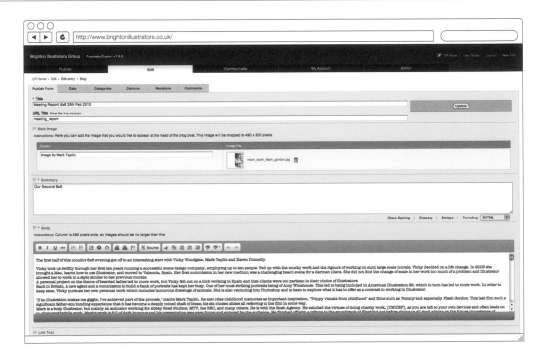

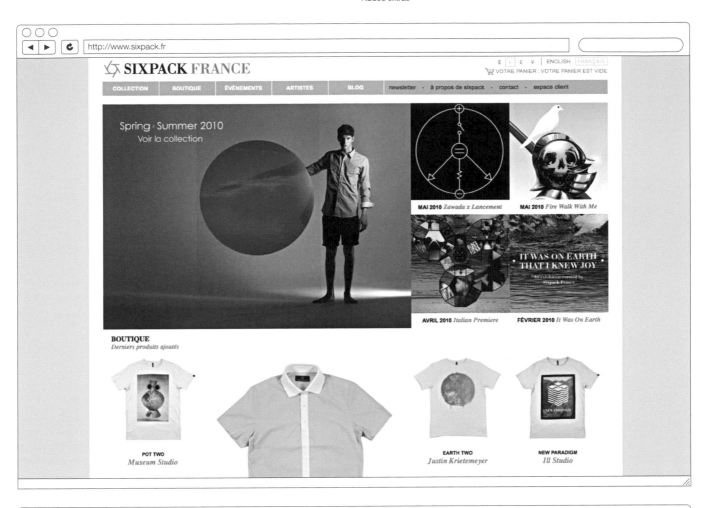

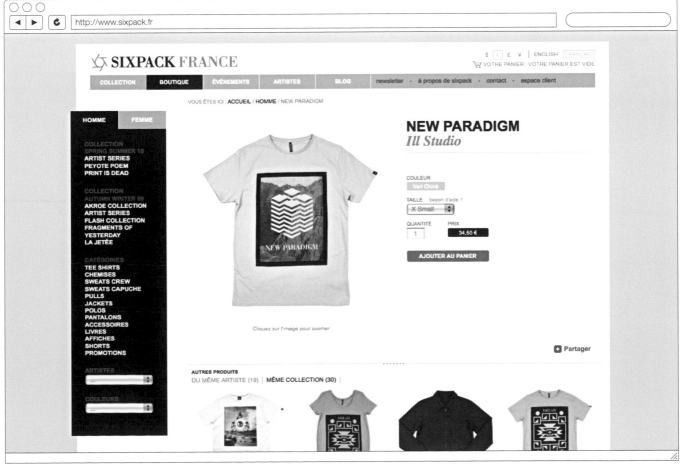

**6.18** Kokoro & Moi, a multidisciplinary
design consultancy based in Helsinki,
Finland, was founded in 2001 by designers
Teemu Suviala and Antti Hinkula. Their
vibrant website incorporates Twitter and
dynamic colourful thumbnails arranged in
reverse date order, like in a blog, leading
to more detail on their projects. They also
have a Facebook page

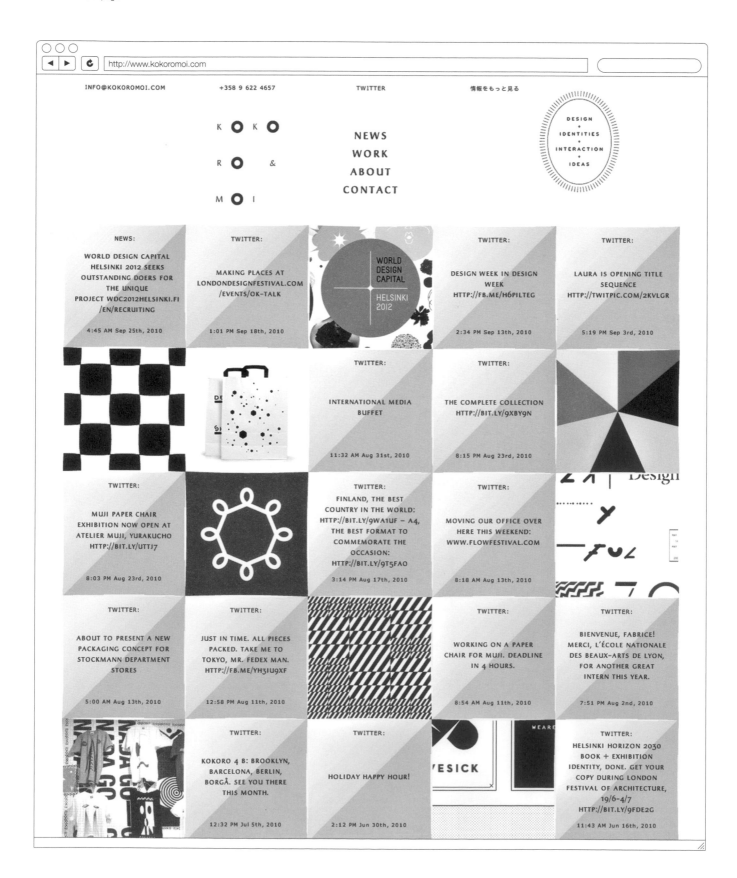

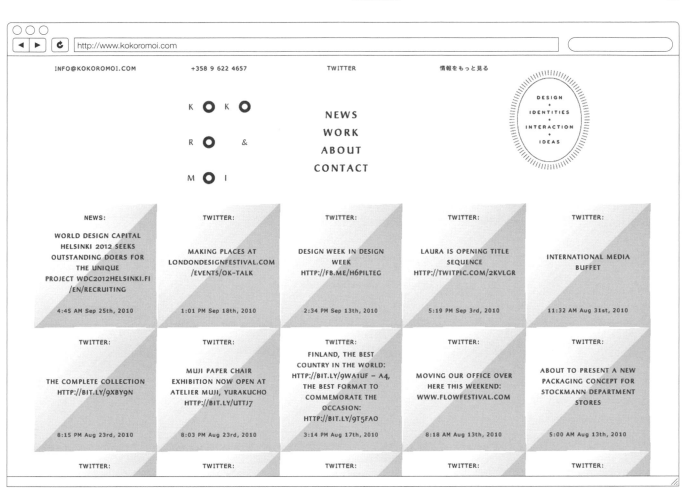

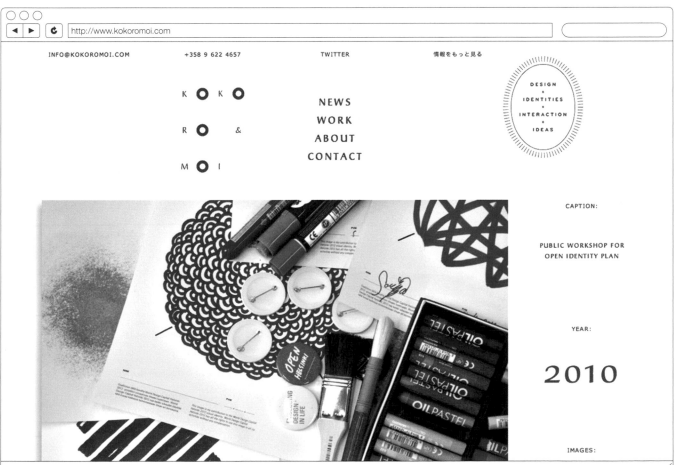

**6.19** Duane King's inspirational Thinking for a Living website has been created to work on the smaller screens of mobile devices, as well as on larger screens (see page 121). Being WordPress-based, there are programs such as MobilePress, a free WordPress plug-in, that can make your blog mobile-friendly

**6.20** FIELD (www.field.io) – the experimental website for the generative art projects of London-based Marcus Wendt and Vera-Maria Glahn – also lends itself to the constraints of mobile devices

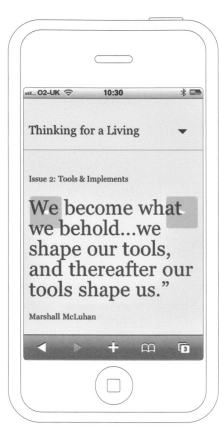

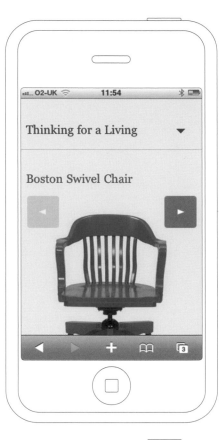

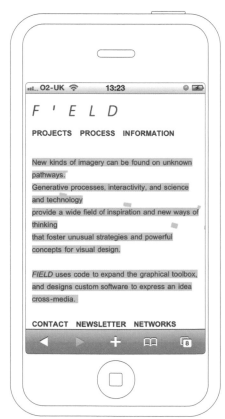

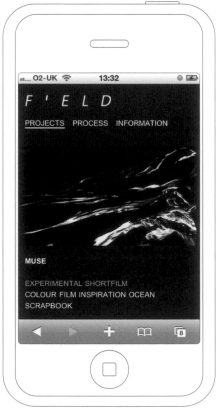

# Websites for handheld mobile devices

More and more mobile devices, such as smart phones, can be used to access websites while you are on the move. Apart from the iPad (Fig **6.21**) and similar rival devices that use Google's Android operating system, most have small screens – from 128 x 160px to 320 x 480px – and utilize a relatively large menu-choosing device: the human finger.

Consequently, websites specifically for mobile devices should be clear and legible, and have simple, foolproof navigation (Figs **6.19** and **6.20**). If you have designed your website using CSS, with the XHTML content logically organized, then it may be just a matter of adding another style sheet using the `<link>` command – some handhelds don't recognize `@import` – and they won't have to download linked style sheets, an important saving when bandwidth is tight.

If you place the handheld style sheet after the screen style sheet in your code, use `display: none` to hide navigation columns, floats, big images, advertising, and whatever else you don't want to send to the tiny screen of the mobile device. The code in the `<head>` section should look something like this:

```
<link rel="stylesheet" type="text/css" media="screen"
href="screen.css" />

<link rel="stylesheet" type="text/css" media="handheld"
href="mobile.css" />
```

If however, mobile phone access is an important part of your client's business, then a separate long and thin one-column site will have to be built from scratch (Fig **6.22**).

Most mobile users will access a website using a search, so browser detection (PHP scripts can be found on the web) can be used to choose the appropriate CSS or redirect to the separate website, usually identified by the domain .mobi or by a subdomain such as mobile.yoursite.com, m.yoursite.com or www.yoursite.com/mobile.

Your mobile-friendly website can be tested on various models of mobile phone using an emulator such as http://mtld. mobi/emulator.php. It is also possible to see how a website will look on a handheld device using the Opera desktop browser,

**6.21** The Apple iPad has a larger screen than most mobile devices and can display conventional websites – but be aware that navigation needs to be clear, simple and finger-sized

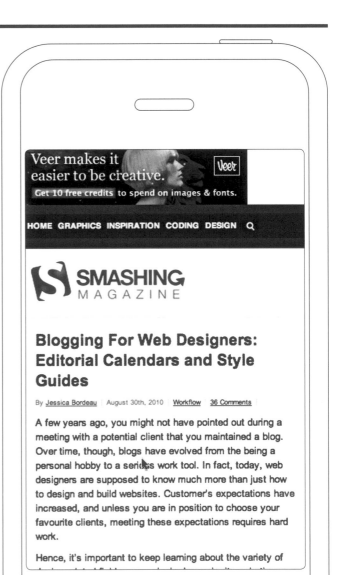

**6.22** Websites for mobile devices should have a simple one-column layout with fewer and smaller images, and clear navigation on the top and bottom of the resulting long, thin page – as in m.smashingmagazine.com, the mobile version of *Smashing Magazine's* website

in small-screen view. It is essential that you validate your code, as mobile browsers will be less capable at recovering from invalid code than their more forgiving desktop counterparts.

Here is a checklist of other important factors to consider:

• Remove unnecessary content: keep headers small and restrict the size and number of images. A website designed for a large landscape desktop screen will not work well on a tiny portrait phone screen. Avoid JavaScript and any multimedia, and remove unnecessary ads. Forget any fancy font information – there are so many different devices out there, most will end up using their own defaults anyway.

• Satisfy your users' needs quickly: mobile users want information fast at any location or time, to find directions for a restaurant nearby, for example.

• Keep navigation simple and concise: put menus at the top and bottom of every page so they are never far away. Breadcrumb-type navigation saves space and is efficient to use. Include a Back button on every page and make sure your image `alt` tags are descriptive, in case the actual images are not loaded.

• Provide obvious feedback: your pointing device is used both for scrolling and selecting hot links, so make the appearance of the link change dramatically – use a contrasting background colour, for example – to reassure the user that it has been properly selected.

• Keep user input simple: entering text on a mobile phone can be painfully slow and error-prone, so allow users to input information by making selections instead.

Non-mobile-friendly CSS properties to watch out for include:

• Float and display: because these properties are traditionally used to create multi-column layouts, they would require mobile users to scroll or zoom, and many mobile devices cannot scroll horizontally.

• Padding and margin: since screen space is limited on mobile devices, you should reduce these to a minimum or remove them altogether.

• Background image: images used for decorating a website for desktop browsers tend to be pretty big files and can have a detrimental effect on a mobile device, so they ought to be removed or replaced.

This brings us almost full circle: the basic one-column website that uses browser defaults as described in Chapter 2 would work fine on mobile devices. If mobile devices play a part in your future, you may go on to develop 'apps' – small programs developed specifically for smart phones. As a starting point there are ready-made apps available, such as those at www.chrismayerapps.co.uk/buycode/ that allow you to create e-books by adding your content to templates. This could be yet another avenue into creating accessible portfolios and improving further your visibility on the web.

# Web 2.0, HTML5 and the future

And so we arrive full circle. Web 2.0 is rather an optimistic term, giving an impression of an entirely new version of the web, one that is interactive, collaborative, democratic and sociable, compared with a passive and static Web 1.0. The term was first used by Darcy DiNucci in her 1999 article 'Fragmented Future'; World Wide Web inventor Tim Berners-Lee was not impressed – this was how he intended the web to be in the first place. Social networking sites such as Facebook have driven the change, making the web accessible to millions, adding a whole new way of communicating to our lives and establishing worldwide communities based on shared interests and hobbies.

A common comparison is Web 1.0's Encyclopedia Britannica versus Web 2.0's Wikipedia: Britannica. The former relies on experts to create articles and publishes them periodically with a price tag; Wikipedia trusts anonymous users to build content and edit it, which is available free to the user. Web 2.0 sites are typified by the following features (Andrew McAfee coined the mnemonic SLATES):

- Search: The ability to find information via keywords
- Links: Making connections between sources of information
- Authoring: The ability to create and update content individually or collaboratively: in wikis, where users can expand, undo and redo others' work; in blogs, where posts and their comments build up over time
- Tags: Categorizing content by adding user-defined single-word descriptions
- Extensions: Using software that makes the web an application platform rather than simply a document server
- Signals: Using syndication technology such as RSS to notify users of content updates

## RSS and Twitter

RSS (Really Simple Syndication) is an XML-based web feed format. Using a desktop reader such as NetNewsWire (for Macs) or FeedDemon (for PCs), you can be kept informed of any new items appearing on blogs, forums or news websites, and if the synopsis looks interesting, click to be taken to the full article on the website. Browsers also now support RSS feeds, and there are versions of the readers for the iPhone.

Another source of hot news is Twitter, which can be a very powerful self-promotion tool. Although restricted to 'tweets' of 140 characters, by using a URL shortening service such as bit.ly or tinyurl.com, you can inform your followers of any news as it happens. Retweeting other interesting messages helps you build up your audience. Like Facebook groups, Twitter has become a great campaigning device, able to gather support very quickly. Unlike blogs, which are archived, tweets are ephemeral and disappear almost as soon as they appear.

It is relatively easy to incorporate an RSS or Twitter feed into a blog, using Alex King's Twitter Tools on a WordPress blog for example. If you have a static website (for the all-time best photos in your portfolio, for example) and a blog, then as well as linking to your blog from your website, you can show visitors to it the most up-to-date postings by incorporating an RSS feed on your website. This will take some PHP or JavaScript programming, but using software such as Magpie RSS or a service such as feed2js.org, it can quickly be created. All you need is the URL of the blog's feed, for example:

http://janedoephotography.wordpress.com/feed/
or
http://www.janedoephotography.co.uk/blog/rss.xml

Your last three or four tweets can also be embedded on an HTML page using a Twitter widget by cutting and pasting some JavaScript. The containing box can be customized by size and colour, but may look out of place in a particular layout.

**6.24** The web pages for the Brussels and Paris offices of the Belgian design studio Salutpublic both incorporate an embedded Google map to help clients pinpoint their locations

**6.25** The website of Milan-based designers La Tigre (see also page 22) often uses embedded Vimeo videos to describe projects in movement and sound. Vimeo is considered by some to be of higher quality and less cluttered than YouTube, and using an external host for multimedia results in faster loading

## Photos, YouTube and Vimeo

The HTML code to embed a photo in a web page that was once found on the All Sizes page is now only in Share This. To get to it, go to the main photo page, click Share This, choose the size you want, and then choose Grab the HTML/BBCode and copy the code generated into your web page (Fig 6.23). BBCode is standard message board code, for use in Forum posts. You can also add a box containing, say, the last three Flickr photos you uploaded, by installing a Flickr 'badge', again by copying the code generated; or a slideshow, by starting the slideshow, hitting the Share button top right, and copying and pasting the code. Similarly, why host video clips when you can first upload them to YouTube or Vimeo and then cut and paste the code into your HTML (Fig **6.25**)? You can even embed Google maps into your pages by copying the code provided (Fig **6.24**).

## HTML5

HTML5 is the successor to HTML4.01 and XHTML1.1, in development at the time of writing, and will incorporate features like video playback and drag-and-drop, which have previously been dependent on third-party browser plug-ins such as Adobe Flash. New tags will replace generic block `<div>` and inline `<span>` elements with more descriptive ones such as `<nav>` (website navigation block) and `<footer>`. New elements include the multimedia elements `<audio>` and `<video>` that avoid the need for Flash, and deprecated tags such as `<font>` and `<centre>` will be completely outlawed, with CSS taking over their function.

Whatever the potential of new developments, always remember, like an over-elaborate cake, your website could become too rich – so exercise restraint and only add the bells and whistles that genuinely enhance the user's experience of your website.

**6.23** Flickr's Share This is where you go to get hold of the code to embed images, in this case one of medium size (450 x 338px), into your website, saving you the trouble of uploading it twice

http://www.salutpublic.be

## Salut Bruxelles

Bruxelles / Paris / Staff / Clients / Blog

Map | **Sat** | Ter | Earth

Imagery ©2010 DigitalGlobe, Aerodata International Surveys, Cnes/Spot Image, GeoEye - Terms of Use

**Salutpublic Bruxelles**
86 rue Le Lorrain
B-1080 Bruxelles
E contact (at) salutpublic.be
T +32 (0)2 3740169

## public

Bruxelles / Paris / Staff / Clients / Blog

Salutpublic est un studio de graphisme fondé
à Bruxelles en 2002. Résolument tourné vers
l'international, Salutpublic forge sa pratique
autour du design de livres, des identités
architecturales, du design graphique et de la

---

http://www.latigre.net

## LA TIGRE DESIGN&DIRECTION

**HELLO,
WE ARE LA TIGRE**
La Tigre 2009/2010

In order of appearance: La Tigre paper-toy // Label, sticker and business card // A3 poster-brochure // "Tales From the Basement" video.

*In ordine di apparizione: Il paper-toy de La Tigre // Etichetta, adesivo e bglietto da visita // Poster-brochure in A3 // Il video "Tales From the Basèment".*

### SELECTED PROJECTS

—Il Sole 24 Ore Infographics NEW
— Panorama Best Shopping
— Panorama Best Shopping #2
— Panorama Best Drive
— Panorama Best Watches
— Correndo per il Mondo Videos
— Infographics for IL Magazine
— Ferrari Assicurazioni Identity
— Federlegno Annual Report
— Edison Trading Video Report
— Milano Film Festival #14
— Milano Film Festival #13
— Design Pubblico
— Officine Libra Art Project
— Andrea+Roberta Wedding Card NEW
— Mariposa Pasta Shop
— Rasori Stock House Look NEW
— Enciclopedia della Battuta
— D Magazine Special Pages
— Mixa Magazine
— Zaf Brand Image Design
— Pedrali Magazine
— Progetto Triuggio Journal
— Fifa World Cup Calendar 2010 NEW
— Sul Palco dell'Idroscalo Book
— 9707 - Dieci Anni Hardcore a Milano
— La Tigre Selfpromotion NEW

### PROFILE

### CONTACT

### BLOG

# Glossary

**Accessibility**
The degree to which a website can be understood by as many people as possible, including those with disabilities

**Achromatic**
In colour schemes, the absence of **hue** and saturation – just black, white and the greys in between

**Achromatic greys**
Made from mixing just black and white together with no other colour

**ActionScript**
**Flash's** object-oriented programming language

**Additive colour**
Colour created by superimposing light. Adding together (or superimposing) the three primaries – red, blue and green – will produce white. The secondaries are cyan, yellow and magenta (see **transmitted colour**)

**Analogous colour scheme**
Colour scheme based on a pie-shaped slice of three or more **hues** located next to each other on the **colour wheel**, usually with one hue in common: yellow-orange, yellow and yellow-green, for example

**Animated GIF**
A simple sequence of images combined into a single image file to produce an animation, but without sound

**API**
(application programming interfaces) An interface that facilitates interaction between different software programs, similar to the way user interfaces facilitate interaction between humans and computers

**ARPAnet**
Advanced Research Projects Agency network – a forerunner of the internet

**ASCII (American Standard Code For Information Interchange)**
A text-only format of 256 codes used to represent alphanumeric characters, with no additional information about size, font or spacing

**ASP (Active Server Pages)**
A scripting language that allows web pages to be compiled 'on the fly' from a constantly updated database

**Behaviour**
In Dreamweaver, this is a **JavaScript** combination of an event and the action triggered by that event

**Blog (weblog)**
An online journal with most recent entries first, which can be customized

**<br />**
A line-break **tag**: as it has no end tag, we add a space and slash inside the tag

**Breadcrumbs**
A navigation aid usually appearing horizontally across the top of all web pages and comprising hierarchical links to the parent pages of the current one, separated by greater-than signs (>), providing a trail for the user to follow back to the **home page**

**Browser**
A **'client'** computer program that allows you to view and interact with **WWW** pages on the **internet**. An example is Firefox

**BTW**
By the way

**CGI (Common Gateway Interface)**
An interface between web **servers** and their clients (browsers)

**Client**
In a client–server arrangement, the client – the web **browser** – requests data from the **server**, or remote host computer

**CMS (content-management system)**
A form-based interface that allows non-programmers to input content to a website

**CMYK**
In graphic design, a colour system in which successive printings of cyan, magenta, yellow and black (black is referred to as 'key') visually mix to produce a wide gamut of colours – also called four-colour printing or full-colour printing

**Colour blindness**
Deuteranomaly is the most common colour deficiency, resulting in a reduction in sensitivity to the green area of the spectrum

**Colour tetrad**
Four colours, equally spaced on the **colour wheel**, containing a primary, its complement and a complementary pair of inter-mediates. Also any organization of colour on the wheel forming a rectangle that could include a double split-complement

**Colour triad**
Three colours spaced an equal distance apart on the **colour wheel** forming an equilateral triangle. Itten's 12-step colour wheel is made up of a primary triad, a secondary triad, and two intermediate triads

**Colour wheel**
An arrangement of colours based on the sequence of **hues** in the visible spectrum arranged as the spokes of a wheel. The most common is Itten's 12-step colour wheel

**Complementary colours**
Two colours directly opposite each other on the colour wheel. A primary colour is complementary to a secondary colour, which is a mixture of the two remaining primaries. Complementary colours accentuate each other in juxtaposition and neutralize each other in mixture

**Complementary colour scheme**
Built around two hues that are opposite one another on the **colour wheel**. This scheme is intrinsically high contrast and intense, to the point of creating vibrating colours

**Cool colours**
Colours have associated temperatures: blue and green we associate with ice, water and crisp salads. On the Itten colour wheel, these are the yellow-green to violet segment (see **warm colours**)

**CSS (Cascading Style Sheets)**
The language used to describe the look and formatting of a document written in a markup language, such as **XHTML**

**Deprecation**
A term applied to methods and **tags** that have been superseded and should be avoided as the feature will be removed in the future. This gives programmers time to bring their code into compliance with the new standard

**Dingbat**
A symbol or ornament such as ❤ or ☞ treated as characters in a font

**<div>**
**HTML tag** that creates containers in which to place layout elements

**DOCTYPE**
A declaration at the start of every web page that tells the browser what version of the **markup language** the page is written in

**Domain**
Your unique web address. Top-level domain types include .com for commercial organizations and .edu for educational institutions

**Double complementary colour scheme**
Two sets of complementaries – if they come from equidistant places on the **colour wheel**, this is termed a **quadrad**

**Drop cap**
A large initial letter dropping into the lines below and signalling the beginning of the text

**Earmarks**
Distinguishing features of a typeface used for identification, named after the ear of a lower-case g

**ECMAScript (European Computer Manufacturers Association script)**
A programming language used for client-side scripting on the web. **JavaScript** and Flash's **ActionScript** are dialects of it

**E-commerce**
Shopping website created on the fly from databases, usually designed using **PHP** or **ASP**

**Email**
Electronic mail

**Escape entities, or sequences**
The left angle bracket (<), the right angle bracket (>) and the ampersand (&) have special meanings in **HTML** and cannot be used 'as is'. You must enter their escape sequence instead: &amp; for example, is the escape sequence for &

**FAQ (Frequently Asked Questions)**
A list of questions and answers. Newbies are encouraged to consult the FAQ before posting, so as not to annoy the old hands

**Favicon (favourites icon)**
The tiny 16px square icon you sometimes see when you add a web address to a bookmark list or see the **URL** in your **browser's** toolbar

**Flame (verb)**
To post a harshly critical message in public on **Usenet** or send very long abusive messages via **email**

**Flash**
Adobe (formerly Macromedia) Flash is a programming language for producing animations and complete websites, based around key frames and a timeline

**Float**
In **CSS**, any elements following a floated element, such as an image or `<div>` tag, will wrap around it. To cancel this effect apply the `clear` property

**Font**
A complete set in one size only of all the letters of the alphabet, complete with associated **ligatures** (joined letters), numerals, punctuation marks and any other signs and symbols

**Font masters**
A set of type designs in one or more sizes that are scaled (enlarged or reduced) to create all the intermediate sizes

**Font metrics**
The information about horizontal spacing built into a typeface by its designer

**Frames**
A deprecated method of creating a web page comprising different segments, with each frame containing and displaying a separate **HTML** document

**FTP (File Transfer Protocol)**
A protocol that lets users transfer files between computers, uploading your website to a server for example

**FYI**
For your information

**Gamut or colour space**
The range of colours that can be reproduced by a colour display, an output device or a particular colour printing method – some colours available on a computer screen may not be printable using the **CMYK** process

**GIF (Graphics Interchange Format)**
A common format for graphics containing flat areas of colour (see also **JPEG**)

**Grid**
A network of horizontal and vertical intersecting lines that provides a framework to guide designers as to where they should place elements

**Hardcopy**
An output from a computer system that you can hold in your hand – usually a paper proof

**Heading**
In **HTML**, `<h1>` through `<h6>` tags, largest to smallest, should be used in turn, not missing out a number

**HLS**
The three attributes of colour: **hue**, luminance and saturation (see **HSB**)

**Home page**
Your own **WWW** site, or the index. html initial page of a website from which all others branch

**Host**
The computer on which your website 'lives' in order to be accessed over the **WWW**

**House style**
Standards of consistency concerning spelling and use of English (or any other language) as laid down by a particular publisher, or to be used within a particular publication

**HSB**
The preferred terms for the three attributes of colour: **hue**, saturation and brightness

**HSL**
In Photoshop, the three attributes of colour are known as **hue**, saturation and lightness (see **HSB**)

**HTML (Hypertext Markup Language)**
Text-based language used to create and communicate **WWW** pages

**HTML5**
The proposed next standard for HTML 4.01 and XHTML 1.0, which aims to replace proprietary plug-in-based rich internet application (RIA) technologies such as **Flash** using new `<audio>` and `<video>` elements and **API**s (application programming interfaces)

**htaccess (hypertext access)**
A directory-level configuration file that enables server-side code such as **SSI** to work

**HTTP (Hypertext Transport Protocol)**
The protocol of the **WWW**

**Hue**
Common name of a colour and its position in the spectrum as determined by the wavelength of the ray of light, for instance red, blue, yellow and green

**ICANN (Internet Corporation for Assigned Names and Numbers)**
Body responsible for **domain** names

**IMHO**
In my humble opinion

**Inheritance**
The property of **CSS** for 'children' to take on the attributes of their enclosing 'parent' **tags**

**Internet**
A network of networks based on the **TCP/IP** protocols; a community of people who use and develop those networks; and a collection of resources that can be reached from those networks

**Intranet**
A local network, such as one within a corporation, using the same tools as the internet: **email** and **WWW** pages, for example

**IP**
Internet Protocol

**ISP (Internet Service Provider)**
The company that connects your computer to the internet and often provides the webspace to host your website

**JavaScript**
Formerly LiveScript, this is an implementation of the **ECMAScript** language used to provide enhanced user interfaces and dynamic websites

**JPEG (Joint Photographic Experts Group)**
A common format for graphics containing continuous tones of colour, such as photographs (see also **GIF**)

**LOL**
Laugh out loud

**Justified**
Type set with edges that are aligned both left and right. Justified setting requires hyphenation and variable spacing between words

**Kerning**
Adjusting the spacing between pairs of letters, such as between T and A, to improve the aesthetic appearance (see also **Tracking**)

**K–P distance**
The distance from the top of a letter k to the bottom of a letter p

**L*a*b**
A device-independent colour model proposed by the Commission Internationale d'Eclairage: L is for luminance; a and b are chromatic components – a for green to red, and b for blue to yellow

**Leading or interline spacing**
The space between lines of type; in letterpress printing these were once strips of lead

# Glossary

**Ligature**
Two or more letters, such as fi and ffl, joined together into one character

**Literals**
In proofreading, spelling mistakes or transpositions of letters caused by typing errors

**Logical style**
Styling text according to its meaning, using tags such as `<em>` and `<strong>`, instead of typographical tags such as `<i>` and `<b>` (see **physical style**)

**Mailing list**
An **email** discussion group, in which a message sent to the list server is broadcast to anyone 'subscribing' to the particular list

**Markup language**
A system for annotating text in a way that is syntactically distinguishable from that text, examples are **XML**, HTML and XHTML

**Measure**
The width of a line of type – usually the column width, specified in mm or ems

**Monochromatic**
Colours of one **hue**; the complete range of value from white to black

**Munsell tree**
A system for naming colours developed by Albert Henry Munsell, related to the **HSB** system, where the 'trunk' has 10 brightness steps of grey from black at the bottom to white at the top. Radiating out from the trunk are different saturations of colour. **Hues** are situated around the outer edge

**MySQL (Structured Query Language)**
A database used to design **e-commerce** websites, with languages such as **PHP** and **ASP**

**Neutral colour**
Colour that has been reduced in saturation by being mixed with grey or with a complementary colour. The sensation of hue is lost or dulled

**Nesting**
In **CSS**, placing a `<div>` **tag** inside another `<div>`, or a **table** within another table

**Newsgroup**
A 'bulletin board' of articles on a specific topic, arranged in threads (see also **Usenet**)

**Owen Briggs method**
A **CSS** workaround that uses a combination of ems and percentages to prevent inheritance producing unwanted reductions in text size

**`<p>`**
In **HTML**, the paragraph **tag** that should enclose any paragraphs or single lines of text

**Packet switching**
Data is broken down into 'packets' and sent off by different routes within a network of computers towards their destination, where they are eventually reassembled

**Partitive colour system**
Based on the perceptional relationship of colours, in which there are four (not three) fundamental colour hues: red, green, yellow and blue. The Swedish Natural Colour System (NCS) is based on these observations

**PDF (Portable Document Format)**
A document format that uses a reader such as Adobe Acrobat to recreate the appearance of fonts and spacing in your page layout

**PHP (Hypertext Preprocessor, formerly Personal Home Page)**
A scripting language that allows web pages to be compiled 'on the fly' from a constantly updated database

**Physical style**
Styling text according to its typographical appearance, using **tags** such as `<i>` and `<b>`, instead of logical tags such as `<em>` and `<strong>` (see **logical style**)

**Pixel**
Short for picture element, this is the dot on a computer display. The resolution (sharpness) of a display is measured by the number of pixels horizontally by the number of scan lines vertically, for instance 1280 x 1024px

**PNG (Portable Network Graphics)**
A lossless, portable format coming into use that provides a patent-free replacement for **GIF** and can also replace many common uses of TIFF

**Primary colours**
The brain accepts four colours – red, yellow, green and blue – as primaries, and this is reflected in the composition of modern **colour wheels**. These are also the basic **hues** in any colour system that in theory may be used to mix all other colours. In light, the three primaries are red, green and blue; in pigments, the three primary colours are red, yellow and blue

**Pseudo element**
**CSS** selector that identifies which part of the text CSS should apply to, for instance `:link` and `:first-letter`

**Quadrad**
A **double complementary** colour scheme using two sets of complementaries from equidistant places on the **colour wheel**

**Ranged left/right**
Ranged left is a method of setting type in which the type is aligned on the left-hand side and ragged on the right. Ranged-right type is ragged on the left and aligned on the right

**RGB**
The **primary colours** of light are red, green and blue. **Transmitted colour** is light direct from an energy source, shining through coloured filters on a theatre spotlight or displayed on a computer screen

**Roman**
Normal type, as opposed to italic or bold; also a kind of type with **serifs** such as Times New Roman

**RSS (Really Simple Syndication)**
An **XML**-based web feed format that keeps you informed of any new items appearing on **blogs**, forums or news websites

**RT*M**
Read the * manual (clean version!)

**RTF**
Rich text file – use in preference to a native Word file

**Sans serif**
A typeface without **serifs**

**Serif**
The mark that terminates the ends of the letters in some typefaces

**Server**
The computer at the **ISP** or hosting service that provides space for your website. In a client–server arrangement, the **client**, for instance the web browser, requests data from the server

**Set solid**
Type set without leading, for example 10 point on 10 point

**sIFR (scalable Inman Flash Replacement)**
A **Flash**-based method for inserting **fonts** that may not be on the end-user's computer into web pages, as developed by Mike Davidson, based on the work of Shaun Inman

**SLATES**
Acronym coined by Andrew McAfee to describe **Web 2.0**: Search, Links, Authoring, Tags, Extensions, Signals

**`<span>`**
**HTML tag** for making localized changes to style – to change the colour of a particular word, for example

**Split complementary colour scheme**
Any **hue** plus the two colours either side of its complementary. Contrast is less marked than with a pure complementary scheme, but more intense than the double complementary scheme

**SSI (Server Side Include)**
A method by which a **server** can call in code containing frequently changing content – a menu for example – and place it in your website

**Statement**
In **CSS**, the instruction or rule of the form `selector {property: value;}` that tells the **browser** how to style the text affected

**Syntax highlighting**
In programs such as Dreamweaver, using different colours in the code to distinguish tags from text

**swf (ShockWave Flash)**
Output file format for **Flash** animations

**Tables**
A grid of rows and columns (rather like a spreadsheet) filled with content and transparent **GIFs** – once used to create layouts, but now **deprecated**. These should only be used to create actual tables within a **CSS** layout

**Tag**
**HTML** code that the **browser** interprets 'on the fly' as the web page arrives from the server to the client. Tags usually have a start and an end that 'contains' the item in question. The first part of the tag turns an attribute on and the second turns the attribute off. Tags are surrounded by angled brackets (the 'less than' < and 'greater than' > symbols) and the closing tag is usually preceded by a slash ( / ) symbol

**TCP/IP (Transmission Control Protocol/Internet Protocol)**
The standards that enable computers to pass information between each other on the internet

**Tetradic colour scheme**
A scheme based on a square – the **hues** are equally spaced and will comprise a primary, its complement, plus a complementary pair of tertiaries

**Tint**
A **hue** mixed with white

**Tone**
A low-saturation colour that is produced by mixing a **hue** with a shade of grey or its complement

**Tracking**
Adjusting the spacing between all letters (as opposed to **kerning**, which only adjusts the space between pairs of letters)

**Transmitted colour**
Light direct from an energy source, or shining through coloured filters on a theatre spotlight or displayed on a computer screen. The primary colours of light are red, green and blue (**RGB**). Light colour is inherently **additive**

**Triadic colour scheme**
Three equally spaced colours on the **colour wheel**, forming the vertices of an equilateral triangle. A primary triad provides the liveliest set of colours; a secondary triad is softer, as any two secondaries will be related and share a common primary: orange and green, for example, both contain yellow

**URL (Uniform Resource Locator)**
The unique address of a **WWW** page, of the form http://www.ISP.com/index.html, also known as URI (Uniform Resource Identifier)

**Usability**
The extent to which a website can be used with effectiveness, efficiency and satisfaction within a specified context of use

**Usenet (Unix User Network)**
Home of newsgroups, not part of the **WWW**

**VBScript (Visual Basic Scripting)**
A language similar in function to **JavaScript** used with **ASP**

**Virtual server**
A self-contained section of a host's server computer that acts as your own server

**WAI (Web Accessibility Initiative)**
Organization promoting accessibility

**Warm colours**
Colours have associated temperatures – red and yellow we associate with fire and sunlight. On the Itten colour wheel, these are the yellow to red-violet segment (see **cool colours**)

**WCAG (Web Content Accessibility Guidelines)**
The guidelines for making web content accessible, as published by **WAI**

**Web 2.0**
**WWW** enhanced by social networking applications such as Facebook, Flickr and Twitter. Coined by Darcy DiNucci in her 1999 article 'Fragmented Future'

**Webmail**
**Email** accessible from a **browser** rather than an **email** client, at an internet page for example – for instance Hotmail or Gmail

**Websafe colours**
216 colours that will be displayed by any **browser** without resorting to dithering (optically mixing two or more colours)

**Wrapper**
In **CSS** a `<div>` **tag** that encloses the whole layout, setting its overall width

**WWW (World Wide Web)**
Interconnected internet 'pages' viewed by a **browser**, such as Firefox, containing text, images, sound, movies and hypertext 'hot links' to other pages

**wysiwyg ('what you see is what you get')**
A screen-based representation of a **WWW** page in a program such as Dreamweaver or Freeway that approximates what you will see as a finished product in a browser, as opposed to a list of computer code

**W3C**
World Wide Web Consortium

**WOB (white on black)**
Reversed-out type

**X-height**
The height of a letter x in a particular typeface – a typographic measurement that ignores the height of the ascenders and descenders

**XHTML (Extensible Hypertext Markup Language)**
A stricter form of **HTML**

**XML (Extensible Markup Language)**
A generalized meta set of rules for encoding documents in machine-readable form. **HTML** and **XHTML** are more specific examples related to web design

# Books

### Reference manuals

There are many manuals available, for instance the 'Nutshell', 'Missing Manuals' and 'For Dummies' series. While there are some on general HTML and CSS, many others are aimed specifically at single specific items of software, such as Dreamweaver (*Dreamweaver for Dummies, Dreamweaver CS3: The Missing Manual*, etc.)

Rachel Andrew, *The CSS Anthology: 101 Essential Tips, Tricks & Hacks*, third edition, SitePoint, Melbourne, 2009

Craig Grannell, *The Essential Guide to CSS & HTML Web Design*, second edition, Friends of ED, New York, 2007
The author has an art and design background and the style is direct and accessible

Patrick Lynch and Sarah Horton, *Web Style Guide: Basic Design Principles for Creating Web Sites*, third edition, Yale University Press, New Haven, CT, 2009

David McFarland, CSS: *The Missing Manual*, Pogue Press/O'Reilly Media, second edition, Sebastopol, CA, 2009

Eric Meyer, *CSS Web Site Design Hands on Training*, Peachpit Press, Berkeley, CA, 2006

Jennifer Niederst Robbins, *Learning Web Design: A Beginner's Guide to (X)HTML, StyleSheets, and Web Graphics*, third edition, O'Reilly Media, Sebastopol, CA, 2007

Jennifer Niederst Robbins, *Web Design in a Nutshell*, third edition, O'Reilly Media, Sebastopol, CA, 2006

Jeffrey Zeldman and Ethan Marcotte, *Designing with Web Standards*, third edition, New Riders, Berkeley, CA, 2009

### Design principles

Jason Beaird, *The Principles of Beautiful Web Design*, SitePoint, Melbourne, 2007

Mark Boulton, *A Practical Guide to Designing for the Web*, Five Simple Steps, Penarth, 2010
Also available as a free e-book from designingfortheweb.co.uk/book

Jill Butler, Kritina Holden and Will Lidwell, *Universal Principles of Design: 100 Ways to Enhance Usability, Influence Perception, Increase Appeal, Make Better Design Decisions, and Teach through Design*, Rockport Publishers, Gloucester, MA, 2007

Steve Krug, *Don't Make Me Think: A Common Sense Approach to Web Usability*, second edition, New Riders Press, Berkeley, CA, 2005

Penny McIntire, *Visual Design for the Modern Web*, New Riders, Berkeley, CA, 2007
Short colourful book, focusing on design principles rather than coding

Jakob Nielsen, *Designing Web Usability*, New Riders, Berkeley, CA, 1999

### Inspiration

Hillman Curtis, *MTIV: Process, Inspiration and Practice for the New Media Designer*, New Riders, Berkeley, CA, 2002

Dave Shea and Molly E. Holzschlag, *The Zen of CSS Design: Visual Enlightenment for the Web (Voices That Matter)*, Peachpit Press, Berkeley, CA, 2005

Fig Taylor, *How to Create a Portfolio & Get Hired: A Guide for Graphic Designers and Illustrators*, Laurence King Publishing, London, 2010

### Portfolio books
These are books full of screenshots with little if any commentary or information on how designs were achieved

Guenter Beer, *Web Design Index 9*, Pepin Press, Amsterdam, 2010

Paz Diman (ed.), *Web Design Handbook, BooQs*, Antwerp, Belgium, second edition, 2009

Julius Wiedemann, *Web Design: Navigation*, Taschen, Köln, Germany, 2009

# Websites

There are many website resources, mostly free. The hardest part is finding the one that you need and that is at the right level. Note that web addresses often change, so if the link doesn't work, try putting the key words into a search engine such as Google.

## Accessibility and usability

Accessibility guidelines
www.w3.org/TR/WCAG10/

BBC accessibility website
www.bbc.co.uk/accessibility/

Usability guru Jakob Nielsen
www.useit.com

## Blogs

Blogger
www.blogger.com

Tumblr
www.tumblr.com

WordPress
wordpress.com

## Colour schemes

Colour scheme designer
colorschemedesigner.com

Colorspire
www.colorspire.com

Kuler
kuler.adobe.com

Online colour calculator
www.telacommunications.com/
nutshell/rgbform.htm

Websafe colours
www.lynda.com/hex.html

## Inspiration and tips

Don Norman's jnd ('just noticeable difference') website
www.jnd.org

A demonstration of what can be accomplished using CSS
www.csszengarden.com

A List Apart website
www.alistapart.com/articles/
practicalcss

Stuart Nicholls's CSSplay
www.cssplay.co.uk

Jeffrey Zeldman Presents
The Daily Report
www.zeldman.com

Dave Shea's weblog about design and the web
mezzoblue.com

Eric Meyer's Geek Talk
meyerweb.com

What is Web 2.0?
oreilly.com/web2/archive/what-is-web-20.html

## Software helpers

Aviary (open-source alternative to Photoshop)
aviary.com

BBEdit
www.barebones.com

CSSEdit
macrabbit.com/cssedit

Dreamweaver
www.adobe.com/products/
dreamweaver

Favicon plug-in for Photoshop
www.telegraphics.com.au/sw

Freeway
www.softpress.com

KompoZer (open-source alternative to Photoshop)
www.kompozer.net

Nvu (open-source alternative to Dreamweaver)
www.nvu.com

PageSpinner
www.optima-system.com/
pagespinner

Style Master
www.westciv.com/style_master

The GIMP (open-source alternative to Photoshop)
www.gimp.org

## Standards

The World Wide Web Consortium (W3C) – an international consortium working to develop web standards
www.w3.org

W3C's Markup Validation Service
validator.w3.org

W3C's CSS Validation Service
jigsaw.w3.org/css-validator

Full list of country domains
www.iana.org

See what your website looks like in different browsers
browsershots.org

## Templates

CSS layouts and web templates
www.code-sucks.com

Listamatic – code for menus
css.maxdesign.com.au/listamatic

The Layout Reservoir
www.bluerobot.com/web/layouts

RapidWeaver
www.realmacsoftware.com/
rapidweaver/index.php

## Tutorials

Definitions and tutorials on HTML, CSS and much more
www.w3schools.com

Adobe's 'Digital Design: Foundations of Web Design' – PDF-based, making use of Adobe programs such as Dreamweaver
www.adobe.com/education/
instruction/teach/digitaldesign.html

Excellent tutorial aimed at Style Master users, which can be adapted for manual design
www.westciv.com/style_master/
academy/hands_on_tutorial/index.html

Tutorial on the CSS float property
css.maxdesign.com.au/floatutorial/
index.htm

Using coloured boxes to build CSS layouts
www.maxdesign.com.au/articles/
process

Dave Raggett's short guide to styling your web pages
www.w3.org/MarkUp/Guide/Style

Owen Briggs method of font sizing
www.thenoodleincident.com/
tutorials/box_lesson/font

How to fool the server into thinking a .html file is a .shtml file using .htaccess
www.andreas.com/faq-ssi.html

JavaScript tutorial
www.w3schools.com/js/default.asp

@font-face tutorial
hacks.mozilla.org/2009/06/
beautiful-fonts-with-font-face

## Typography

Entity codes and escape sequences
www.w3schools.com/tags/ref_
entities.asp

Font replacement using sIFR
www.mikeindustries.com/blog/sifr/

Fonts common to Macs and PCs
www.ampsoft.net/webdesign-l/
WindowsMacFonts.html

Google font directory
code.google.com/webfonts

# CSS Properties

This is an abridged list; a complete list can be found at www.w3schools.com/css/css_reference.asp.

**The CSS column** indicates in which CSS version the property is defined (CSS1 or CSS2).

| Property | Description | CSS |
|---|---|---|
| *Background Properties* | | |
| background | Sets all the background properties in one declaration | 1 |
| background-color | Sets the background colour of an element | 1 |
| background-image | Sets the background image for an element | 1 |
| background-repeat | Sets how a background image will be repeated | 1 |
| *Border Properties* | | |
| border | Sets all the border properties in one declaration | 1 |
| border-bottom | Sets all the bottom border properties in one declaration | 1 |
| border-bottom-color | Sets the colour of the bottom border | 2 |
| border-bottom-style | Sets the style of the bottom border | 2 |
| border-bottom-width | Sets the width of the bottom border | 1 |
| border-color | Sets the colour of the four borders | 1 |
| border-left | Sets all the left border properties in one declaration | 1 |
| border-left-color | Sets the colour of the left border | 2 |
| border-left-style | Sets the style of the left border | 2 |
| border-left-width | Sets the width of the left border | 1 |
| border-right | Sets all the right border properties in one declaration | 1 |
| border-right-color | Sets the colour of the right border | 2 |
| border-right-style | Sets the style of the right border | 2 |
| border-right-width | Sets the width of the right border | 1 |
| border-style | Sets the style of the four borders | 1 |
| border-top | Sets all the top border properties in one declaration | 1 |
| border-top-color | Sets the colour of the top border | 2 |
| border-top-style | Sets the style of the top border | 2 |
| border-top-width | Sets the width of the top border | 1 |
| border-width | Sets the width of the four borders | 1 |
| *Dimension Properties* | | |
| height | Sets the height of an element | 1 |
| width | Sets the width of an element | 1 |
| *Font Properties* | | |
| font | Sets all the font properties in one declaration | 1 |
| font-family | Specifies the font family for text | 1 |
| font-size | Specifies the font size of text | 1 |
| font-style | Specifies the font style for text | 1 |
| font-variant | Specifies whether or not a text should be displayed in a small-caps font | 1 |
| font-weight | Specifies the weight of a font | 1 |
| *List Properties* | | |
| list-style | Sets all the properties for a list in one declaration | 1 |
| list-style-image | Specifies an image as the list-item marker | 1 |
| list-style-position | Specifies if the list-item markers should appear inside or outside the content flow | 1 |
| list-style-type | Specifies the type of list-item marker | 1 |

| Property | Description | CSS |
|---|---|---|
| *Margin Properties* | | |
| margin | Sets all the margin properties in one declaration | 1 |
| margin-bottom | Sets the bottom margin of an element | 1 |
| margin-left | Sets the left margin of an element | 1 |
| margin-right | Sets the right margin of an element | 1 |
| margin-top | Sets the top margin of an element | 1 |
| *Padding Properties* | | |
| padding | Sets all the padding properties in one declaration | 1 |
| padding-bottom | Sets the bottom padding of an element | 1 |
| padding-left | Sets the left padding of an element | 1 |
| padding-right | Sets the right padding of an element | 1 |
| padding-top | Sets the top padding of an element | 1 |
| *Positioning Properties* | | |
| bottom | Sets the bottom margin edge for a positioned box | 2 |
| clear | Specifies which sides of an element where other floating elements are not allowed | 1 |
| float | Specifies whether or not a box should float | 1 |
| left | Sets the left margin edge for a positioned box | 2 |
| right | Sets the right margin edge for a positioned box | 2 |
| top | Sets the top margin edge for a positioned box | 2 |
| visibility | Specifies whether or not an element is visible | 2 |
| *Text Properties* | | |
| color | Sets the colour of text | 1 |
| direction | Specifies the text direction/writing direction | 2 |
| letter-spacing | Increases or decreases the space between characters in a text | 1 |
| line-height | Sets the line height | 1 |
| text-align | Specifies the horizontal alignment of text | 1 |
| text-decoration | Specifies the decoration added to text | 1 |
| text-indent | Specifies the indentation of the first line in a text-block | 1 |
| text-shadow | Specifies the shadow effect added to text | 2 |
| text-transform | Controls the capitalization of text | 1 |
| vertical-align | Sets the vertical alignment of an element | 1 |
| white-space | Specifies how white-space inside an element is handled | 1 |
| word-spacing | Increases or decreases the space between words in a text | 1 |
| *CSS Pseudo-classes/elements* | | |
| :active | Adds a style to an element that is activated | 1 |
| :first-letter | Adds a style to the first character of a text | 1 |
| :first-line | Adds a style to the first line of a text | 1 |
| :hover | Adds a style to an element when you mouse over it | 1 |
| :link | Adds a style to an unvisited link | 1 |
| :visited | Adds a style to a visited link | 1 |

# HTML / XHTML Tags

**DTD (Document Type Definition)** indicates in which HTML 4.01 / XHTML 1.0 type (S = Strict; T=Transitional) the tag is allowed.

This is an abridged list of tags; a complete list can be found at www.w3schools.com/tags/default.asp.

'Deprecated' means that the tag is still allowed, for now, to take care of older websites, but is likely to be withdrawn in the future and should not be used for new websites.

| Tag | Description | DTD |
|---|---|---|
| <!--...--> | Defines a comment | ST |
| <!DOCTYPE> | Defines the document type | ST |
| <a> | Defines an anchor | ST |
| <b> | Defines bold text | ST |
| <blockquote> | Defines a long quotation | ST |
| <body> | Defines a document's body | ST |
| <br /> | Defines a single line break | ST |
| <caption> | Defines a table caption | ST |
| <center> | *Deprecated.* Defines centred text | T |
| <cite> | Defines a citation | ST |
| <col /> | Defines attribute values for one or more columns in a table | ST |
| <colgroup> | Defines a group of columns in a table for formatting | ST |
| <dd> | Defines a description of a term in a definition list | ST |
| <div> | Defines a section (division) in a document | ST |
| <dl> | Defines a definition list | ST |
| <dt> | Defines a term (item) in a definition list | ST |
| <em> | Defines emphasized text | ST |
| <fieldset> | Defines a border around elements in a form | ST |
| <font> | *Deprecated.* Defines font, colour and size for text | T |
| <form> | Defines an HTML form for user input | ST |
| <h1> to <h6> | Defines HTML headings | ST |
| <head> | Defines information about the document | ST |
| <hr /> | Defines a horizontal line | ST |
| <html> | Defines an HTML document | ST |
| <i> | Defines italic text | ST |
| <img /> | Defines an image | ST |
| <kbd> | Defines keyboard text | ST |
| <li> | Defines a list item | ST |
| <link /> | Defines the relationship between a document and an external resource | ST |
| <map> | Defines an image-map | ST |
| <menu> | *Deprecated.* Defines a menu list | T |
| <meta /> | Defines metadata about an HTML document | ST |
| <noframes> | Defines an alternate content for users that do not support frames | T |
| <noscript> | Defines an alternate content for users that do not support client-side scripts | ST |
| <object> | Defines an embedded object | ST |
| <ol> | Defines an ordered list | ST |
| <p> | Defines a paragraph | ST |
| <param /> | Defines a parameter for an object | ST |
| <pre> | Defines preformatted text | ST |
| <q> | Defines a short quotation | ST |
| <s> | *Deprecated.* Defines strikethrough text | T |
| <script> | Defines a client-side script | ST |
| <select> | Defines a select list (drop-down list) | ST |
| <small> | Defines small text | ST |
| <span> | Defines a localised section in a document | ST |
| <strike> | *Deprecated.* Defines strikethrough text | T |
| <strong> | Defines strong text | ST |
| <style> | Defines style information for a document | ST |
| <sub> | Defines subscripted text | ST |
| <sup> | Defines superscripted text | ST |
| <table> | Defines a table* | ST |
| <tbody> | Groups the body content in a table | ST |
| <td> | Defines a cell in a table | ST |
| <tfoot> | Groups the footer content in a table | ST |
| <th> | Defines a header cell in a table | ST |
| <thead> | Groups the header content in a table | ST |
| <title> | Defines the title of a document | ST |
| <tr> | Defines a row in a table | ST |
| <tt> | Defines teletype text | ST |
| <u> | *Deprecated.* Defines underlined text | T |
| <ul> | Defines an unordered list | ST |

* Table tags should now only be used for tabular matter, not for layout.

# Index

# Credits

1.1 Hey web: Hey Hey blog: Johnny Kelly, Happy Socks, Stefan Karchev;
1.2 Jason Kristofer & Patrick Riley; 1.5 Who Is; 1.6 Photo by John Dilnot,
website design Alan Fred Pipes; 1.7 UNIQLO UK (Ltd); 1.9 LA TIGRE
Studio Associato; 2.1 Designer: Noah Harris, Interaction Designer: James
Stone. Images by Carl Burgess, Kyle Bean, Lernert&Sander, Lynn Fox,
Pleix, Zeitguised, Ben Hibon, David Wilson, Dave Cornmell, Kristofer Strom;
2.4 Cargo Team: Folkert Gorter, Josh Panqell, Rene Daalder, Jon-Kyle
Mohr, Richard Cacares; 2.13 Mas Entero. Website designed by Magnus
Jepson, Tomas Aparicio and Alejandro Gallego Lozano; 2.14 MilieuGrotesque,
coding by Thomas Michelbach/NoMoreSleep. Graphic concept & design
by Timo Gaessner/123buero in corporation with Alexander Meyer/XYZ.ch;
p49 bottom Effektive Website (http://www.effektivedesign.co.uk) Effektive
Blog (http://www.effektiveblog.com) Cargo Platform (http://www.
cargocollective.com) Tumblr (http://www.tumblr.com) Mag Theme (http://
magtheme.tumblr.com/) 3.1 Design: Base Design, Website development:
Tentwelve; 3.13 ©2003-2010 Nitrocorpz Design LTDA; 3.14 Hey web: Hey
Hey blog: Johnny Kelly, Happy Socks, Stefan Karchev; 3.16 Design;
Gavillet & Rust, photography: Olivier Pasqual; 3.17 With permission of
www.disabilityartsonline.org.uk; 3.18 ©BBC; p80 fig1+2+4 Creative
director, Partner Edenspiekermann: Robert Stulle;  Design Director: Sven
Ellinger; Web Developer: Alex Coles. Fig3 Berliner Philharmonie GmbH,
Webdesign by Edenspiekermann. Creative Director, partner Edenspiekermann:
Robert Stulle; Design Director, Interaction design: Sven Ellingen; Graphic
design: Okan Tustas; Interaction Design: Marcus Scheller; 4.1 Studio von
Birken, Creative Direction & Art Direction: Katia Kuethe, Programming
Claus-Christoph Kuethe; 4.4 Konst & Teknik & Martin Ström; 4.12 Editing
House: Dias Contados, Web Designers: Mario Eskenazi, Esiete; p104 top:
Personal and commercial works by M. Giesser. (Image #7 "Vormberichten"
cover designs completed at Dietwee Communicatie en Vormgeving)
bottom: "Vormberichten" cover designs completed at Dietwee Communicatie
en Vormgeving; p105 Website designed and produced at Polimekanos-
Joseph Kohlmaier and Shoko Mugikura; 5.4 Graphic Design: Quinta-Feira,
Developer: Bielsystems; 5.5 CD:Kashiwa Sato, AD/Flash Developer/Sound:
Yugo Nakamura, D: Keita Kitamura, Programmer: Erika Sakai, National Art
Center Tokyo CD/AD/D: Kashiwa Sato, Photo: Mikiya Takimoto; 5.17
Created by Duane King, Ian Coyle, Frank Chimero and Shane Bzdok; 5.19
Au Revoir Simone/Designed Memory; p130 fig 5: Samsung Player Star
Shooting by Khuong Nguyen; 6.1 Creative Director: Robin Souter, Digital
Strategist and MD: Peter Veash. And the wonderful people at BIO;
6.2 Warp: Creative Direction: Universal Everything, Design & Development:
Remote Location; 6.7 Client: Elisava Design School Agency/Concept: Soon
In Tokyo, Creative Direction: Angelo Palma, Javi Donada Copywriter:
Angelo Palma, Art Director: Javi Donada, Designer: Thiago Monteiro,
Programming: Jesus Gollonet Direction/Animation/Compositing: Johnny
Kelly & Matthew Cooper, Production Assistant: Joe Pelling, Additional
Compositing: Yu Sato; 6.11 Vitamina, Energia Creativa & GROM. Guido
Martinetti, Cristina Stroppiana, Manuela Garbo, Nicoletta Torielli; 6.13
Matthew Dent – Illustration work – http://www.matthewdent.co.uk, Cargo-
Website coding and design-http://cargocollective.com, Artprojekt-Logo
(not created by Matthew Dent) NIKE78-Logo (not created by Matthew Dent);
6.17 Web Design by LUNETTES NOIRES – www.lunettesnoires.net – All
images SIXPACK FRANCE – www. sixpack.fr – Photography by AKROE
and JULIETTE VILLARD; 6.19 Created by Duane King, Ian Coyle, Frank
Chimero and Shane Bzdok; 6.21©Apple; 6.25 LA TIGRE Studio Associato